MIRIAM ADAHAN

RAISING CHILDREN TO CARE

A JEWISH GUIDE TO CHILDREARING

FELDHEIM PUBLISHERS

Jerusalem / New York

First printing, January 1988
Second printing, July 1988

Copyright © 1988 by Miriam Adahan

Published by Feldheim Publishers Ltd. in conjunction with
Gefen Publishing House Ltd.

Feldheim Publishers Ltd.   Philipp Feldheim Inc.
POB 6525 / Jerusalem, Israel   200 Airport Executive Park
Printed in Israel   Spring Valley, NY 10977

Library of Congress Cataloging in Publication Data

Adahan, Miriam.

Raising children to care:
a Jewish guide to childrearing / Miriam Adahan

p. cm.
Bibliography: p.
Includes index.

ISBN 0-87306-456-9:

1. Child rearing—Religious aspects—Judaism.
2. Jews—Families—Religious life. I. Title./
HQ769.3.A33 1988 649'.7—dc19   88-4246 CIP

Printed and bound at Keterpress Enterprises, Jerusalem.
Typesetting by Gefen Publishing House Ltd.

*To parents everywhere
who give of themselves so that
their children will experience
the true Jewish spirit of
tolerance, loving-kindness and
the dignity which evolves
from self-discipline.*

*To my mother,
Anne Dann Luborsky* תחי׳
*who maintained her faith and love for me
through many troubled times.*

Seek at an early age to influence (your child's) inner life.... Accustom him...to be honest, gentle and compassionate. Open his heart to the love of all things that share existence with him.... Teach him early to feel himself under the personal eye of God...and to love and respect God's children. When he commences to hear from you or to read of the history of his ancestors and he begins to understand his mission as a Jew, then inspire him with respect and love for and pride in his Jewish mission...so that he should rejoice...and feel gratitude and love for all the world. Train him to be sociable so that he may respect the life, the health, the body, the property, the joy, peace and honor of his surroundings, that he may respect every creature around him...and willingly contribute to the welfare of others.

But do you know the great instrument which you have in your hands for giving him this training? Your own example! Parents...become friends to your children in those (teenage) years. Let thy son and daughter have no greater or closer friend than father and mother. Parents too have no greater or more natural friends than their children when grown up. Son and daughter must pour out their hearts into yours, and should heaven and earth abandon them, they must ever find loyal support, at once kindly and stern, in father and mother... as they grow older, they must be treated differently and you must become friends to them in order that they may be friends to you.

(HOREB, pp. 412-14)

To reach this level with our teenagers, we must begin early to establish a relationship of mutual trust and respect. That is the purpose of this book.

בע"ה
ח' אייר תשמ"ז

The undersigned welcomes the opportunity to endorse and commend Miriam Adahan's second major work, *Raising Children to Care: A Jewish Guide to Childrearing.*

Her first work, *EMETT: A Step-by-Step Guide to Maturity Established Through Torah*, offers guidelines to the adult Jew on how to refine his or her emotional faculties.

Raising Children to Care addresses itself to the importance of finding and maintaining the subtle point of balance between authority/love, external discipline/self-motivation and self-interest/altruism in the raising of a Jewish child.

In the opinion of the undersigned, the authoress has again produced an admirable Torah guide for our troubled times.

Rabbi Nachman Bulman
Kiryat Nachliel, Migdal HaEmek
Israel

Acknowledgments

I am deeply grateful to Hashem for instilling in me the ability and the desire to write this book and for bringing me to Torah observance, the Guiding Light of my life, and for the great blessing of my four beautiful children.

I thank my husband, Carmeli, for his support and my children (presently sixteen, eight, six and four) for providing the raw material for this book — especially my daughter, Dalya, who has been so understanding and helpful.

My deepest appreciation to Rabbi Chaim Dov Altusky, *rosh yeshivah* of Torah Ohr, Jerusalem, for his painstaking review of this book and many helpful comments. Also, to Rabbi Zelig Pliskin, a very astute and empathic counselor, who reviewed it so carefully and whose books have been a source of great inspiration to me. My thanks to Susan Weiss, my friend, neighbor (and lawyer), who reviewed the first edition, to Wendy Horowitz-Chopra, who edited the final edition with such meticulous care, and the lovely people at Gefen Publishers.

I am grateful to my dear friend, Rebbetzin Chana Boas, whose enthusiasm and encouragement for the initial manuscript gave me the courage to make it public.

I want to thank Irene Klass, editor of the Women's Section of *The Jewish Press*, who encouraged my efforts by publishing much of the information in this book.

And my thanks to Bracha Steinberg at Feldheim Publishers who edited this, as well as my EMETT book, with unusual patience, above and beyond the call of duty.

My great thanks to the thousands of Orthodox women who have attended EMETT groups over the past ten years and whose dedication and devotion to motherhood have inspired me so greatly. After my coming from a secular world where material comforts and personal accomplishments were paramount, these women provided a welcome change with their examples of selflessness and abounding faith. These women have shared their joys and woes with me. I treasure their feedback, especially when they tell me of their successes, such as, "Miriam, it worked! I kept a list of the good deeds which my troublesome child did for the last few days and read them to him each night. And he behaved so much better!" Or, "Miriam, intead of slapping my little one when he misbehaved, I bent down, cupped his face in my hands, looked into his eyes and simply said very firmly, 'We don't do that in our house.' He then cooperated without a fuss! Before, I certainly would have gotten enraged and slapped him." If there is a little more joy in the world because of these classes, I have received the greatest possible reward.

It would be most helpful to readers if this book is used in conjunction with my first book, called *EMETT: A Step-by-Step Guide to Emotional Maturity Established through Torah.* I hope that mothers will form support groups throughout the world to help each other navigate through the often turbulent times which motherhood inevitably brings, and to share their joys as well. We need each other to share and to care.

Miriam Adahan, Sivan 5747

Table of Contents

Introduction

The book of Shemuel I tells the story of the prophetess Chanah, who was barren. Her husband, Elkanah, had a second wife named Peninah, who had many children and who taunted Chanah about her childlessness. In desperation, Chanah refused to eat. Elkanah tried to comfort her, saying, "Why is thy heart grieved? Am I not better to thee than ten sons?" But one did not make up for the other. Nothing could take away the "bitterness in Chanah's soul," and she continued to cry. Finally, she went to the priest, Eli HaCohen, and vowed to him that if she would have a son, "I will give him unto the Lord all the days of his life...." Eli assured her that her prayers would be answered and she went away happy. In time, she bore a son whom she called Shemuel. When she weaned him at the age of two, she took him to Eli and said,

> For this child have I prayed. And the Lord has given.... Therefore...as long as he lives, he shall be devoted to God.
>
> (SHEMUEL I, 1)

The *raison d'etre* of an Orthodox woman is her family. As little girls, we pray that we will be "...a joyful mother of children." (*Tehillim* 113). From the time we learn we are pregnant, the prayers do not stop, as we ask for an easy birth and a healthy child. After the child's birth, we continue to pray that our children should not suffer from serious illnesses or mental harm. We pray that they should be devoted to Torah and good deeds, have good character traits, be self-confident, joyful and responsible.

At times, we may think with exasperation, "For **this** child I prayed???" And the answer is, "Yes!" Hashem has given us these particular children with their particular weaknesses and strengths. Each one is given to us not only for us to help him with his *tikun*, but for him to help us with ours as well. Each child challenges us in his own special way. And it is in loving them when we feel least loving or they are least lovable that we make the greatest spiritual progress. So we pray for ourselves as well as for them:

* For wisdom to answer our children's questions, to deal with the many conflicts which arise, and to guide them correctly so that they live up to the ideals of Torah,

* For self-discipline when anger wells up within us and we want to crush their spirits with criticism or beatings,

* For cooperation from our spouses so that our children will grow in an atmosphere of love between their parents,

* For creativity, so that we will find positive solutions to the many crises and conflicts,

* For blindness to the minor irritations, aches and pains and insignificant mistakes and inconveniences,

* For insight into the hearts and minds of our family members,

* For patience...and more patience...and still more of the same,

* For empathy, so that they know we care deeply about what they think and feel,

* For courage to set firm limits, so that they feel safe, secure and protected,

* For gratefulness, so that in the midst of pain and frustration we do not forget the ecstasy of holding them for the first time, the joy of their first steps, or the blessing of their existence,

* For strength and health, so that when we are tired or in pain we can remain functional and vigilant,

* For joy and laughter and enthusiasm, so that they will feel confident about facing life with faith and positivity,

* For silence, so that we do not destroy their spirits with harsh words, ridicule or shame,

* For acceptance of them as they are at this moment, so that they will feel encouraged to grow,

* For love, not only of our children, but of our own inner child as well, which is also in need of time, understanding and expression,

* And especially for faith at all times in Hashem's ever-present love, mercy and wisdom in all that He gives us.

To be a mother means to be more or less in a continual state of prayer. This is the hidden source of our own strength, courage, wisdom and love.

Preface

A number of factors gave me the impetus to write this book. First was my own experience as a mother. I realized quite soon how ironic it is that the job of mothering, which requires so many complex skills, has no formal training. I myself, with two degrees in psychology, a love of children, and many years of experience as a counselor, thought motherhood would be a cinch. How wrong I was! I found myself quite unprepared for the realities of life. My first child was a fragile five-pounder who was almost perpetually awake during her first year of life. Then came three boys in quick succession (after the age of thirty-five) who never ceased to amaze me with their exuberant, often aggressive energy and variety of needs and demands. All my book learning did little to help me with the logistics of doing the endless household chores and trying to be a loving, creative mother while still keeping a part of myself involved in my beloved EMETT work, all in the midst of the exhaustion which resulted from babies who preferred to sleep during the day and be up most of the night, and the allergic ones who needed special care. This book was partly the result of my attempts to figure out how to remain functional and caring in the midst of these stressful times.

Second was my training as a counselor, where I witnessed the tragic effects of early childhood abuse and neglect. I saw many children and adults who were self-destructive or destructive of others, who could not function in a responsible manner in the world, and who could not love or allow themselves to be loved.

The one thing my academic training had done was to instill in me a profound awareness of the great importance of the earliest years of life in terms of providing a strong foundation for future mental health. During the first year of existence, a child establishes a basic sense of trust in people **if** his physical and emotional needs are satisfied by attentive and affectionate parents. His future capacity to love — to invest himself emotionally in others in a giving manner — is rooted in the parents' prompt response to his cries of distress and their ability to fulfill his need to be touched, soothed and protected from harm. During the second and third years, the child develops self-confidence if he is allowed to master the disciplines and skills appropriate to his age. Thus, the child's feeling of being loved by both father and mother and his feeling of success in social relationships and school will, to a large degree, determine how he relates in the future to his or her spouse, children, and the world in general. This is when the foundation for love, joy, a sense of trust in others and responsibility are established.

The relation of the child to his parents provides the model for the child's relations with both God and man. It is during the formative years that the parents' love carves a vessel in the child's soul which will enable him later to internalize the wisdom of Torah, and for him to model the fundamental principle of Judaism, *gemiluth chesidim*, which is "its beginning and its end" (*Sotah* 14a). Without this vessel, Torah practice remains mechanical and devoid of the true spirit of love.

Obviously, we cannot possibly satisfy all of our children's needs, nor would we want to, for they must learn to be self-sufficient, self-disciplined and unselfish. A child who cannot delay gratification will become a spoiled tyrant. However, in order to become self-disciplined in a non-punishing manner, a child must first have a strong foundation of loving care.

Unfortunately, conflicting opinions and unsound advice have confused many modern parents. Some withhold affection and attention from their children out of fear of spoiling them. Such parents constantly interpret their children's undesirable behavior and demands as attempts to exploit or manipulate them.

How opposite this is from the Torah view, where parents are encouraged to be protective and affectionate. For example, Rabbi Eliezer Papu says that a mother will be severely judged for making her baby cry unnecessarily to be fed. (See *Pele Yoetz*, section *Yonkai Shadayim.*) These early years are like the roots of a tree. If the roots are damaged, the entire structure remains disturbed to some degree. Therefore, anything that would hinder your ability to create a secure and loving home, such as if you or your husband are often hysterical, impatient or angry, is cause for you to seek immediate help.

Another reason for writing this book was my ten years of

experience as an EMETT group leader, when I realized how widespread the problem of low self-esteem and guilt was among mothers. Mothers will talk about how difficult it is to feed, toilet-train or dress their children, but they rarely talk about how inadequate, enraged, frightened and helpless they feel when they are unsuccessful at getting their children to cooperate or to do what they think should be accomplished quickly and easily. I found that mothers would question themselves anxiously: "Why do I always feel that I can never do enough for them?" "What's wrong with me that my child still sucks his thumb/kvetches so much/still wets his bed?" "Why do my neighbor's children help her so willingly and mine don't?" "How come my sister gets her kids to sleep so easily and dressed so easily in the morning while I'm so discombobulated?" They often concluded, "I or my children must be failures." With such a thought in mind, the mother would then feel discouraged and unloving and the home atmosphere would become tense and joyless.

Finally, writing this book helped me deal with my grief over the loss of my last two pregnancies. I felt that if I could not hold another little *neshama* in my arms, at least I could give mothers something of value to hold in theirs. And so, as is my habit, I turned my loss into a gain.

A Caution About Books on Mothering

The one thing which I do not want to happen when parents read this book is for them to feel more anxious or inadequate than they already may. You may think, "This book is too idealistic. I cannot possibly put all this into practice. It's asking too much of me." If this is your attitude, think of the high moral standards which Torah demands of you! It is better to have an ideal to work toward than none at all!

Mothering books often make the job seem easy, as if all problems can be quickly and neatly solved and as if all other mothers are successful the minute they try to put the author's advice into practice, after which the children become perfect angels. The reality is far different. We all have moments when complex demands are overwhelming or when we simply cannot utilize the suggestions mentioned here even if we would want to. Therefore, enjoy the book for what it can give you, even if it is only a different attitude. When you feel ready, put one or two suggestions into practice each week. By the end of a year, you will have made noticeable improvements.

Don't work for perfection. Perfectionism creates anxiety and mistrust, which is the opposite of what this book hopes to accomplish. You should reread this book a few times in order to internalize those concepts or suggestions which are foreign to your nature. Be patient as well as persistent as these new understandings become a part of your life.

The second problem which may arise from reading this book is that you may want to put changes into practice immediately, and become frustrated and angry about the resistance and conflicts with those who believe in a harsh, punitive approach to children. You may be accused of "spoiling" your children or ascribing to "psychological nonsense."

The most effective method of getting family members to appreciate your ideas is for you to become a staunch, self-disciplined model of calm, non-hostile assertiveness, loving-kindness and creativity. Those who have minds to understand and hearts to feel will eventually learn from your example. If you become hostile and hysterical, you are likely to become the object of ridicule and will not be taken seriously. The Torah sources mentioned here may be effective in dealing with others' objections, but do not be surprised if others have their own sources which seem to say the very opposite of what you believe is the most effective way to raise children. One-liners are sometimes effective:

> "Whatever you mention gets strengthened. So let's mention the good that we and our children do instead of criticizing so much."
> "Instead of getting so emotional about this situation, let's focus on a solution."
> "We can't teach patience by being impatient."

Do not try to teach in the heat of anger. You'll do more damage than good. When you find a calm moment, discuss the ideas in this book and allow for feedback and discussion. Don't force your ideas on others, as this will arouse greater resistance. Assure those around you that children brought up in a respectful, loving atmosphere may be more lively, curious, talkative and somewhat more demanding in the beginning than those brought up in suppressive, authoritarian homes. However, in the long run, they become adults who can feel fully, love generously, act courageously and think creatively.

The third problem which can arise from reading books on mothering is that you may become hypersensitive and overly anxious about your children's every passing mood, grimace, cry or act of non-cooperation. Instead of being more relaxed, you may be more distressed as you wonder, "Am I doing enough? Does his thumb-sucking/psoriasis/bed-wetting/ or failure to eat as much as I want mean that he has a serious problem?" "Am I being too strict or not strict enough? Should I spank more or less, yell, give him a lecture, give in more often or less often, ignore him, take away privileges when he misbehaves or simply talk to him sternly?" You can easily become so confused and overwhelmed by taking everything so seriously that you are unable to act with calm firmness. Realize that there are no "ultimate" right answers or solutions which always work. If you are uncertain about whether or not a problem falls into the category of "passing stage" or "permanent disability," ask an expert. But don't torture yourself with self-doubt over every minor upset.

Most parental mistakes are not fatal, and most children brought up in Observant households are caring, disciplined people. A mother who is generally loving will convey that love to her children even though she yells, blunders and loses control at times. A hit or a yell is like a withdrawal from a "love bank." If you have a healthy bank account, occasional withdrawals will have no lasting impact on the child's personality. Children must be subjected to prolonged abuse in order to suffer serious psychological damage. Wounds heal quickly in an atmosphere of unconditional love and honest communication. Refuse to take trivial mistakes seriously so that you can maintain an atmosphere of joy, respect and stability.

It is a commonly held misconception that if anything goes wrong with a child, it's the mother's fault. But you are not the only influence on your child. Teachers, peers, your husband, relatives, siblings, as well as his own innate predispositions and life experiences all contribute to forming his personality. So go easy on the guilt! In particular, the role of the father is often minimized. Often fathers do not recognize (or do not want to recognize) their crucial role in their children's psychological development. If you have a non-supportive husband, both you and your children cannot help but suffer.

Also, you may not be able to control the major childhood stresses, which are: death of a family member, chronic severe illness, divorce, lack of space, marital disharmony, or the verbal or physical abuse to which your child may be subjected when you are not around. You can only hope that, despite such traumas, your child will still grow up into a caring person because of your personal example.

Unless you or someone else is being deliberately abusive or neglectful, be "generously forgiving" (*Isaiah* 55:7) of yourself, your children and everyone else you come in contact with.

MIRIAM ADAHAN

RAISING CHILDREN TO CARE

A JEWISH GUIDE TO CHILDREARING

ONE

The Importance of Self-Respect

It is a cardinal principle that a person cannot love others unless he loves himself first. Yet many will say, "How can I love myself when I have so many faults? Isn't self-love a sign of arrogance? How can I inspire myself to improve if I don't constantly put myself down?" True, introspection is certainly necessary to identify areas of weakness. However, excessive shame (i.e., low self-esteem) leads to discouragement, anxiety and, inevitably, hostility toward others, for one will seek to blame and shame others to the degree that one feels ashamed of oneself. Yes, a person should feel appropriately ashamed for any conscious sins or deliberate acts of carelessness or lack of loving-kindness. But one should not feel ashamed of one's very being, nor for anything which is beyond one's control, including one's own or other people's present level of competency, maturity or awareness. This would constitute excessive shame. And excessive shame distances us from others, preventing us from loving them:

> *Only a person who feels inwardly good about himself will be able to fulfill the mitzvah of, Love your neighbor as yourself.*
>
> (AHAVATH MAISHORIM, p. 109, VAYIKRA 19:17)

Because excessive shame is so psychologically destructive, parents and teachers are warned,

> *It is forbidden to shame a child who is old enough to feel embarrassment.*
>
> (MITZVOTH HA'L'VOVOTH 4:5)

1

Just as God loves us despite our imperfections, so too, must we love ourselves and each other, even though we are all far from perfect. Certainly, you will notice that you are sometimes nasty-tempered, resentful, selfish and discouraged. You may be careless, forgetful, disorganized and impatient. You will notice similar shortcomings in your children and spouse. When you do, act like a physical therapist and prescribe for yourself certain spiritual exercises which will make you well again. You do not need to stop loving yourself or others. What you need most at such a time is unconditional love, a love which accepts your limitations with humility, yet which urges you to become more of what you are capable of becoming. In such an atmosphere, self-development is maximized.

Maintain your self-respect and respect for others not in order to become smug, complacent or self-deluding, but in order to maintain calm objectivity as you figure out how best to go about the lifelong task of self-improvement.

Realize that the Godly part of a person naturally and spontaneously impels him toward growth, unless he is crippled by excessive shame, guilt or fear. In classical Hebrew, the word *osher* [happiness] comes from the root, *to make progress* (*Effective Jewish Parenting*, p. 56). This will happen automatically if you have a positive attitude toward yourself.

The Insecure Mother

If a young mother has been brought up in a stable home, with loving parents who provided unconditional acceptance and opportunities to master the skills and disciplines necessary to manage a home, she will certainly have a general feeling of being loved, loving and competent. However, if she has a tendency to be insecure and unconfident, has little experience with children or household management or does not have a supportive husband, she will have greater difficulty feeling good about herself. She may see women with large families who seem to manage so easily, while she has so many difficulties accomplishing the simplest tasks. She may think: What kind of a mother is it whose children disobey, who can't have the house in tip-top order, who feels so tired half the time, who is not grateful enough for the many blessings which Hashem has granted her, who has dirty dishes in the sink, who can't even keep the checkbook balanced, who doesn't do more with her life, who can't even get the children to bed without screaming or get them dressed in the morning without hitting? A failure! That's what!

The feelings of shame are compounded if there are close family members or neighbors who convey the message of failure with unwanted advice, grimaces, hostile silences or criticism.

The children, too, may voice their complaints or be hostile because the food isn't to their liking or the Purim costume is not as creative as that of some other child, or because someone else's mommy is prettier or better at something than theirs. Mothers are notorious for playing a destructive game called "Comparing and Competing." Even the slightest handicap or difference can induce feelings of failure.

In addition, there are the inevitable illnesses — both her own and her children's — which wear down her resistance and make her think, "See, I just can't manage." With all this, it is easy to adopt an "I'm-not-O.K." attitude. It is a common joke that when anything goes wrong with the children or the marriage, the mother or wife is blamed. But it is no joke when the mother begins to feel discouraged and loses hope about her ability to manage.

The insecure mother should realize that she is fighting a difficult battle and that her greatest challenge is to avoid discouragement and self-pity over the fact that she has to work so hard to do what seems to come so easily to other mothers. Rather, the very act of having to struggle for self-improvement is her way of bringing greater *kedushah* into the world.

To increase self-confidence, it is important to stay out of the negative cycle and stay in the positive one:

SELF-RESPECT AND SELF-MASTERY CYCLE

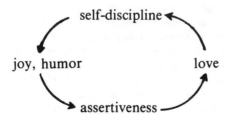

SELF-HATRED AND DISCOURAGEMENT CYCLE

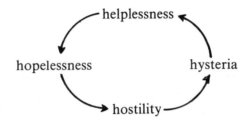

How do you get out of the negative cycle once you are in it? To penetrate the positive cycle, you must perform some act of love, joy, self-discipline or assertiveness, no matter how minor, superficial or insincere it may seem at the moment. For example, you might smile instead of grimacing, even though you really feel lousy, sing or be silent instead of criticizing, leave the table instead of gorging, hug your child instead of ignoring him, or talk instead of hitting. These acts will get you in touch with your inner source of strength and self-worth. **Any act of self-restraint can increase your sense of self-worth.**

An added bonus is that when your children see you struggling for self-improvement, you give them a greater gift than if you pretend to be at the top level of excellence, for you demonstrate to them that they, too, should be involved in a lifelong struggle for ever-increasing improvement of their *middoth*.

> ✿   It was one of those mornings. I woke up feeling fat, which was bad enough. But the baby also had a fever and had hardly slept all night. My four year old was dawdling and didn't want to get dressed, even though it was almost time for the school bus to come. My six and eight year olds were taunting each other and didn't want to eat breakfast. My nine year old stomped around angrily because the white blouse which she needed for school was in the wash. Ordinarily, I would have been screaming at them all from sheer helplessness. Instead, I kept humming *modeh ani* to myself over and over as I got them off to school. The whole atmosphere lightened up as I refused to be dragged down into their negativity and anxiety. When my two year old put up a fuss about getting his shoes on, I was about to hit, but restrained myself and just looked him in the eyes, my face full of frustration. He looked back at me and patted my face and said, "I love you." That was my reward. I realized that all my self-restraint had had a positive effect on them. I felt so proud of myself. I even restrained my desire to overeat after they left!

Be patient! Just as it takes time to restructure your body with physical exercises, so, too, does it take time to restructure your psyche and habit patterns.

How To Maintain Self-Esteem

Self- esteem is based on **love** (of self and others) and **mastery** (over oneself and over important life skills). Since your outer environment may not always provide you with love or a feeling of control, you must learn to rely on yourself to maintain your sense of self-worth no matter what is going on around you. The following will help you to avoid feeling devastated when things do not go your way or others do not give you the love and appreciation which you would like:

First, know that you have intrinsic worth, even if you are imperfect, because you were created *b'tzelem Hashem*, in the image of God (*Bereshith* 1:27). Do not let your self-worth rise and fall according to the condition of your kitchen sink or your children's behavior. Mess and misbehavior do not reflect the state of your being unless you are deliberately and exceptionally uncaring and negligent.

Second, instead of thinking of yourself as a failure when things do not go smoothly, assume that you lack the information, skills, discipline or experience to do better. We all come to motherhood with different aptitudes for the various skills involved in good mothering and homemaking. When you see an area in need of improvement, do not become discouraged. Find out what you can do to change and then do it. Remember, you do not have to be perfect to be deserving of love and respect, for if that were the case, no one would be deserving, since no one is perfect! It is essential that you break the connection between incompetency in certain skills and the condemnation of total failure. Everyone has areas of deficiency. This in no way implies total worthlessness.

Third, conquer that which is difficult. If you have a choice of tasks to do, do the difficult. This builds inner strength and self-respect. For example, if you have the choice of going to the dentist or avoiding that often expensive and unpleasant task, GO! If you wonder whether you should stay home or go to that stimulating class or exercise group, do what will build your sense of self-worth.

Do the things you have been procrastinating about, such as writing those thank-you notes or visiting your child's teacher if there have been problems in class. Doing what is convenient or comfortable may be satisfying in the short run, but will eventually make you feel less self-respect. Should you lie down or do the dishes? Do what is best for your mental and physical health. Activity and difficulty are better than apathy and passivity. Stretch yourself to your limits. You will feel better for your efforts. Of course, if you are ill or weak, then the "difficult" for you may be to rest your body and **not** push yourself. Only you can decide for yourself what is best for you, given your particular circumstances.

Fourth, recognize that the terms *success* and *failure* are relative, constantly changing, and often totally meaningless. Some days, just putting one foot in front of the other and getting minimal housework done is a major accomplishment. Success may mean screaming instead of beating, or giving a light slap instead of a strong hit. Respect your limitations. Do not think of yourself in absolute black/white terms. We all stumble and fall. No one stands still. No one knows what pressures or problems are impinging on you at any given moment. No outside person can evaluate you as a success or a failure. That is between you and God.

Fifth, have realistic standards for yourself, your children, and your husband. Do not expect everyone always to be understanding, helpful or appreciative or that you will never feel resentful and unloving. You will. That's normal.

Sixth, focus on your goals. What do you want in life? You want to be a compassionate, disciplined mother and have compassionate, disciplined children. Monitor your thoughts and actions. Do not give importance to petty annoyances or minor aches and pains. Ask yourself, "Is this thought or this action going to bring me closer to my goal in life?" The goal of a Jew is that his life be a living example of Torah values. If what you are doing or thinking is not in accordance with those values, stop. Change your thoughts and your behavior.

Seventh, strive for balance. You need to nurture your children, work hard, but also find time for yourself. Remember,

> *If I am not for myself, who will be for me? But if I am only for myself, what am I?*

(AVOTH 1:14)

You don't win any extra brownie points in Heaven by suffering needlessly or neglecting yourself. Self-punishment is not a sign of mental health.

A man should aim to maintain physical health and vigor . . . for it is impossible for one to understand . . . and meditate . . . when he is hungry or sick or when any of his limbs is aching.

(HILCHOTH DEOTH 3:3)

Eighth, let the people around you know how important positive reinforcement is for everyone in the family, yourself included. Take a strong stand against criticism. Carelessly given criticism is spiritual poison. What comes out of your mouths should be as kosher as what goes in.

Ninth, focus on the positive. There are so many moments of cooperation and joy in any family, times when you see your children helping each other, being responsible and loving, times of laughter and humor. Keep a mental photo album of these memories so that you can recall them when things are not going well. If you are having difficulties with a particular child, realize that sometimes the most difficult children turn into the most creative, dynamic adults. The more intelligent the child, the more apt he is to be very active, curious and inquisitive. Realize that you, your husband and your children will go through many stages and phases and that if you remain loving and confident about yourself, you will eventually see positive results in your endeavors.

Tenth, be realistic. All emotionally honest parents feel inadequate at times because we are! We all make mistakes and fail. We are not omniscient, omnipotent or omnipresent. We do not have all the answers. Do the best you can. Accept your limitations while striving to do your utmost. You are not a failure; you are simply inexperienced or exhausted!

Low Self-Esteem and Dysfunctional Patterns

A child needs three things from his parents: a) loving-kindness, b) strictness and c) encouragement toward mastery and independence. When a parent is motivated by love and is self-loving, he will usually find a balance between all three, adjusting to the child's ever-changing needs on a moment-to-moment or day-to-day basis. One of the factors which can undermine your own best intentions to be a balanced parent is the kind of parenting you yourself had as a child. When a child is not properly nurtured by his parents, he feels helpless, angry and ashamed. When he becomes a parent, these feelings are then projected onto his own children, and often his spouse as well. If your parents were unusually mean, disinterested, anxiety-ridden, sickly or depressed, you may have a tendency to force your children to give you what you never had, such as a feeling of power, freedom and love. You may become hostile toward them when they do not satisfy your needs. This then causes them to become confused and hostile to protect themselves against the hurt of what they perceive as your rejection of them. A vicious cycle is set in motion which may make you feel that your best intentions to undo your past and have a good relationship with your children will never succeed. Three main dysfunctional patterns result from an emotionally impoverished background. (If you see yourself in these patterns, do not panic. This book will help you restructure your thinking and your behavior and to heal yourself by treating your children differently than you were treated.)

The Tyrannical Pattern. This is the parent who demands excessive control over his children. He demands obedience not for the sake of his children, but for his own sake, so that he can feel powerful and dominant. Just as his needs were ignored as a child, so does he now ignore the needs of his children. To overcome the feelings of helplessness he experienced early in life, he or she now demands unconditional obedience, becoming enraged over any difference of opinion or independent action on the children's part. They must jump when he snaps his fingers to prove how powerful he is. Every petty act of clumsiness or every minor mistake is magnified and called attention to, often accompanied by humiliating name-calling or punishments. When his children fail to measure up to his standards, he feels that he himself has failed, which then causes him to be even more harsh, and to crush any opposition to his will. He or she pressures them relentlessly, regardless of their distress or desires, in order to prove his or her worth and impress the neighbors, relatives and the world in general. Contempt toward the children is freely expressed as he builds himself up at their expense.

The Over-Protective, Indulgent Pattern. This parent conveys his inner anxiety to his child by being compulsively approval seeking, overly involved and indulgent. It is usually the mother who falls into this "Martyr Mom" pattern — the woman who feels guilty for thinking of her own needs at times and too inadequate to ask to be treated with respect by family members. She often feels confused and helpless, and sees her children as the powerful ones. She creates dependency by overdoing for her children, then turning on them angrily or withdrawing from them bitterly for being so demanding, after which she feels guilty for her anger, and tries to appease them indulgently again. She wants so much to win her children's love that she is afraid to alienate them with strict rules or by enforcing reasonable demands. She does not realize that, although it may appear that children want an unlimited amount of freedom, they actually crave strict guidelines to make them feel safe. Their excessive demands and misbehavior are attempts to test her in the hope of getting her to establish firm limits. When they don't get the discipline they need, they get angry at the parent. Just as the harsh parent thinks that the source of his children's problem is that he has not been harsh enough, this parent thinks she just hasn't given enough. She will often remain masochistically "nice" in the face of the child's or spouse's aggression and hostility.

The Aloof Pattern. This parent does not feel connected emotionally to his children. He is detached and disinterested. He is often physically unavailable as well as emotionally distant. He complains about their demands for attention and sees those demands as attempts to exploit and manipulate him. His frequent message to them is, "Go away. Leave me alone," a message which is usually given with hostile impatience. Having never been loved himself, he does not know how to connect to or care about his children. Such a father will rarely be home. He will find endless excuses to avoid interacting with them. A mother of this type will be preoccupied with cooking, cleaning, outside projects, or her own illnesses, and will see her children as a burden who prevent her from doing what she really wants to do in life. This is a tragic attitude. Children are not simply bodies which need to be clothed and fed. They are emotional, intellectual and spiritual beings who require development and guidance in all of those areas. Unfortunately, for some parents this is too great a burden, and they do not hesitate to let their children know it.

No parent has the perfect balance all the time. We all goof, and maybe exert too much pressure here or too little there. However, what we should try to do is stay out of the "combination pattern," being indulgent one minute and hostile or aloof the next. There is nothing wrong in telling a child firmly, "I need to be alone," or, "I know you can do it yourself." When motivated by love and sensitivity to the child, the parent's wishes will usually be respected. But when a parent is motivated by the excessive desire for power, approval or freedom from demands, the child will suffer. A child needs to feel that his parents love him. When parents display the above patterns, he learns that *love* means being hurt, rejected and neglected. In his future relationships with his spouse and children, these early patterns may reassert themselves. Much effort is necessary to overcome them.

An awareness of these dysfunctional patterns is not meant to provoke anger toward parents or to justify the continuation of harmful behavior. Rather, it is meant to give the reader insight so that he or she can become more sensitive to his or her children's need for proper guidance and discipline as well as attention and nurturance.

Changing deeply-rooted patterns is a long struggle, one which usually requires outside support. Do not hesitate to get such help if you recognize your tendency toward one of the above extremes. You have bad habits. But you are not a bad person. These habits are like a physical handicap, requiring that you be more diligent and disciplined than the average person in order to live a normal life. If you tend to be excessively controlling, watch for opportunities to encourage independence and to talk lovingly to your children. If you tend to be indulgent, be proud of yourself every time you act with firm authority, or say "no" without guilt or defensiveness. If you tend to be uninterested in your children, set aside time with each one to find out what is going on in their hearts and minds. Make ten-or fifteen-minute appointments and stick to your decision to not let anything interfere with your conversation with them.

It is very tempting to seek out those particular authorities or Biblical statements which may seem to justify one extreme or another. Thus, a tyrannical type will quote numerous statements justifying a harsh, punishing approach to child-rearing while those who have difficulty forming emotional relations will find instances in which indifference to the family is recommended for the sake of spiritual growth. This is a misuse of Torah principles, which value loving-kindness as the highest manifestation of true service to God.

If you have negative tendencies, it is especially important for you to master the concept of averageness, as explained in *EMETT*. When you strive for averageness you will find that your standards will automatically rise in those areas in which you have been deficient, and that you will become more accepting in those areas where your perfectionistic standards have made you anxious and condemnatory. The next time you are in a panic or feel like a failure, focus on what is positive about yourself, and realize that it is just fine for you, your children and your husband to be average or "normal range." As you work to master this concept, you will achieve greater peace of mind and joy.

TWO

Confronting the Transitions from Non-Parenthood to Parenthood

Your world changes drastically when you become a mother. You experience new heights of joy and love. You also sometimes feel anxious, insecure, discouraged, resentful and angry. You never suspected that you had such stamina and love, as you trudge wearily once again to a crying child in the middle of the night or tend to his needs at the end of a fast-day or when you are sick with a fever. You never thought you could love so deeply and tenderly. You also never thought that you could have such ugly, violent impulses when your children pick on each other for the umpteenth time or when the baby cries for hours, no matter what you do to try to get him to stop. There are times when you think you are losing your health, your youth, and even your sanity. It is important to be honest about your feelings, and not be ashamed or guilt-ridden over the fact that you are not always joyous, appreciative or loving. You are human. And to be human means to have a multiplicity of feelings, with contradictory ones sometimes arising at the same time.

Old freedoms are lost and new areas of weighty seriousness and responsibility descend on you. Suddenly you must be a teacher, psychologist, nutritionist, doctor, economist, chef, entertainment director and spiritual guide. It is an awesome task which can never be performed to perfection. We can only do our best from moment to moment and remember to feel blessed to have been given this honor to care for these precious beings. We strive for balance, strive to be patient and loving, rather than hysterical, critical or hostile, strive to juggle the variety of needs and demands given our external pressures, internal stamina and level of awareness and maturity.

The more you understand what is happening to you, the more likely you are to be able to grow into your new role with ever-increasing self-confidence. The following ten transitions are faced by all women when they become mothers. Depending on your personality, aspirations, previous life experiences and physical stamina and health, you will face them easily or with more difficulty. Knowing that other mothers have survived these passages will, hopefully, give you the confidence that you, too, can successfully confront and overcome the same obstacles. You will discover that your doubts and fears are faced by many other mothers. You are not alone.

The following list is not meant to be discouraging, but rather to help you face the realities of these changes. Crises and conflicts are inevitable. With the help of this book, you will learn to view them as similar to birth contractions, which you were taught to accept with as much calm confidence, faith and patience as possible. By confronting the difficulties which arise in the course of your daily life, and finding positive solutions to them, you will develop strengths and resources which previously had lain dormant.

1. From Social Fulfillment to Social Isolation

Before motherhood, your life revolved around the stimulation, excitement, and fulfillment of school, peer relationships, and social events. This is especially true of the year or two before marriage, when the excitement of engagements, weddings and parties is high. There is constant peer interaction at that time. Now, suddenly, you are alone much of the day, isolated from friends and family, and from the activities which gave you something to look forward to each day. The stress of loneliness and the lack of projects which spark enthusiasm can produce major, emotionally distressing changes.

  ⅋ I had no idea that a baby would so completely take over my life. She blocks out everything else. Of course, I love her and am so grateful to have her, but sometimes I feel stifled in this little apartment all alone. I'm supposed to be happy and fulfilled, but I feel at times like I'm going crazy. Then I feel ungrateful and guilty for having these thoughts.

  ⅋ I'll be dragging myself around, feeling miserable, full of self-pity and lethargy when a friend will arrive and suddenly I brighten up. I feel like a new person. I have someone to talk to! An adult! A normal, grown-up human being. My entire attitude changes, and then I realize that I was suffering from social isolation. It's hard to cope with the aloneness at times.

⅋   It's easy for others to say,"Get out of the house!" Ha! Easier said than done. Get out? By the time I get the bags packed, coordinate their nap times, and change their diapers, sometimes I'm too exhausted to leave, or someone needs yet another diaper change or has suddenly fallen asleep again. It's more trouble than it's worth, especially since I don't have a car and have to *schlep* on buses.

⅋   There is no place to go with my three little ones which will please my two older ones as well. They all want something different. I have no family here and I'm tense if I walk into a friend's house because I'm worried that they'll break something. Many people with small children are already overwhelmed with their own messes and don't want any more. The tension of having to watch over three little ones who are all going in different directions drains me. If I go into a store, the owner gives me mean looks as if there's going to be a disaster at any second.

⅋   Baby sitters? First, they're hard to find. All the other mothers seem to want to go out at the same time. Then, they often don't show up for some reason. They have their own lives — school, parties, school examinations, etc. Sometimes their mothers need them at the last minute and they don't bother to tell me that they can't come or they call just as I'm about to leave and say they're sorry that they can't show up. When I do go off, I wonder if the baby sitter will remember to turn off the gas, feed them, change their diapers, and give them time and attention. Will she understand their baby talk or will they end up getting hysterical because she doesn't understand? What if one falls down or two get into a fight or the little one loses his beloved pacifier? It's awfully hard to get out when you don't have a really reliable person to care for them. My social event of the day is when I take out the garbage.

Yes, you miss your friends and your old way of life, even though you love your children. You miss the carefree time when you could leave the house at a moment's notice. Your life has become more restricted. The trips, vacations, and visits to which you looked forward all your life may be more burdensome than pleasurable. The direction of your energies is inward, not outward. Now you wait and hope for people to come to you. And very often they don't. Your loneliness is very real. Lack of adult, peer interaction may, at times, make you feel despondent, irritable and easily upset.

Furthermore, your husband may not be available to help, or, if he is around, may not be the type who gives of himself willingly.

> ❦ When I was a child, our home was always full of guests and happenings. We were a large family and there were so many comings and goings and always people to talk to. Now there's just my husband and my two small children. When my husband comes home, he wants peace and quiet. He's not a big communicator. It took me a long time to accept that this was not a sign of rejection by him, but, rather, that he doesn't really connect to people all that much. That's just the way he is. I accept him, but I do feel very lonely.

> ❦ Thankfully, my husband is the type who loves children of any age. He loves nothing better than to come home and play with the kids, read to them, bathe them or whatever needs to be done. All day I look forward to when he'll come home. My problem is during the day when I feel so locked into this tiny apartment. Just getting down four flights of stairs and back up again is a major undertaking. Unfortunately, when he does come home, he is only there for a short time and has to run back to his studies. I'm proud that he is studying in a kollel, but I wish we had more time to share.

> ❦ When I went to the hospital to give birth to my third, it was in the middle of the night. I didn't want my two other children to awaken in the morning and not find my husband there. So I took a cab alone and told him to get the kids off and come to the hospital in the morning. But things went quickly and I gave birth without him. It just wasn't the same, having the baby without him there. I still feel sad about not being together then. As time goes on, I see that there are many things I must endure alone. However, I do feel stronger and more competent now. A few years ago, I felt so weak and helpless in comparison to where I am now. Now, if I'm alone, I tell myself, "God is always with me. I am never really alone." Then I close my eyes, take a deep breath, and experience His presence.

The problem of isolation is most severe among young mothers of several small children. As the children get older, they become less physically draining and more intellectually challenging. You can have meaningful discussions about Torah, about feelings and concepts, their hopes, interests and fears. It is far easier to go away from them without fearing that they will be traumatized by your absence. In the meantime, you can only keep reminding yourself that the joy of creating a strong and healthy family unit becomes a worthwhile *trade-off*, a sacrifice you make for all that you are getting in return.

2. From Relative Control, Order and Predictability to Unpredictability and Disorder

One of the most predictable things about babies and children is their unpredictability. Although some babies have a set, orderly routine for eating and sleeping by six weeks, others may take six months to a year to have a reliable schedule. Even then, they may go off schedule when they are sick, teething, or upset about something. Toilet training may go smoothly for weeks and then the child will regress for some reason. They have periods when they eat heartily and other times when they hardly seem to eat at all. As they get older, you are faced with the unpredictability of their moods, crises, stages, and the violent impulses which they may exhibit when they are hungry, tired, frustrated or in pain. All human beings like to feel that they are in control of their lives. It gives them confidence and a feeling of power. With young children around, you will not always have that desire fulfilled.

> ✿   I never knew when my baby daughter would sleep for the first eight months of her life. I could put her down, thinking she was in a light trance and certain that she would wake up soon. So I would keep myself up, thinking that she would be up before long, and she would sleep for two or three hours. Yet, when I thought she was in a deep sleep and I would finally fall into bed exhausted, she would invariably wake up! Wow, was I frustrated and exhausted as well!

> ✿   In addition to the normal events, I have an allergic child who has many special needs. I need extra time to prepare his foods, take him to the doctor and make sure that he doesn't put any milk or wheat products into his mouth. Every day is packed with demands, crises and a need for me to be extremely vigilant.

> ✿   The chemistry between my two oldest boys has been explosive since the younger one was born. For two years, I never left them alone with each other for a second. I didn't leave the room without taking one of them with me. I'm still anxious about the two of them being together because they are so provocative and competitive. At times, I feel like I'm living in an emergency room atmosphere.

Adequacy is usually associated with control, and most of us feel inadequate when we do not feel fully in charge of our lives. Yet, being around children means that you will never have all the control you might want over them physically, emotionally or mentally because they are separate beings with needs and demands which often differ from your own. To some extent, you must break the connection between adequacy and total control, or you will end up feeling inadequate every time they misbehave or balk at cooperating with you.

If you have an excessive need for control over others, learn to let go a bit. If you are the opposite type, tending to be indulgent and undisciplined, force yourself to take charge and make the environment as orderly and as scheduled as possible so that you can meet your obligations and not have to function with a feeling of chaos. The most important thing for you to control is your own negative thoughts and harmful impulses. A reasonable amount of external disorder can be tolerated in order to keep the atmosphere humane. However, if you step over that thin boundary between reasonable disorder and unacceptable chaos, you will find yourself feeling more tense and overwhelmed. Do what you can to be disciplined, but retain your flexibility and tolerance.

3. From Predominantly Intellectual Pursuits to Hard Physical Labor

For at least twelve years of school, a young woman is praised for her intellectual accomplishments. Parents and teachers beam when she does well in school, and the pride she feels in her learning is a major source of pleasure to her. When children come along, there is a sudden switch as her life becomes full of messy diapers, food preparations and endless clean-ups. The transition from head to hands is harder for those women who have high academic aspirations, have delighted in intellectual stimulation in the past, and do not find much satisfaction in doing mundane, routine chores. They miss the challenge and excitement to which their brains were accustomed. Almost all mothers admit that they had no idea how little time they would have for themselves and how hard they would have to work once they became mothers, even those who had a great deal of experience and responsibility as baby sitters for their own younger brothers and sisters or other children.

> ♪ I don't mind the hard work. I'm a hard working person. What bothers me is the boredom of doing such menial tasks over and over and over again or getting interrupted time and again when I'm trying to finish one project and not having the satisfaction of ever feeling that I've completed anything.

❀   It hits me most on the holidays, especially the fast-days. As a
teenager, I would spend all day in *shul* praying. I used to feel so spiritual
after these times. Now, I just don't have time to do the studying I want.
It's like I'm on a merry-go-round and can never get off because I have to
stay on top of things, like the floors and the laundry and shopping. I
don't have time for my inner world because my outer world is always
pulling on me. I finish one meal and think, "What will I cook for the
next?" There is always laundry and mending to be done, or things which
the children need. It is a real struggle not to lose touch with the part of
myself which used to love learning and to keep myself from turning into
a kind of blank, empty type who's only concerned with the most
mundane matters.

❀   I wish I could be learning more with my children or doing creative
activities which will teach them about the greatness of Torah and the
wonders of nature or just sitting and talking or reading to them. But
often I find myself swamped with endless messes and chores. I should
push myself more, but there are times when I feel that my brain has
turned to soggy noodles. I don't want to feel dull and dumb. But there is
really very little time for other things right now.

There is no question that most household chores are tedious,
mundane and boring. Doing dishes may not be nearly as satisfying
as the pride you felt when you learned something new or were
developing a talent. The desire for intellectual stimulation is a very
valid and important human need.

You need spiritual elevation as well. As a mother, that inspiration must come, to a large extent, from within yourself. You have
to be your own spiritual teacher throughout the day. Even while
doing the dishes, you can focus on ways to improve your own and
your children's *middoth*. You can also take advantage of excellent
cassette libraries which offer stimulating lectures which can accom-
pany you as you go about your household tasks. You need to keep
your mind honed by finding time to read, even if only for a few
minutes each day. Find at least one inspirational class a week
which you can go to so that you do not feel that you are stagnating
mentally or spiritually. Assert your right to have this need fulfilled,
for you will then be a happier mother.

Although many household chores could be done by a maid, it
takes intelligence to have the right attitude toward your work and
to coordinate your many jobs. You are not only a cook, laundress
and cleaning lady. Your primary role is as an educator, and this is
something which you can do throughout the day with your child.

As you go about your chores, you can talk to your children, sing to them, make some loving connection with them, talk Torah to them. Many of our great women role models brought their babies to the nearest *Baith Midrash* so that the beauty of Torah could permeate their children's spirits even before they knew how to talk. Your home is a miniature *Baith Hamikdosh*, a holy sanctuary. With this thought in mind, every act you do becomes elevated, no matter how trivial that act may be. This thought may seem laughable when you have umpteen loads of laundry to fold or a mountain of dishes to clean, yet the right attitude will keep you grateful and happy instead of bitter and resentful.

4. From Future Orientation to Day-To-Day Focus

Before having children, a woman focuses on achievements in school and on the excitement of an upcoming vacation, graduation, marriage or birth. There is always some dramatic event in the near future which holds the promise of a major life change, of heretofore hidden mysteries to be revealed, of wonderful surprises, and of dramas to be played out with oneself as the star. Nothing can compare to the thrill, glamor and excitement of being an engaged woman, then a bride, and finally awaiting the birth of a child. In comparison to those peak experiences, sitting at the park with other mothers, or cleaning yet another chicken for the holidays, may seem dull and unchallenging.

> When I was pregnant, I felt special, like a queen. This wonderful, mysterious miracle was unfolding inside of me. Everyone treated me as if I was so special. All my thinking was focused on my due date. I'd wake up in the morning thinking, "How many more weeks? How many more days? What will it be like — the birth, the baby, the hospital?" It was all so new and mysterious to me. I guess I got used to the excitement like a drug. Now I have to wean myself away from it and not feel bad about the days which stretch out, one after the other, with endless cooking, cleaning and routine chores to be accomplished. I have to make my child my most exciting and challenging project.

Most young women do not realize how much they have lived their lives in excited anticipation of earth-shaking changes. One major lesson which can be learned from this experience is how important it is to have goals to which one can look forward with excitement and enthusiasm. In Hebrew, the word *enthusiasm* comes from the word *flame*. Indeed, without this enthusiasm, life looks gray and dull. Yet with goals, the very same life is filled with excitement and promise. Your body comes alive. You awaken in the morning with a sense of purpose and drive. Once the goals of marriage and the first few births have been accomplished, a woman must focus more than ever on making moral and spiritual excellence a primary goal. Self-improvement may not seem as dramatic a goal as marriage, but it can provide the daily challenges which give every minute a heightened importance.

Motherhood is a profession. It requires expertise in child development, nutrition, basic medical care and many other areas to cope properly with your family's needs. Think of ways to develop yourself, your mind and your skills. You can also learn and perfect your creative talents for various crafts. Think of the things that used to make you happy and used to fill you with enthusiasm. Find out how you can bring those things into your life now. Don't lose your sense of joy. There is always so much to be accomplished, both internally and externally.

5. From Dependency on External Rewards to the Need for Internal Endorsements

Before you had children, you got some acknowledgment for working on a term paper, doing the dishes or babysitting — a mark, praise, money or at least a word of thanks. As a mother, however, you work harder than you have ever worked before and with greater *mesiruth nefesh*. But now there is often no one to notice, let alone praise you for your efforts. No one praises a mother for changing diapers, cleaning floors, putting the laundry away or getting up twenty times a night with a sick child. There is no paycheck or public acknowledgment. Because a mother usually lacks tangible rewards, she may feel unappreciated, even bitter. The fact that others do not notice her efforts or praise her work may make her think that they do not value what she is doing or that they take her for granted. As a result, she may not value her efforts either. She may have the erroneous opinion that only her husband is doing really important work, or that only women who work outside the home or make a name for themselves in public are deserving of special acknowledgment.

It is sometimes difficult for a woman to wean herself away from the childhood pattern of being dependent on other people's approval or of the very common human desire for recognition. Yet she must learn to be satisfied mainly with the internal endorsements she must give herself as the most important form of recognition, knowing that Hashem takes heed of all her acts, even if no one else does! She may still look to others, such as parents, in-laws, her husband and children, for assurance that she is appreciated, but she should see these external endorsements as a nice extra and not rely on them to give her a sense of self-respect. That is something which must come from within.

    ‣ My husband does not realize how important his words of encouragement and praise are to me. I keep telling him how our Sages counseled husbands to praise their wives and gladden their wives' hearts because women are often so overwhelmed with worries over health, education and finances. But my husband usually forgets. I realize that he has difficulty expressing his love to me verbally. He thinks that I should know that he loves me and that he appreciates me without him having to tell me. But I want to hear the words.

    ‣ I'd like to hear some positive words from my mother and mother-in-law about how I'm doing. But all I get is advice, which often implies that I'm not doing very well at all in their opinion. One particular relative is not a feeling-type person. She thinks that a good mother is one who has a clean house and clean children and no more. I'll never live up to what she wants me to be. I wish people who gave advice would first ask me if I want it! They don't realize that advice can be a very subtle form of criticism.

    ‣ One morning, I took all the kids to the zoo and back on the bus. I was so exhausted when I came home that all I wanted to do was sleep. But I couldn't because the baby napped at the zoo and was ready for action. So I stayed up all afternoon, cooked and cleaned and kept the kids occupied so that they wouldn't make noise and disturb the neighbors during "the quiet hours." Then my husband came home and was upset that I had forgotten to go to the bank. I was ready to explode. Instead, I read off my endorsement list of all I had accomplished that day. My kids were laughing, and so did my husband in the end. Even if no one else endorses my efforts, I'm going to do it out loud if I have to! It always adds a little humor to our lives as well.

As a mother, you no longer look for prizes, gold stars or other material manifestations of appreciation. You look for rewards of a higher level: the smiles, hugs and looks of love and signs of growth in *middoth* and understanding in yourself and your children. Most of all, you are aware that the sanctity of the Jewish people is in your hands because the family unit is the cornerstone of our religion. This is our supreme task — the one which is our greatest reward in and of itself. The greatness of mothers is precisely that they do the majority of their acts of self-sacrifice in private, with no expectation of external acknowledgment.

6. From Nurturee (Taker) to Nurturer (Giver)

From the time you were a young child, you were the constant center of attention from yourself, if not your parents, peers, and teachers as well. You thought about your skin, your figure, your hair, clothes, marks and plans for the future. Now the tables are turned. You are the one who has to think of others' needs most of the time. You are the one to whom others turn for guidance, reassurance, advice, as well as physical necessities. You have to be there, in sickness and in health.

> I come from a large family and, as one of the oldest, had a great deal of responsibility. But my mother also wanted me to have a childhood and did not want to burden me too much. I remember that even if I had some important chore to do, if I had a bad stomachache or an important test to study for, she would usually let me off the hook. I never felt that I had to shoulder the responsibilities all by myself. Now it is different. There's no one to turn to but me. It is truly awesome.

> I was spoiled as a child. Mom was always there. She did all the cooking and cleaning. Even made my bed. I'm just not used to working or giving so much. I come home and expect the house to be cleaned and the meals made. Then I remember that I'm the one who has to do it! Now I have to work hard no matter how I feel.

> We had invited some very stimulating guests over. I wanted to sit and listen to the conversation, but I had to be up serving and taking care of the children. I was jealous that they could sit and enjoy the meal while I was running around barely being noticed by anyone. Only now can I appreciate all my mother's efforts, all the giving that she did for us!

> When I haven't slept well, or am sick, I get scared about the fact that I have no one to turn to for help or to get the meals on the table. Part of me feels that I myself am still a child who was having fun playing house but who suddenly has been given more responsibilities than I can handle. My husband works long hours during the day and then studies

at night. There's just so much time he can take off. The fact is that all these responsibilities are on my shoulders. It is a great strain at times. But it is hard to explain this to my husband. I think maybe he's afraid that if I let go for a minute, I'll never get myself back together again. But the fact is that then I could be more of an adult, knowing that he is there to turn to.

While no mother should deliberately work herself into a state of exhaustion or allow herself to become a doormat, she should strive to emulate the ways of the saintly,

> ... *whose giving is maximal and their taking minimal. Even the little they take is essential for them, since it enables them to maintain the giving .... Selfishness ... is the root of all the evils of the world.*
> (STRIVE FOR TRUTH!, vol. I, pp. 120-23)

It is in giving that we best emulate God. It is in giving that we receive the most. Who but a mother has as many opportunities to express this Divine attribute! At the same time, she should also give others the opportunity to demonstrate the same to her. Remember, the Talmud stresses the importance of not only studying Torah but also doing acts of kindness (*Yevamoth* 105a and 109b).

7. From Private Efforts to Public Performance

During the years before motherhood, a girl and young woman can keep her failures relatively private. Few people know of the arguments she has with her parents or the grades she receives in class. But as a mother, her deficiencies all seem to be displayed in public. There is no place to hide from the shame of a child who throws a tantrum in the supermarket or bites another child at nursery school. And when "Mrs. Perfect" walks in and sees pretzels and toys strewn all over the floor, there is no one else to blame as she lamely tries to make apologies for the lack of order. Teachers may call her in for conferences and complain about this or that deficiency in her child. Neighbors may complain about a child who hits another or isn't sharing his toys. Your parents or in-laws may keep harping on the fact that this one isn't yet trained or that one is overweight or another is withdrawn or unruly. You are subjected to grimaces, advice and criticism.

⚘ It started when I couldn't nurse the baby in the hospital. Everybody kept giving me advice, like there was something wrong with me. I felt like I was already a failure as a mother so soon!

⚘ I dread going to the doctor for fear that he'll give me one of his looks when he notes that my daughter's weight still isn't up to what it should be for a child her age. People always give you these looks as if to say that you are a failure because the child is skinny or fat or has a runny nose or is crying or isn't turning over when he is supposed to, or, when he gets to school, is not at the top of his class.

⚘ When I bring my daughter late to kindergarten, I can feel the judgmental eyes on me as if they're thinking, "Oh yes, that's the mother who can't get it together to get her child here on time."

⚘ As a divorced mother, I am often a target for people's criticism. My children have behavioral problems in school. They suffered greatly from the terrible tension which I could not avoid before and after the divorce. When I go to a school conference, my heart pounds with feelings of anxiety and shame. I try not to look as distraught and incompetent as I feel. I just can't give my children what I don't have, and I don't have the time or money to sit with each one for one or two hours each day or pay for tutors.

Young people in their twenties and thirties are usually very absorbed in proving themselves to each other and the outside world. The young mother wants to prove that she is at least as good, if not better, than her own mother and to show herself and her peers that she is a capable mother and homemaker. Unfortunately, many women try too hard to please that insatiable inner tyrant called success. That tyrant can never be fully satisfied. The constant, competitive pressure to prove that, "My kitchen is the cleanest/my children are the smartest/my home is the nicest," makes the entire family anxious and tense because perfection is an unattainable goal. Nothing we attempt is ever without error, especially child-rearing and homemaking. No home is perfectly spotless. No child can measure up to a parent's perfectionist standards. The tension of not living up to your own or other people's goals can have a paralyzing effect on one's ability to learn, love or function to the best of one's capacity. The passion for perfection is built on a false dream and a childish hope that one must be totally perfect and successful in whatever one endeavors in order to be deserving of love and respect. This false notion must be eliminated.

When you stop trying to prove your worth by performing for

others, you function with greater ease and efficiency and are less touchy about others' disapproval. You will be more loving toward others when the fierce competitive struggle for that false sense of superiority no longer consumes you. Leave your judgments of inferiority or superiority up to God, not man.

> *True honor is possessing intrinsic worth. The less confidence one has in one's own true value, the more one needs the consolation of other people's approval. Yet if one does not have it [a feeling of intrinsic worth] then [other people's opinions will not help].*
>
> (STRIVE FOR TRUTH!, vol.II, p. 12)

8. From an Idealized Version of Motherhood to a Realistic One

Most young women have an idealized vision of how they are going to be as mothers. They expect that they will not have the problems and conflicts with their own children that they had with their mothers. They expect that they are going to be at least as competent as their mothers, if not more so. Usually, they imagine that they will be superior. Then the reality hits.

> ❦ I didn't realize things would be so hard. I didn't think I'd have so many sleepless nights and so many conflicts about what to do, like when to give in to the kids or when to be strict, when to shrug off an illness as minor and when to go to the doctor, or when to interfere and when to let them work things out on their own. I thought I knew all the answers and that I would cope so easily, quickly and efficiently with whatever problems arose. Boy, was I wrong! Only now do I understand what my own mother went through!

> ❦ I thought that I would always have everything in order, unlike when I was a child and felt too ashamed to bring friends over because the house was such a mess. I thought I'd never get hysterical or impatient. I thought I would be in full control all the time. It's not so easy.

> ❦ I thought that parenting came naturally. I didn't realize how much knowledge, creativity, stamina, patience and wisdom it takes to be a good parent.

> ❦ I never thought that my relationship with my husband would go through such drastic changes after motherhood. I thought we would be closer than ever before and be able to maintain that wonderful, thrilling feeling we had when I was pregnant with my first, and that it would last

forever. Then came the baby and I was so absorbed in her that my husband felt left out, I suppose. Or maybe he just went through the natural process of becoming more and more absorbed in his studies. The more needy and tired I became, the more he stayed away. I had felt so good when I was pregnant. Afterwards, I was more demanding and was depressed for a period. I hadn't expected that that would happen.

You expected motherhood to bring you honor, stability, love, freedom, joy and maturity. You do get a lot of that. What you didn't bargain for was boredom, conflict, crises, depression and fury. Thankfully, these moments are counterbalanced by the many satisfactions which we also experience: the delight in our children's eyes as they help us prepare for a holiday or watch us light Shabbath candles; the pleasure of seeing them cooperate together and help each other; the miracle of touch as they reach out to us for warmth, reassurance and love; the joy of seeing them grow into responsible, caring people. The reality is that there are both ups and downs and that we must learn to ride the waves of both.

9. From Submissiveness to Assertiveness

The feminine ideals which most girls are encouraged to develop during their formative years include such traits as flexibility, nurturance, submissiveness, selflessness, compliance and gentleness. Girls are praised for being self-sacrificing and carrying out other people's orders. Others are in positions of power and the display of dominance is very much frowned upon. Boys, on the other hand, are socialized to be independent, forceful and authoritative. Yet a mother must have these qualities as well, as she must often be unyielding and tough. She must be an assertive defender, protector and disciplinarian. This transition is a difficult one for many mothers. It is particularly problematic if the wife is expected to be very submissive to her husband and then must switch to be assertive with her children.

     Disciplining my children is the hardest part of parenting for me. I don't know how to be firm without being hostile at the same time. Either I come down on them like a ton of bricks or give in meekly to their demands. I often feel helpless in the face of their tricks and aggressive demands. They just don't listen to me like they listen to my husband, and they listen to me even less when he's around! I don't seem to have the voice, the self-assurance or the whatever it is that he has. This is one thing you can't fake. They know if you have it or you don't.

  It's precisely when the kids are most in need of control that I'm most tired or spaced out. If I've been up since 5 or 6 A.M., I'm wiped out by dinner time when they are the most rowdy. That's also when the baby is most cranky. I just can't divide myself into seven pieces. I have to force myself to be authoritative or everything goes to pieces.

  All the books tell me that I must be loving but tough, be consistent yet flexible. People tell me that I have to make firm rules and stick to them. But the truth is that I don't know how to structure a home, don't know which rules to be firm about and which ones to give in on. I don't know how often to bathe them or when, what is the best time for them to go to sleep, or how much to demand of them and at what ages to make changes in those demands or expectations. Some mothers seem so self-assured and decisive. But I seem to have a different nature and am full of doubts and confusion. I hope I improve as my children get older!

Wishy-washy orders, hysteria, begging and hysterics are marks of weakness. You can know this intellectually, yet not know how to go about making the necessary changes in your approach to proper discipline. You are growing and changing along with your children. Patiently allow these changes to come about as you work on disciplining with strength, conviction and love. This is certainly the most difficult aspect of motherhood.

10. From Carefree Spontaneity to Vigilant Seriousness

Before children, when you wanted to go, you went. When you felt like eating, you ate. When you felt like sleeping, you could usually sleep for as long as you wanted and without worrying about what was happening in the outside world while you slept. Now things have changed. You have to stay unselfishly vigilant because caring for small children is often a life-and-death matter. And this demand usually takes place around the age of twenty, precisely when a woman is just emerging from the period of greatest self-preoccupation and self-centeredness.

  When I was first married, my husband and I would often just spontaneously go visiting or go for a walk. Now, these things have to be planned. As each new child came along, we had less and less time for each other. We were growing apart, like strangers. When I mentioned this to a friend, she suggested we go away for a day together. At first, I couldn't imagine how I could possibly make all the necessary arrangements or ask friends to help me for what seemed like a luxury. But it wasn't a luxury. It was the best thing I could have done for our marriage and, as a result, for our children as well. I needed to get away from the seriousness of being with the children, my preoccupation with household chores and the tension of just being at home all the time.

   🏵   I taught school and lived with two other girls before I was married. It was a very carefree time. I felt so independent and capable. Now, with three small ones, I feel so dependent on my husband for help and companionship. It gives me tremendous joy to be a mother. But I am also much more serious than I was and much more in need of others.

   🏵   There's always so much to do! I found that I was neglecting my older children because of the immediacy of the younger one's demands. I realized that I did not know what was going on in their lives. So I had to schedule times to be with them, to develop a relationship. Planning had never been a strong point with me, but I now force myself to make appointments to be with each child alone for even a few minutes each week. We play checkers or just talk. It's important for both of us.

   🏵   My mother always used to tell me that nothing could keep me home for long. As a teenager, I was always on the go. But that was before I had twins! Before they came along, when my kids were bored, we'd just get out, even if it was only to the supermarket to go up and down the aisles comparing prices and talking about the different foods. But now with very active nine-month-old twins, I just can't take my brood out like I used to. I think that some women are better able to "contract themselves" into a home-bound environment while more expansive types have more difficulty. It's a matter of nature.

Transitional Coping Tools

Although there are no quick solutions to the foregoing transitions, the following attitudes will increase your feeling of competence and confidence:

* Develop a relationship with God. Pray. Talk to God. In Hebrew, the word *faith* is *emunah*, which comes from the root, *to practice.* Indeed, faith is something which we must constantly practice. Don't put yourself down for not always having 100 percent unquestioning faith. At times, you will doubt and fear. Use these moments of apparent distance to become even closer to our greatest Source of Strength.

* Do things that make you happy. Motherhood requires self-sacrifice, not self-destruction! Don't forget about your own emotional and intellectual fulfillment. Do take classes and keep your friendships, as well as making time for the development of talents.

* Keep things orderly enough for peace of mind, but not so orderly that you lose it! The sparkle in your child's eyes is worth more than the sparkle on the windows. No one feels comfortable in a sterile house, nor in one which is chaotic. Find a healthy balance, but don't worry if you lose it once in a while. It is easy to become petty-minded, focusing on the sink and the floors instead of on your priority, which is loving-kindness (especially if you have very critical, fastidious relatives!).

* Learn from other women, but don't compare or compete. Each mother has her own talents, skills, experiences and physical stamina.

* Don't be ashamed to get help. It is a sign of good mental health to know your limits and to care enough about yourself, your marriage and your children to seek help if you feel weak and overwhelmed, or you find yourself getting hysterical and hostile toward those you love most for an extended period of time.

* Be patient with yourself. Patience is one of the foremost signs of true spirituality and good mental health.

* Be continuously grateful for your children. Gratitude is the source of joy. There is only one thing worse than having children who make a lot of noise, demands and dirt, and that's not having children to bring all that commotion and joy into your life. Yet gratefulness is a difficult *middah*, for it is the nature of man to be dissatisfied with what he has: "He who has one hundred wants two hundred" (*Koheleth Raba*, 1:34). Gratefulness is a habit which needs to be cultivated.

The difference between a resentful mother and a happy one is mainly in her feeling of gratitude. The word *Yehudi* (Jew) comes from the root, *to give thanks*. This is the source of our strength as a people. However, overcoming our natural selfishness and self-preoccupation takes time. By cultivating a spirit of gratefulness throughout the day, both in happy times and stressful ones, we are far better able to cope with the frustrations and disappointments and maintain a loving spirit. This is a discipline which requires lifelong effort.

>   When I first became a mother, I wondered how I would be able to use my musical talents, considering the many demands on my time and energy. I wondered if I would feel resentful at not having time to practice and develop my talents. It did take a while to make the adjustment. I now see my creative impulse expressing itself through my children. It takes tremendous effort to react creatively with them. My degree in Early Childhood Education had made me aware of the tremendous importance of my being there during their formative years. When I sit at the piano and sing songs with them, I feel great. I have traded one joy for another.

A Major Coping Tool: Joy

Through joy and humor man can make the transition from smallness to greatness. One can then study and attach himself to God.

(BEN PORATH YOSEF, 49b)

The great master, Rav, would engage his students in humorous talk before serious study, saying that humor opened the mind and helped them to learn with great ease (*Pesachim* 117a). How true this is! With humor we can jump from petty concerns over insignificant matters and gloomy self-preoccupation to greater clarity of vision and rationality. One of the foremost signs of good mental health is a sense of humor, something which can easily be lost when you are sleep-deprived or inundated with tedious, mundane chores. Obviously, you could not be expected to have a sense of humor about matters which involve danger or which others are taking seriously. However, as long as there is no real and present danger to your own or your family's mental or physical well-being at the moment, strive to elevate yourself throughout the day with cheerful thoughts and plans which will bring joy to yourself and your family members. Think of *simcha* as your best friend. Your children will feel loved by you if they see that you are happy to be with them and happy with your life. Love and joy are strongly related. Therefore, cultivate this *middah* throughout the day.

> *The divine Presence comes to rest upon one only through his rejoicing in a mitzvah.*

(SHABBATH 30b)

Find ways to make "smile time." Your children may not

remember this morning's breakfast, but they will remember that you laughed together. Furthermore, there is an "inner child" within us all which needs to play at times. Make time for zoos, museums and parks. Let them enjoy Jewish singers with their own Fisher-Price tape recorder, which is almost child-resistant. Have a dress-up box for rainy days or those long three-day holidays when they can put on plays illustrating stories from the lives of our Sages. *Olomeinu* magazine and *The Jewish Press* are excellent sources for inspiring stories.

It is also important to have equipment available so that they can have a positive outlet for their pent-up physical energies. A mini-trampoline, measuring about three feet around, is a great favorite. Keep a supply of boards and nails for them to hammer, as well as craft material, such as clay and paints. Children also love playing games such as checkers and other board games.

Teach them to find humor in non-dangerous situations. Laughter is the greatest stress reducer. [Of course, you should teach your children not to laugh at other people's pains or to make light of truly serious situations.]

Maintain Self-Esteem with Self-Endorsements

The smallest victory that you win over [the yetzer hara] regard as important that it may be a step to a greater victory.
(DUTIES OF THE HEART, p.23)

Another essential coping tool is endorsements. An endorsement is a kind of mental pat on the back for all those victories which you win each day over the temptation to be mean, selfish, lazy or hostile. Few will notice, much less reward, your most heroic efforts to provide love, safety, stability, order, cleanliness and food to your family. You will give up your sleep, your quiet time and your energy to them. You will serve them when your legs ache and your back hurts, when you are fasting and weak, when you are upset and discouraged, as well as when you are healthy and happy. To avoid feeling bitter and angry over the lack of acknowledgment and appreciation, get in the habit of giving yourself endorsements throughout the day. If you are going through a particularly difficult time, it is enormously helpful to actually jot down in a notebook the various things which you did throughout the day which manifested positive *middoth*. You can wear a pretty pendant or other piece of jewelry to remind yourself to keep your spirits lifted with these endorsements. Right now practice looking at your ring or your watch or something else which you normally wear and think, "I endorse myself for . . ." Make a conscious effort to do this throughout the day for the next two days and soon it will become a natural part of your life to have positive thoughts about yourself. In this way, you will habituate yourself to have positive thoughts about your children and all others.

The more you learn to endorse yourself, the less dependent you will be on those around you for praise. After all, we are not in this world to be honored, appreciated, understood or made comfortable. It is nice when we get these extras, but they are not the essence of our existence. Our major purpose in life is to serve God by taking care of our family members in a manner befitting His most beloved of all creations. To do so takes great self-discipline and constant work on our *middoth*. Every act of self-restraint increases our inner strengths.

Like any discipline, the art of endorsement must be practiced hundreds and thousands of times in order to become a part of your very nature. Remember, you do not give yourself endorsements in order to become arrogant, but in order to maintain your feeling of self-esteem which, in turn, helps you to become more tolerant and loving of your children. There is **always** something for which you can endorse. This is something you can do at any time of the day or night instead of doing the opposite, such as prognosticating fearfully into the future or going through your list of hurts and complaints! The rest of this chapter is devoted to explaining four kinds of endorsements.

1. Endorse for Bearing Discomfort

In an age in which comfort and convenience are glorified by many, we must remember the importance of learning how to bear discomfort and even affliction without losing our *emunah* and *bitachon*. Hardship builds strength of character and self-confidence if you face obstacles with faith and courage. Show your children how you bear discomfort without excessive complaining by adopting a positive attitude toward aches and pains, disappointments, disorder and distress.

❀ I must have very intelligent children because they are very active and curious! When I'm in the midst of one of those "emergency room moments." as I call them. I tell them out loud that I'm endorsing myself for bearing discomfort with a positive attitude and that they can all endorse for something out loud too. We focus on how we are building inner strengths by learning from life's disappointments and difficulties instead of grumbling about them.

2. Endorse for Effort, Not Success

Doing is the chief thing.

(AVOTH 1:17)

Motherhood would be a lot easier if we were all omniscient, omnipotent and omnipresent! But we are not. We are human and, therefore, imperfect. Instead of bemoaning our failures, whether they happen to be in what we cook or how we act, we can endorse for our efforts to live our lives in a Torah-true manner, even though we do not always succeed. We will have minor accidents, be forgetful, make meals which no one likes, sew outfits which don't fit, say the wrong thing, and be insensitive at times. All we can do is try our best. No one can achieve 100 percent success all the time. When we don't. we can endorse for our efforts.

3. Endorse for Avoiding the Four Cs

At any time, endorse yourself for avoiding condemnations, criticism, complaints and comparisons. If such "toxic language" pops into your head, then endorse for not using it out loud and for diverting your attention to constructive endeavors and thoughts. Endorse for disciplining your mind. If you are the type who thinks you are about to have a nervous breakdown any minute, then endorse for thinking to yourself, "As time goes on, I will gain in inner strengths and endurance." If you are the type who tends to brood endlessly over other people's shortcomings or their lack of respect and appreciation for you, endorse for forgiveness, compassion and tolerance.

4. Endorse for Small Gains

You can endorse for the small gains you achieve in becoming more aware and self-disciplined. Character development is not a dramatic one-time event, but rather a series of minor changes. If you are busy endorsing, you can't be blaming and condemning yourself for not having reached perfection. Each and every positive act will bring you closer to your goal of becoming more calm, loving and confident. Even if you don't feel that way at the moment, you can *wear the mask* of whatever state you wish you were able to achieve, even though you have not yet done so in reality, such as the mask of love or calm confidence. It is also important to add some positive muscular act, such as smiling or moving energetically, in order to convince your mind of your desire for greater mastery.

Minds are shaped by deeds.

(SEFER HACHINUCH, precept 16)

What this means is that any positive act, no matter how forced or insincere, can overcome the negativity in your mind, if only for a short time.

> ⚘   My dentist said that the bottles of apple juice to which my two year old is so attached have been causing widespread decay. I had to hold her in the chair while he worked on her because she was so upset. I wanted to be with her while the dentist worked on her, so I pretended not to be bothered by her cries so that he would let me stay. At first, I was shaking inside because she was so distressed. But as I pretended to be calm, I actually did feel better.

> ⚘   I've done a lot of favors for a neighbor because she has no car and I do. Yet when I asked her to watch my two young ones for a short while this morning, she said she couldn't do it, without giving what I felt was a valid reason. I turned away angrily at first, but then endorsed myself for giving her the benefit of the doubt and for thinking of mitigating circumstances in order to forgive her.

> ⚘   My doctor told me that I have to stop drinking caffeine because it is making me nervous and interfering with digestion. I have to endorse every time I want so much to reach for a cup of coffee but take something more nutritious instead. I had to endorse myself those first few days as I went through withdrawal symptoms and got myself used to more nutritious food.

> ⚘   I wanted to scream at my two oldest children because it was late and they still weren't in bed. It took a supreme effort on my part to tell them that as soon as they were in bed, I would sit with each one for five minutes and talk about the day's events. All I really wanted to do was to

be alone. But I wore the mask of love just to keep myself from going to pieces. It worked! I did feel more loving toward them once the lights were off and I relaxed as I sat by their bedsides and talked to them. I thought I was at the end of my rope, but I found that there are always a few inches that I didn't know about.

You will find that when you endorse yourself, your children will too:

    ☘   I was very upset at my husband about something and ran into the bedroom, slamming the door and locking it behind me. I was sitting there fuming and crying. Suddenly, from underneath the door, came a note written by my daughter in her newly learned, first-grade handwriting. On it was written, "Endorse yourself, Mommy. I love you." It was like a burst of sunshine in the darkness to see that note. I pulled myself together and thought about all the things which were positive in myself and my life, and I was then able to deal with the problem calmly.

THREE

Tactics to Gain Cooperation

We are obligated to teach our children good character traits. This is an awesome responsibility, especially since we ourselves are not always shining examples of these traits!

Mom, the Doctor

A mother must be like a doctor, seeing defects and providing the right medicine. Yet, just as a doctor must often guess at the diagnosis, so must you. A child's mind is complex. There may be a dozen different reasons why he is bed-wetting, withdrawn, hostile or doing poorly in school, etc. Furthermore, even the finest doctor is not allowed to operate on his own children because his emotional involvement may affect his mental clarity. That is why a teacher or neighbor may have more objectivity than you do about your children's problems or how to manage them. Do not expect to always have calm objectivity. This is especially true when you are deprived of sleep, ill or dealing with seventeen minor crises at the same time!

The following chapter will help you to build a "pharmacy" of remedies to treat many of your children's problems. Add to it as time goes on. The greater your understanding and the more tactics you have acquired, the more constructive you will be.

When you see a problem, you have three choices, any of which are manifestations of love if done with the proper motivation and in consideration of the child's needs:

1. Detachment (33% of the time): You take a "wait and see" attitude, or ignore the problem, knowing that it is insignificant and will fade faster if you pay no attention to it. This is good for minor squabbles, temporary bad moods, and minor aches and pains. (Note: the dysfunctional pattern is to go to the extreme and be emotionally cold all or most of the time.)

2. A Show of Affection - "TLC" (33% of the time): The child is in distress. You may not even know what is wrong, but you do know that he needs your reassurance and perhaps physical touch. Whether you are dealing with a collicky baby or an older child who is having trouble in school or with his peers, or a child who is merely upset, you reassure him that you care with a hug or a few minutes of "holding time." You feel with him, share his pain, listen to him and show your concern. (Note: the dysfunctional pattern is to be overly anxious and indulgent all or most of the time.)

3. Loving toughness (33% of the time): You calmly but assertively enforce the need for strict obedience to rules, regulations and good manners. (Note: the dysfunctional pattern is to be dictatorial and cruel all or most of the time.)

Don't let anyone tell you what you should "always" do in a particular situation. There are no "alwayses" in child-rearing. For example, with a cranky child you might first try detachment, then move to TLC, then realize that he may be sick or is simply bored and needs a change of environment. No one thing will work all of the time.

Focus on Your Goal

Rabbi S. R. Hirsch defines holiness as the attainment of moral freedom (*Vayikra* 4:24).

> . . . *the whole purpose of your creation is just this, to eradicate [negative]* middoth *and evil dispositions and to change them for good ones. You are capable of doing so and obligated to do so, and no excuses will avail you. Granted it is not easy to go against one's nature, yet you certainly possess the power to prevail and fulfill your mission valiantly, since God does not act as a tyrant toward His creatures.*

(LEV ELIYAHU, p. 213)

No matter what you are doing or thinking or what is going on around you, your task is to work on your *middoth* and be an inspiration to others to work on theirs. Therefore, throughout the day, ask yourself, "Are my thoughts and my actions getting me closer to this goal?"

Kibud Av V'Ame: Teaching Children to Respect You

We have an obligation to teach our children to respect us.

Honor your father and your mother.
(SHEMOTH 20:12. DEVARIM 5:16)

Every man shall have awe of his mother and his father.
(VAYIKRA 19:13)

Ironically, one of the most important factors in helping your children learn to respect you is to give up the notion that you **need** their respect for your own personal sense of satisfaction or self-importance. You don't. A spiritually elevated person is supposed to flee from honor (*Avoth* 6:6). However, respect for you **is** a fundamental obligation and an essential need of your children, for **their** physical, mental, emotional and spiritual well-being. If you think you need their respect for your own sense of worth, then you put yourself in a position of dependency on them which will make you quite angry, if not furious when you don't get that respect. The result will be that you cannot properly teach them how to respect you because you are too enraged to think clearly! However, when you focus on your child's need to develop respect for his elders, and for you in particular, for *his* good, not yours, then you will be able to help him perform this mitzvah in the proper spirit of firm, but loving strictness.

A very young child has no concept of the profound meaning of respect as rooted in the appreciation for the essential dignity and Godliness of every human being, regardless of his status or shortcomings. When a child is frustrated, he naturally tends to turn against the target of his frustration, thinking that that person is hurting him deliberately or is inferior in some way. He then thinks that he has the right to treat that person with disrespect for being "bad." Therefore, great patience should be exercised during the early years, as you instill in him the awareness that all of Hashem's creations deserve respect, even if you do not like those creations at the moment.

All living things resist external threat. So, too, does a child. If you continually approach him with a threatening demeanor, he will adopt an oppositional pattern. This is normal and healthy. It shows evidence of a sense of integrity and selfhood. Therefore, parents are warned by our Sages not to be excessively harsh in demanding honor, as this constitutes " ... a stumbling block before the blind," *(Vayikra* 19:14), since the child will naturally be provoked to silent hostility or overt aggression in order to protect himself. Rather, the parent "should forgive ... and shut his eyes, for a father has a right to forego the honor due him" (*Yorah Daiah* 240:l9). Nevertheless, a parent must be strict about requiring respect, for this forms the foundation for the performance of all religious obligations. God accounts honor shown to parents as though it were shown to Himself (*Mechilta* on *Shemoth* 20:12, *Sifra* on *Vayikra* l9:3). Obviously, there is a great difference of opinion as to what constitutes excessive strictness. This is especially true in religious matters, where the tendency to be coercive is so strong. In these cases, it is wise to consult a kindhearted and experienced Rav who can help you differentiate between issues which call for firmness and those which require flexibility.

Honor for one's parents is considered the most difficult of all the mitzvoth in the Torah (*Yerushalmi Peah* 1:1). Consider how difficult it has been for you to fulfill this mitzvah in its entirety, to always speak in a pleasant voice to your own parents, to serve them cheerfully at all times, to run quickly to do their bidding and never to argue with or contradict them, to mention only a few of the obligations involved (*Sefer Haharedim, Yorah Daiah* 240:4, *Chayai Adam* 67:3). This should help you to be more patient and compassionate in training your children to have respect for you.

What you want to avoid is a vicious cycle in which mutual respect becomes impossible. This is what happens when you become hostile toward your child because of his misbehavior. Your hostility makes him feel that he is unloved. Since the love of a parent is the child's foremost emotional need, he reacts to being hurt by wanting to hurt you back, to test you, to see if you really do not love him. The only way for him to test your love is to misbehave and see if you will still love him anyway. However, if you again interpret his testing as a sign of having failed as a parent or as having a failure for a child, you will again become enraged, which makes him feel even more unloved. The vicious cycle is manifest in constant battles between the two of you. Once a child feels hated, you have lost your most powerful weapon in the development of a strong, internalized sense of ethics and morality. This is why this present chapter focuses on non-violent methods of winning cooperation in a manner which allows the child to retain his feeling of self-esteem and strengthens the love between you.

Do not assume that you have to be a model of perfection in order to be deserving of your child's respect. On the contrary! The fact that our children see our imperfections (often more clearly than we see them ourselves!) yet must respect us nevertheless, becomes the basis for his ability to be tolerant of and respectful toward all human beings, including those he may not like or agree with. The way of a *tzaddik* is to be unconcerned about one's own *kavod*, yet to be extremely scrupulous about preserving the *kavod* of others. This is the lesson you demonstrate as you patiently and respectfully teach your children the particulars of this mitzvah.

Realize that some children will have more difficulty with this mitzvah than others. For example, those with a strong drive for power, whether this comes from inner anxiety or an innately aggressive nature, may seem more oppositional and defiant because their very natures make it more difficult for them to accept external authority. If it is any consolation, you can read stories about the childhoods of many outstanding leaders and rabbis who were described by their parents as having been unusually headstrong and troublesome as children. Many young people who survived the Holocaust remember being told by their parents that they were difficult to handle as children. What may seem exasperating to you may be a sign of great character strength, leadership potential and perseverance. [If the opposition is extreme, and is combined with chronic unhappiness and cruelty, seek immediate help for the family.]

Do not automatically assume that your child is showing deliberate disrespect when he misbehaves. He may be so hungry, tired, or upset that he simply does not have control over his impulses at that moment. On the other hand, do not allow your compassion for him to keep you from being strict about the importance of respect.

When he has calmed down, discuss the event with him and ask him how he could have responded in a more respectful manner. Ask yourself, "I see that this child is in distress. How can I best help him to be more aware of his obligation to be respectful?"

If your child is unusually disrespectful, he might be feeling like a failure in school, in his peer relationships, or in your eyes. Find out if this is the case. Remember, children need to feel successful in what they are doing, both socially and academically, or they feel greatly distressed. Or, it may be that he feels you have been treating him in a disrespectful manner and that, therefore, you deserve the same in return. For example, you may have responded angrily when he asked for something to eat before going to sleep. You may have said with hostility, "Tough for you! You weren't here when I served dinner, so you can go to bed hungry. I don't care." He did not know how to tell you that his stomach is not on a schedule like yours or that he was so absorbed in what he was doing that he did not feel hungry before. He simply thinks you are being cruel for no reason. (What does he know of varicose veins and aching backs!) So, a few hours or days later, he gets the chance to hurt you back. Neither of you may make a connection between the two events, but it is there.

If he is continuously disrespectful, do some detective work. Look into your own actions. Certainly, if you do not feel like making him a meal, you can give him a light snack which does not take much work, just to demonstrate *chesed*. Or, you can explain to an older child that you cannot spend your whole day in the kitchen and that if he doesn't come when called, he can make his own meals and clean up after himself. All this can be done in a respectful tone of voice which will not arouse antagonism.

Remember, respect for ourselves and each other is our greatest protection against mental illness. Beneath anger is always pain. If you are not being respected, you are in pain. So is your child. Heal the relationship instead of getting angrier.

Obedience

Habituate [your child] early to obedience, to sacrifice his own satisfaction and enjoyment for something higher.

(HOREB, p. 412)

One aspect of honoring parents is obedience. Children need to learn obedience for two reasons. For one, their lives might depend on immediate obedience to a command such as, "Don't touch that," or "Stay on the curb!" Also, it is important for a child to feel that there is a strong guiding hand which will keep him from getting out of control. He needs that protective barrier provided by his fear of punishment as well as his love of you. Obedience to parents early in life becomes the foundation for the ability to be obedient to the will of God.

However, parents should realize that obedience is a skill which must be allowed to develop slowly. Parents can become very grim and so excessively demanding about this that the atmosphere in the home becomes joyless and tense. It is crucial that parents avoid unrealistic demands as they train their children in this mitzvah. Certainly, there are times when a child must carry out a parent's command immediately. However, there should be a balance between the use of commands and instances when explanations and praise can be used to gain cooperation. When the "joy level" goes down for an extended period of time, that is your cue that something is very wrong with your relationship.

The following section is not meant to make mothers feel guilt-ridden or inadequate if they don't use creative solutions all the time. Try the 50-50 approach. That is, 50 percent of the time, you will probably find yourself requiring instant obedience, such as: "Get those dirty clothes off the floor and into the hamper!" "Be quiet right this second!" "Right to bed and not another word!" The other 50 percent of the time, you can try a creative tactic. It doesn't have to be elaborate. For example, to a four year old, "It makes Hashem so happy when you say a *brachah*." Or, "If you hang up your coat without me telling you to, you get a point." These solutions create an atmosphere in which you encourage a child to obey because he loves you and wants to please you.

The life of an Orthodox Jew is governed by many rules and regulations. These give us dignity and strength. Fear of punishment is the lower level from which we obey these commandments. But the higher level is the level of love. We must strive to instill a desire for obedience more from love than fear, for when the coercive external pressures are absent, the fear may disappear, along with the desire to do what is right.

Achieving an Air of Authority

Both men and women need help in becoming assertive, men because they are often unnecessarily aggressive and women because they tend to fear the use of power and feel guilty afterwards. In order to be assertive without being hostile, you have to state your goals clearly and differentiate between aggression (which usually involves hostility and excessive force without regard for the needs and feelings of others) as opposed to assertion, which implies getting what is rightfully and realistically due you without crushing the other person's spirit in the process. Assertion avoids the polarities of dominance/submission or winner/loser implied in the aggressive power play.

One effective method of gaining cooperation is the "Broken Record." You simply tell the person over and over, very matter of factly but firmly, what you want. For example, "The dishes must be washed right now." If he balks, makes excuses ("I have no strength," is a popular one even though he may run out the door a minute later with a friend), or argues ("But I didn't make the mess," "But I did them last night," etc.), do not get locked into a power struggle. Simply repeat the message again calmly but firmly. "The dishes have to be done now." Or, "No sleep-overs on school nights." You might practice this exercise with store clerks. You say, "I want my money back," despite their protests that no one else had trouble with this item or that it is really quite satisfactory despite its performance in your home.

If you are a basically unassertive person, don't expect overnight changes. Also realize that you might go to the opposite extreme at times and become hostile and aggressive as you try to find the right balance. Take control wherever you feel it is possible, whether it is asking a child to hang up his coat or telling a critical person to stop inflicting this pain on others. Aggressive displays make you feel out of control and lower your self-esteem, whereas assertiveness promotes a feeling of control, thereby building self-respect.

Positive Motivators to Good Behavior

Your goal in motivating a child to do something, whether it is washing his hands before eating, saying his prayers, or keeping his belongings neat, is that he should eventually want to do these things of his own volition, because they are proper and right. The best way to do this is to associate responsible behavior with positive feelings.

You have the choice to motivate a child to behave properly with positive techniques or with negative ones. Negative ones include the threat of punishment, physical pain (slaps, pinches, beatings, etc.), or emotional anguish due to name-calling, criticism and other forms of rejection. Some children walk around with permanent black-and-blue marks on their bodies or their psyches from such treatment. True, you often get short-term cooperation quickly with these methods. However, the long-term effect of chronic negative conditioning is some degree of psychological dysfunction in the ability to love others and/or master essential skills in order to function effectively.

Your other choice is firmness with love. While force is often necessary with young children, you should be in control of yourself when using it.

An overly strict, exacting, short-tempered, impatient person cannot teach.

(AVOTH 2:6)

Your job is to teach your children good *middoth*, particularly self-mastery. You can hardly do that if you are screaming like a maniac! While anger is often an initial response to many of your children's acts, you can control the manifestation of that anger and work to change your attitude so that minor upsets no longer provoke a strong emotional response.

Those of an irate disposition, their life is not considered living.
(HILCHOTH DEOTH 2:3)

Life with an angry parent is a nightmare. The same is true of a man or woman whose spouse is short-tempered. The following section will help you maintain control, both internally and externally.

Make Good Behavior Rewarding

The various following techniques may seem contrived at first. You may think, "I don't have time for this nonsense!" "I'm not at all creative!" "I'll just end up hysterical anyway." "All they need is one good smack and they do what I want, so why bother with games?" In the long run, however, using positive associations will save you a great deal of work because the child integrates the desired behavior and it becomes part of his very nature. He will want to do the right thing on his own initiative, not because he is being forced by external pressures. Therefore, you will need less nagging and less arguing as the child cooperates willingly more and more often. No child rebels against something which brings him pleasure. Therefore, try to associate desired behavior with positive feelings or some pleasurable outcome. This is especially true when the issue concerns our beloved religious rituals and traditions.

>   We used to have terrible pre-Passover panics. But this last time, I sat down with my older children and we made lists of what each one needed to do. I promised them a night out at their favorite kosher pizza place if we finished everything on time and in a happy mood. It worked!

>   My three year old wouldn't let me brush his teeth. I decided I would show him who's the boss and held him down, closed his nose and brushed. However, the next few nights, he put up even more of a struggle, and I needed more force. The following day, I decided to change tactics. I let him choose his own good-tasting toothpaste and toothbrush all for himself. I let him squeeze the toothpaste on the brush himself when we got home. I drew a chart with a ladder. At the top was an ice cream. I told him that he could put a star on each of the rungs of the ladder. When he got to the top, I would get him an ice cream. He held the stars in his hand while I brushed. After that, he brushed willingly.

>   When I was a child, I was forced to practice piano from the age of six until I was sixteen. My first teacher used to hit my fingers with a wooden ruler when I made a mistake. I hated practicing and did so only because I was forced. After ten years, I was finally allowed to stop. Nevertheless, I always loved music and when my six year old expressed an interest in piano, I signed her up for three months of lessons. I also rented a piano instead of buying one so as not to have the pressure of forcing her to play against her will. When she started with her lessons, I was shocked to discover that I could not remember any of the musical notes. That made me realize that when children learn something against their will, especially if they feel unsuccessful, the learning does not become internalized. Therefore, with my daughter, I make the experience a pleasant one. I sit with her and give her a great deal of praise and show my joy in seeing her play. I give her a treat at the end of a practice session and put stickers on the pieces she has learned. If, at the end of a year, I see that she really dislikes playing, I will stop and perhaps start again when she is older or try another instrument if she wants. At least I have done my job in exposing her to one creative outlet.

No mother can be calm and creative 100 percent of the time. Nor can we expect that children will always feel happy about what they have to do. This would be unrealistic and not even advisable, for we all have to learn to do things we may not necessarily want to do, and do them without grumbling. Do not set yourself up for failure by thinking you always have to make tasks pleasant. Not only do you need time to develop creative skills, you also need the right environment in which to put them into practice, which you will not always have if you are under a great deal of stress. On the other hand, do not try to excuse yourself by thinking, "I'm too overwhelmed to find time to love my children or be creative." You can develop your creativity by using the chapter in this book on goal setting. And you can find a minute here and there to bring a positive attitude, humor, and loving concern into your relationships, even if those moments are not as often or as long as you would like.

Training Children for Sensitivity to Adults

Children often say and do things which are quite insensitive. There you are, climbing up the stairs with three heavy bags of groceries and a baby in your arms, and your three year old says, "Mommy, hold me." Or, you are sitting exhausted in a chair, hardly able to move, and your child says, "Teach me how to ride my bike." These are wonderful opportunities for you to teach him to look at people's faces and their body language for cues as to how others feel. Thus, you might say:

"Look at my hands. Am I capable of holding you right now?"
"Look at my face. Does it look to you like I want to get up right now, or do you think I need a few minutes to rest?"

Your children will not be sensitive to your needs, moods and feelings unless you train them to be. And you cannot do that if you are insensitive to them.

Self-Esteem Builders for Children

The way to educate youngsters is to elevate them by pointing out the greatness that can be theirs if they utilize their potential.

(OHR YECHEZKAIL p. 219)

Self-esteem is the basis for good mental health. It requires an interplay between input from you and others in his environment and output from him, in terms of demands for self-discipline and awareness. For example, you have a responsibility to give him food. He then has a responsibility to bless God for the food, thank you for preparing it, and to clean up after himself. You have a responsibility to show respect and sensitivity to him. He has a corresponding responsibility to do the same to you.

Children who feel good about themselves are generally a joy to be around. They usually behave well on their own, without having to be forced to do so by external authorities. Yet because of their small size, dependent position and lack of skills, children often feel helpless and, therefore, anxious. The more insecure they feel, the more likely they are to resort to non-constructive behavior in order to lessen their anxiety. You can do a great deal to build self-confidence and self-control in your child by looking for opportunities to make him feel better about himself. There is no more important work for you as a mother. For example:

1. Enjoy your children. Show them that you are happy to have them, that you are happy to have the opportunity to teach them and love them. Whether you are learning Torah, shopping with them, showing them the wonders of nature, baking a cake or hearing about what they have learned in school, show them that their presence gives you pleasure. Obviously, there is a certain percentage of time when this will not be so, as can be seen from many of the examples in this book. Accept that perhaps 10 or 20 percent of your mothering time will involve a certain degree of unhappiness and discomfort. However, the "total view" should be positive. If not, something is drastically wrong. When the "joy level" in your home goes down for any length of time, get help. Joy and love are evidences of good mental health. Your children will feel anxious and insecure if they feel that you are not happy with your life and will conclude that you are not happy with them. This means that you must avoid *downing* yourself throughout the day, which is a favorite harmful habit of many mothers.

2. Build your child's sense of his own inner strengths and wisdom. Doing too much for your child conveys a lack of trust in his own abilities. Therefore, when he has a problem, ask him for his own solution instead of jumping in quickly with your advice:

> "You're thirsty/bored/tired? What is your solution?"
> "He hit you? How do you think you could solve that problem in a civilized manner?"
> "Hm ... that's a problem. Close your eyes for a minute and I bet you can come up with a good answer."

Obviously, you should make sure that your child has the capacity to find his own answers. A three year old may not be able to think of what to do when he is bored. A five year old may not know how to make up with a friend. Also, be aware that sometimes a child does not want a solution. All he wants to do is have you share and validate his pain. Thus, when he tells you that he had a fight with a friend, he may only want you to say, "Oh, I'm sorry that that happened. You must feel very bad."

3. Give plenty of positive reinforcement. One research project found that the average parent says twenty-five negative statements to his child for every positive one! That is not a very constructive ratio! It is an all-too-human tendency to notice the negative. As children get older, your relationship with them can deteriorate into, "Do this," "Get me that!" "Stop doing that!" Therefore, make a concerted effort to do the opposite. Think of positive reinforcement as "soul food." This is spiritual nourishment for your child, as important to his mental health as food is to his physical well-being. Like food, you do not want to overdo it. However, get in the habit of mentioning the things your child does which please you so that he will not grow up emotionally malnourished. Look for endorsable behavior:

> "Chaim, thank you for talking to me in a grown-up voice and not whining."
> "Devorah, thank you for hanging up your coat when you came in. That showed that you are responsible and considerate."
> "Yosef, I appreciated it so much when you did your homework so diligently without my having to nag you. You concentrated really well."
> "Malka, you made a beautiful cake for the new neighbors. They were thrilled. That was a big mitzvah."
> "Moshe, you saved me a lot of problems when you let your brother have the window seat and didn't fight him over it."

"Ya'akov, I'm very proud of your patience and persistence in saving your money to buy that Lego set that you wanted."

"Sara, I want to thank you for being so sympathetic and helpful yesterday when I wasn't feeling well. You really came through for me."

"Yosef, I'm very proud of you for telling me the truth about being *fleishig* when I offered you some cream pie. It took a lot of inner strength to be honest."

Never seek to put your child down. Always look for ways to build him up. Give him *success experiences*. There are endless opportunities to praise your children throughout the day. They often come when you call, cooperate when you ask, are quiet at least part of the time when you are on the phone, remember to hang things up and are loving and helpful to each other at times. The more you do this for them, the more they will want to do this for you and each other as well.

> ☞ My seven year old helped his younger brother with a task, then ran to me and said, "See, Mom, I gave Eliahu a success experience."

Train yourself to look for the good. By mentioning them often, you give them and yourself as well constant reminders of the many good experiences which you have together. Put little "love notes" in your children's lunch bag. Tape one to the bathroom mirror so he sees it when he first gets up in the morning. Or, put one on his pillow at night. No doubt, you, too, will be rewarded with similar messages of appreciation which they will eventually write to you. Even if you do this only once every six months or once a year, it will be a memory your children will cherish all their lives.

One of the most effective of all techniques is to tape a piece of paper to the refrigerator and to jot down the positive things your children do during the week. Then read it off at the Shabbath table. The glow of joy on your children's faces will be your greatest reward. This is especially effective if you are having trouble with a particular child. Find something (anything!) positive which you can jot down, and then read it to him at night, when all is quiet and he can really appreciate what you have to say. It does not matter how small the act, even sitting quietly while eating, or remembering to close a door. The important thing is that you are forced to focus on what you like rather than what you dislike.

Writing down your words of appreciation is very powerful for children (and grown-ups as well, so don't forget your husband!). There is something about the written word that surpasses the verbal message. Perhaps it is the fact that you have taken the time to put your feelings into writing. Perhaps it is the fact that the person has the opportunity to savor the message alone, in private and to re-read it over and over. The fact that it is something tangible makes it special.

Written notes can also be used to establish or strengthen a habit. Even if you exaggerate a bit you might find that the child responds positively:

> ⊛ When my daughter has not been helping me as much as usual, I find that instead of telling her that she's lazy or inconsiderate, it is far more effective to compliment her on whatever help she has been giving me, even if it is minimal. Almost immediately, she becomes much more helpful.

If a child has done something which displeased you, a note might be more effective than a verbal rebuke, especially if combined with praise:

> ⊛ My son said something which hurt my feelings. Things were too hectic for me to discuss it properly at the time. He would only have been defensive and even more upset. But that night, I wrote him a note telling him that he had hurt my feelings by talking to me in that tone of voice. I told him that I loved and appreciated him and that I gave him the benefit of the doubt and assumed that he did not mean to hurt me deliberately. Then I mentioned my appreciation for his helping me that day by baby-sitting for his little brother and taking out the garbage. The next morning, he came to me and said how sorry he was that he had hurt me and he said he would be more respectful in the future. I accomplished a lot more with my note than with the harsh slap I had wanted to give him at the time.

My daughter, Dalya, at the age of eight, told me, "When you feel proud of yourself, it makes you feel strong inside. It makes you want to do what's right." She was very accurate!

4. Emphasize a special quality. In order to have a healthy sense of self-esteem, a child not only needs to feel loved. He also needs to feel that he is competent. Find something which your child is especially good at. A child who is at the top of his class or is the brightest and most capable in the family will automatically feel good about himself. But there is only so much room at the top, and the child who is not there may suffer from a paralyzing sense of failure. He may try to establish a "negative identity" because he feels that his older brother or sister, or the best child in the class has taken the positive identities. Therefore, he may become "The Whiner," "The Baby," or "The Bully." If you see this happening, look for ways to make your child feel special. He may be good at art, cooking, sewing, music or mechanics. He may be especially good in performing certain mitzvoth. Make sure that he knows that he has something important to offer the world.

> When I was a child, I had three older brothers and sisters and felt bad that I was so little and couldn't do the things that they did. I remember that my mother made me feel better by telling me that she needed my little hands to get into the places behind the stove which were hard to clean. Even that little praise made me feel proud of myself.

> I have a very handicapped child. The child closest to him in age was starting to have many psychosomatic complaints. Despite my very busy schedule, I decided to give that child organ lessons so that I could spend fifteen or twenty minutes a day with him alone, doing something which we both enjoyed. We purchased an inexpensive used organ and it made an enormous difference in that child's attitude. Plus, the music lightened up the atmosphere in the home considerably.

5. Program their minds positively. The child's mind is very much like a computer. You are the major "computer programmer" during their first few years. You watch carefully what you feed their bodies. You should be even more careful to make sure that you "feed" their minds positive images of themselves, marriage and people in general.

> When I was a child, my mother often told me that because I had such a good heart I would always make friends wherever I went. Then, when we had to move, I remembered her words , and to this day, I can remember that I was not as frightened as I might have been because I was so sure that I would have friends in my new school.

> I was a very unconfident child. I just didn't fit in. I was bright, but had few friends and was very nervous. When I was a teenager, I had a really wonderful rabbi for a class. One day, he called me to his office and he told me that he was very proud of my progress in class. Then he told me, "You're the type of person who can accomplish anything you want if you really put your mind to it." The words had an incredible effect on me. I remember many times when I was about to give up in discourage-

ment and then I would suddenly think of what he said, and would tell myself that if I really wanted to accomplish it, I could. From that moment, I could feel a positive change taking place in my attitude toward myself and others. I really did become more confident.

How different such "programming" is from that of those children who are labeled as stupid, unlucky, selfish, sloppy or problematic by parents or teachers who may not realize the long-lasting effect which these words have on a child. It is important to realize that a label like "bully," "nudnik," "slob" or "brat" often becomes a self-fulfilling prophecy from which a child feels he cannot escape. It is also a license to continue doing whatever it is which annoys you. Thus he thinks, "If this is what they think I am, then I guess that is the truth." He comes to think that he is his label.

At the same time, avoid using negative language about yourself. Don't go around saying that you are a "clumsy idiot," weak-willed or other names. Your children may fear that they cannot escape the same labels.

When you do notice negative traits in your children, don't dwell on how "awful" it is for them to be like this. Instead, create experiences which show them that they have the ability to change. For example, if a child has been having difficulty sharing, you might buy a very large bag of pretzels and then ask him to make up little bags to give to his friends. When he does so, praise him for his ability to share. The same is true if he is showing signs of sloppiness, defiance or other unwanted traits. Notice them, but do not make it worse by calling your child names or reinforcing the habit by constantly calling his attention to it. Instead, figure out a program to bring about change.

6. Make your children feel useful and important. Children love to feel important and grown-up. Self-esteem is strengthened when a child faces difficulties and overcomes them successfully. Whether it is a matter of learning *pisukim* by heart or helping a neighbor, your child feels important when he does important work and when he has to struggle to reach a little beyond what he thinks are his limits. He should know how to work hard for the sheer satisfaction of knowing that he is contributing to the family. He should be told, "This is **your** house too. You should want to see it looking nice and clean for **you,** not for me." Make sure that your demands are just a few inches above what he thinks he is capable of reaching. If your standards are too high, he will give up easily and feel like a failure. If your standards are too low, he will never experience the thrill of pushing himself to his limits and finding that those limits have expanded to bring him new strengths and awareness.

Involve your children in community *chesed* programs and projects to help Jews around the world. He might write to a child his age in Russia or in other ways show concern for those less fortunate than himself. Let him know that his contribution counts.

7. Touch, hold and hug your child. Touching your child is a means of showing that you care. You kiss your *mezuzah* and your *siddur* often to show your love of God. Your child needs the same message. In modern times, we have become out-of-touch with the importance of physical contact, as if such demonstrations of affection will spoil the child or make him dependent. A "touch-deprived" child is far more anxious and hostile than one who gets his own particular quota of "touch time." Obviously, you should not go overboard and push yourself on a child. But you should find ways to express the importance of physical affection.

A baby swing is an essential piece of equipment for newborns. Remember, your baby has been soothed by the gentle rocking of your body for nine months while you were pregnant. It was being "rocked" almost continuously *in utero*. A baby swing can provide an extra pair of hands for you while aiding in the development of the baby's neurological system, of which the brain is a part.

> ✍ I play "Hearts" with my little ones. I hug them tight so that we can feel each other's hearts beating. They always scamper off so happily afterward. Sometimes, while nursing my baby, my three year old will have such an unhappy look on his face. Then I tell him that we'll play "Hearts" as soon as I'm finished and that seems to lessen his jealousy. Even my five-year-old daughter will sometimes tell me that she wants to play Hearts. It's really just a long hug. But it seems to satisfy their need for touch.

8. Reassure your children of your love for them. This may sound silly and unnecessary to you if you think that they should automatically know how much you love them by all that you do for them. However, all human beings like to be reassured of the fact that others care for them. What is prayer but an expression of our love for God? Who needs that reminder? We do! The same with children. We need to remind ourselves, as well as them, of our love.

  For about five days in a row, I delighted my kids by saying to them, "I'm making this sandwich for you because I love you." "I'm *schlepping* this bike up the stairs for you for love." "I'm fixing your pants for love." "I'm helping you with your homework for love, etc." After a few days of this, when I asked them to cooperate with me and they balked, I would say, "Do it for love." My message really had a positive influence on them.

  When I light the Sabbath candles on Friday night, I light one for each child. I let them know that each one is a special light, special to me and special to the whole world.

9. Listen to your children. Make eye contact when they talk to you. Care about what they have to say. Take time to talk about the day's events. Listen. Be there for them. Enter their world by sharing their feelings.

10. Respect your child's individuality. It is important to respect your child's individuality and his developmental timetable as well as his particular strengths and limitations. Some children mature more slowly than others. Some children are intellectually oriented, others are more physical. Some children are bossy, others timid and unassertive. Some like to please while others are oppositional and independent. Some are placid and obedient and can sit for long hours without bothering anyone. Others are gregarious and lively, wanting a great deal of contact with others. Some are down-to-earth and practical while others are otherworldly and imaginative. These are God-given differences. Love your child for what he is, not for what you want him to be. Help him understand his own individual path in life and to see himself as not superior or inferior to those who are different from himself.

11. Help your child to save face. Children are easily shamed. Their egos cannot withstand a great deal of hostility from others. Therefore, when he does something wrong, help him to save face. Instead of accusing him angrily of being bad, stupid, clumsy or selfish, ask him questions which will promote greater awareness and sensitivity. For example:

"Is what you are doing right now a mitzvah?"
"Is what you are doing right now good or bad?"

If he has made a mistake, ask him, "What did you learn from that experience?"

📮 My seven year old took too many dishes off the table and they crashed to the floor. I was about to tell him, "I told you so!" and yell at him. But I could see from his face that he already felt so bad. I didn't need to make things worse. Instead, I asked him, "What did you learn from what just happened?" He said, "I should not carry more than I can handle." I hugged him and then we cleaned up the mess.

Your children should know that mistakes and messes call for solutions, not wholesale self-condemnations.

12. Help your child feel good about his body. Provide organized physical activities, such as sports, dance and exercise classes. If the child is small in stature, fearful and insecure or an aggressive, impulsive type, he or she can benefit greatly from self-defense courses as these classes build self-confidence and self-discipline.

13. Protect your child from verbal and physical abuse. Criticism and name-calling are forms of violence, which can hurt even more than pinches and smacks. This includes pinches on the cheek which some adults think are so cute, but which are so humiliating and painful to a child. In this day, when abuse of children is getting such widespread publicity, parents are being made aware of the importance of teaching children to speak up for themselves and say, "I don't like that." "You're not allowed to do that to me." This is important training for every child.

You cannot protect your children completely from violence, but you can, at least, keep abusive behavior out of your home in the same way that you keep non-kosher food out. You take a firm stand and do not allow it in! Criticism is toxic. It destroys more lives than physical illness. As your children get older, you can teach them coping mechanisms to help them face critical people who cannot be avoided or confronted: for example, to give the benefit of the doubt; to be forgiving; to realize that, "The pain of criticism atones for sins" (*Rosh Hashanah* 17a); and that criticism is unpleasant, but not dangerous, as long as you do not have to live with it continuously! You can tell your child that, "The whole world exists on the merit of one who bridles his mouth in the moment of strife" (*Chulin* 89a). Thus, to be criticized and not allow oneself to be dragged down to the other person's level of pettiness and negativity is a sign of greatness. Let your children know that their worth is independent of other people's opinions.

Speak up if your child has an abusive teacher. Even though he may not seem to be bothered outwardly by such abusive behavior or may not be the direct object of such abuse, he will be affected since he is forced to spend many hours in a state of anxiety. If he displays psychosomatic illnesses or irritating habits such as nail-biting, nose-picking or bed-wetting, or is scatterbrained, aggressive or generally unhappy, find out if his classroom environment is an anxiety-provoking one. A very deeply-feeling child will be particularly affected.

> My four year old kept asking me if I was going to lock him in the bathroom if he didn't behave or made a mess. I was mystified as to where he got this idea, as I would not do such a thing. Then one day he said that his kindergarten teacher had done this to another child. When I asked her, she was surprised. First, she said that it happened a few months ago and that she had done it to another child, not mine. However, the terrifying impression of that event had obviously been traumatic for my son even though he himself was not directly involved.

Make a house rule that there will be no violence in the home, other than an occasional slap on the backside of a very young child who might be endangering himself or others. This will force you to find constructive solutions to situations instead of relying on violence, which is often the lazy way out or the mark of desperation.

Don't think to yourself, "He's a boy, so he doesn't need to be treated with sensitivity." Because boys are more prone to stifle their feelings, they are the ones who, most of all, need to be treated in a manner which does not encourage emotional suppression.

However you treat your children, make a firm decision to think, do and say only what will build their self-respect, and your own as well.

Make Written Goals and Contracts

Instead of getting angry when you see your children misbehaving or displaying negative character traits, think of a possible contract which would help them improve. When you have your child's willingness to participate in the change and his signature on a contract which states that he will do so, you have won half the battle. For example:

A.

1. Goal: I will be more organized and neat.

2. Method: I will accomplish this by not throwing my clothes on the floor when I undress at night and by cleaning out the old food in my book bag each day.

3. Signature and date:

B.

1. Goal: I will do better in school.

2. Method: I will do my homework right after dinner instead of putting it off until bedtime. I will take the responsibility for finding a tutor and going to him twice a week.

3. Signature and date:

C.

1. Goal: I will be less grouchy.

2. Method: I will volunteer once a week at a hospital and will keep a "happiness notebook" in which I write down the good things that happen and the mitzvoth which I do. I will share this with Mom every Shabbath.

3. Signature and date:

Make sure that the contract is simple, specific and attainable within the next few days. Also, realize that the later you start making these changes, the more difficult the change will be for the child and the more persistent and creative you both will have to be.

Creative Uses of Clocks and Timers

A sixty-minute kitchen timer and a three-minute egg timer are invaluable tools in gaining cooperation and control. For example:

* As a punishment, have the child hold the three-minute timer while sitting in a corner. When the sand runs out, ask him if he is now able to control himself. If so, then he can come back to play with others.

* Give your children a task and tell them to see if they can "beat the clock," and get it done before the clock rings. For example, they might have to pick up their toys, get their shoes and coats on, or have their hands washed.

* Get them in the habit of doing various tasks when they hear the bell ring. For example, if you have to leave home or are taking a nap, tell a child to wake you up when the bell rings, or turn off the oven, or go out to play.

* Take the timer to the dentist's office. Let him hold it while the dentist is drilling. Tell him that when the sand runs out, he can rinse out his mouth or take a breather. Or, the dentist may say that he will be finished with the drilling in "two timers." This diverts the child's attention, gives him a feeling of control, and makes him feel that the distressing event is time limited.

* Use a timer to keep a young child in bed for longer periods in the morning. If he awakens at 5:30 A.M., go to him and put the timer on for five minutes. Tell him that when it rings, you will come in. The next day, let it go for ten minutes. Keep working up until you get from half an hour to an extra hour's rest, if not more.

* If an older child has to do some task which he finds unpleasant, let him set the timer for five minutes or more. This limits the amount of unpleasantness which he feels he has to endure. Often, once he starts on his homework or the dishes, he will want to continue past the time limit.

* If a young child is cranky and going on and on about some trivial disappointment which you know is totally insignificant to him in reality, tell him that you are going to allow him three minutes of crying time. Before he starts, spend some time making some elaborate preparations, like ceremoniously shaking down the sand and saying, "It's almost time to cry. Wait! A few more seconds. O.K. Now we're ready. Ready ... set ... go .... This is your crying time." Usually, by this time, he will give you a big smile.

* Many children think that their teeth need to be brushed for no longer than ten seconds. Turn over the three minute timer and tell him that he should brush until the sand runs out. Once he gets in the habit of brushing well, he will not need it any more.

Family Conferences

Children from the age of four or five on up love family conferences. Sit down and discuss problem areas such as if they like the food you are making for them, how they feel about the chores they do, and what new chores they can do to help you out, such as making their own lunches or taking care of the little ones. You will be amazed at their receptivity and cooperation. Because you are treating them as adults, they are far more likely to respond in a mature manner. This is especially important as your children grow older and become more and more resentful of commands and orders. You have the opportunity to teach them how to arbitrate and negotiate and express differences of opinion in a respectful manner.

Role Playing

One of the most powerful methods of helping to raise people's level of awareness is to reverse roles and have them take on another person's personality. By the age of five, children can engage in role playing quite successfully. [Note: It is helpful to use props like hats or aprons.]

* If a child does not want to do a chore or his homework, have him play you and you play him. Tell him, "You be the mother. Try to get me to do that chore and I'll resist and give excuses just like you." Then ask him how it feels.

* Let the child be the guest. Invite him in and then start squabbling with a sibling or engage in some other irritating behavior. Ask him how it feels as a guest to have to watch this scene. You can play the child and grab all the toys away from the guest. Or, you might have an older child display bad table manners, such as grabbing the biggest pieces for himself from the serving plate or having a mini-tantrum when he doesn't get what he wants.

* If you have a slowpoke who has difficulty getting out of bed in the morning, then climb into his bed and pretend to be him. Have him be the mother who has to get you out of bed while you very ... very ... slowly ... move ... one ... muscle ... at ... a ... time.

* If your child is being bullied, you play the bully and get him to assert himself or walk away. Or you play him and let him play the bully so that you can get a feel for what your child is enduring or show him how to respond assertively.

* Let your children experience what it is like to be handicapped. One teacher had her pupils wear gloves, cotton ear plugs and thick glasses for a morning in order to feel what it is like to be old. Then they went to an old folks home. The children all said that they were far more compassionate than they would have been without that preparatory exercise.

* If your child is having a problem, you play him while he plays

a wise Rav. Ask him what to do. This will encourage him to come up with his own solutions and insights.

You might also want to try role-reversal with your husband so that you can both gain greater insight into the pressures which you are each bearing.

Remember that in all these interchanges, you not only want your child to become more aware. You also want to experience what he is going through as well.

Rewards

It is customary for a Jewish mother to bake cookies in the shape of the *alef-bet* when her child begins to read, so that he will always associate learning with the sweetness of that early memory. The same principle can be applied as we attempt to imbue them with a love for other healthy behaviors. Certainly, we all want our children to do mitzvoth for the intrinsic reward of doing good. However, do not be afraid to use occasional rewards to instill certain habits in your children, especially around the ages of three to five. This should not be considered bribery, for bribery is an attempt to deceive. You are not trying to deceive your children when you offer a reward. You are simply trying to create a positive association in their minds between a desirable act and a pleasurable feeling, so that they will want to continue that behavior on their own even when there is no reward. For example, if you want them to hang up their coats when they come home or put their dishes in the sink, provide a reward for a few days, such as a star or a point on a chart. Once you see that the behavior has been well-established, discontinue the reward. It is as simple as that.

Adults often forget how exciting it is for a child to receive something tangible for his efforts. A star or a sticker can be as meaningful to him as a paycheck to an older person. It gives him a feeling of importance and control to know that he has acquired something with his own efforts. Even if you meant to buy the child a certain item anyway, such as a new pair of socks, let him feel that he has earned those socks by hanging up his coat for three days in a row, doing a special chore, baby-sitting a younger sibling, or making *shalom.*

If you think that rewards will make children "mercenary" and that they will then not want to do anything for you unless they get some reward, it is well to realize that most of the positive acts which your children perform go unrewarded. The few acts which you do reward are quite minor compared to the more numerous acts of cooperation and consideration, to which you respond with a simple "Thank you," or no comment at all.

You can acknowledge many of their acts of kindness and maturity by simply saying, "That was very responsible," or "Thank you for giving in instead of making a big scene over a trivial item." If you reward one or two habits once in a while, this in itself will not make the child money-hungry or spoiled. Furthermore, the world will soon teach them that most people do want something in return for what they give. Few people work for nothing; even the notion of a heavenly reward is a useful incentive. Finally, if they see you performing acts of kindness with no thought of reward, they will eventually follow your example as they get older. You can remind them that doing a mitzvah is its own reward.

For two weeks, I would give a special snack to my two children if they were quiet during my afternoon nap. After that, I didn't need to give them anything special. They were quiet on their own.

I promised my kids a trip to the zoo if they would dress quickly each morning for a week. I made a chart with a road leading to the zoo and squares on the road. They could see each day that they were getting closer. Soon, they were in the habit of not dawdling.

I paid my eight year old a small amount for baby-sitting his baby brother for the hour before candle-lighting. He was thrilled. I didn't want him to waste the money on junk food, so we went to the hardware store and he decided that he would save his money for a lock and key. By the end of three weeks, he was able to buy it.

The street where we live was always littered with papers. Each Friday, before Shabbath, I offered two of my children as well as two neighborhood boys a popsicle if they would clean up the mess. They were happy to do so. After that, I noticed that they would spontaneously put papers in the garbage cans without being asked to do so.

My kids were fighting over every little thing. Finally, I told them that I would give points to whoever would be *m'vater* [giving in] for the sake of peace. At the time, I didn't know what I would do with the points, but in the meantime, they were happy just accumulating them. Finally, I decided to buy each one an inexpensive eraser. It was certainly worth the half dollar to teach them the joy of making peace.

More Examples of Creative Solutions

🙦 My three year old was having nightmares. I had an old spray bottle into which I put a few drops of good-smelling perfume. I told him that this was a special chemical which kills monsters. The "monstercide" seemed to work and, *Baruch Hashem*, the stage passed in a few days.

🙦 My teenager told me that she had so many resentments toward people and didn't know how to stop thinking these obsessive thoughts. I told her that her mind was like a radio with many stations. The stations could be called, "self-pity," "joy," "caring," "anger," "bitterness," or anything else she wanted. I then told her that when I touched her left shoulder, she should think of a thought which made her feel angry and resentful. She told me of someone who had broken a promise. Then I touched her right shoulder and told her to think of something which made her feel compassion or happiness. She told me she could give the person the benefit of the doubt or think of an upcoming family wedding. I showed her that it was her choice to decide which thoughts to think. Over the next few days, I would touch her on her right shoulder every once in a while to remind her to keep her mind "tuned" to positive thoughts. She would always look up and say, "Thanks for reminding me, Mom." I've done this at a simpler level even with my four year old. It helps me too! I find myself patting myself on my right shoulder when I've done some little act which required self-restraint or which brought joy to the family.

🙦 Before going on a long car trip, I recorded songs and stories on a blank tape cassette. It kept the kids busy during moments of tension and boredom.

🙦 Two of my boys love to make Lego creations but hate to take them apart. I was running out of pieces. So I decided to photograph them proudly holding their constructions. That satisfied their desire to have a permanent record of what they had done. I also made a photo album for each child. When there is a moment of crisis, or a child is unhappy, I give him his own album to look through and he usually calms down quickly.

🙦 One of my children tends to be a little "hyper." He has difficulty sleeping at night, so I taped a very soothing cassette for him. I started with his head and said, "Think of your head and all the hairs on your head. Each one is going to sleep. Now your eyes are feeling heavy and tired. They want to go to sleep too. And your ears and your nose also feel tired and want to sleep. Good. Now think of your neck and your back. You did so much today. Your muscles want to relax and go to sleep." Slowly, over the next fifteen minutes, I went over his whole body. Then I ended with a very slow and boring recital of all the animals in the zoo who were going to sleep, and all of his friends who were now in bed and going to sleep. I also used the opportunity to tell him how much I love him and the good things which he has been doing and how proud I am when he controls himself, etc. After that, whenever he would have trouble going to sleep, he would ask for the cassette. If I had to leave him with a baby sitter, he seemed to feel better having at least my voice with him.

    ☞   Before my husband and I took a two-week vacation without the children, I made up a little book for them with my own drawings on each page of the things we would be doing, including getting on the plane, checking the bags in, sleeping in strange places and seeing certain relatives. Even before I left, they wanted to read the booklet over and over to prepare themselves. Since I gave the book the same number of pages as the days we would be gone, they could see how soon we would be returning.

    ☞   My children tend to come home from school very grouchy, partly from just being cooped up for so long and partly because they haven't eaten well all day. Now, I put on music before they come in, have the mini-trampoline out for them to jump on for a few minutes and also make sure that a meal is on the table, ready to eat. Of course, if I have spent the morning at some doctor's office, then things are much more hectic. But at least I don't blame them any more for having trouble making the transition.

    ☞   I'm not a very good disciplinarian, but I'm getting better since I had a friend of ours, who is a policeman, give me one of his old hats. One evening, I put on the hat and pretended that I was him: firm, no-nonsense, and unemotional. Somehow, I felt more in charge and the kids went to bed without their usual fussing.

    ☞   I couldn't get my older boys to remember to put their dirty laundry in the hamper after their baths. I always ended up picking their clothes up off the floor. So I had my husband put up a basketball hoop just above the hamper. Now, they love to see their dirty clothes go through the hoop and land inside.

    ☞   When it's time to take the dishes off the table, my children do so according to age. The three year old takes off three items, the six year old takes six, and so on. Usually, they're so anxious to be a little bit older that they take off more.

    ☞   Whenever I feel bad about how I'm doing as a mother, I spend a morning at a kindergarten run by a very patient, firm, but loving woman. I always pick up new techniques from her and come home feeling stronger and more enthusiastic about my job as the educator of my children.

    ☞   We have a "family cheer." I ask them, "What are your hands for?" And they say, "To do mitzvoth." "What are your feet for?" "To run swiftly to do Hashem's will." "What is your tongue for?" "To speak holy words and to cheer people up with good sayings." Then, whenever they misbehave, I can remind them to use their limbs properly.

🕸 We had three long blocks to walk. My two year old wouldn't budge from the stoop where he had parked himself. So I told him to wait for me there while I would go halfway down the block. He was to wait until I gave him a signal to run to me. I told him that when he got to me, I would swing him around like a helicopter. I walked to the end of the block, held my arms out wide while he ran to me with a delighted smile. We were home in about six helicopter swings.

🕸 I tape-recorded my children when they were arguing with each other and then played it back to them so that they could hear how they sounded. They stopped arguing long enough to listen, and that broke the deadlock. Then we talked about some problem-solving tactics.

🕸 One day, when my kids were in a good mood, I taught them the "Freeze Game," in which they make all kinds of funny movements and then have to hold the pose for ten seconds when I say, "FREEZE!" This got them used to the game so that when they were being rowdy, I could say, "FREEZE!" and they would stop what they were doing.

🕸 I keep a list of good deeds which my children do on a piece of paper taped to the fridge. When one misbehaves, I go over to the sheet and say, "I'd like to have something good to write down about you right now." This usually makes him want to do some positive act.

🕸 I was so heavy from my pregnancy that I could no longer bend over to get into tight corners. I remembered reading in one of the books of a series called *All of a Kind Family* that the mother hid pennies in hard-to-reach places and told her girls that whatever they found they could keep. I tried it and it worked like magic. They cleaned really well. I used nickels instead of pennies. My children vied with each other to see who would have the opportunity to do the corners that day. I didn't want them fighting with each other, so I let them take turns.

🕸 My three year old had a grouchy face. I knew she just needed cheering up, so I asked her, "Hey, what happened to your happy face? We have to find it." Then I would go looking in the drawers and under furniture until she would suddenly start to smile and I would say, "There it is! You found it!" I would hug her and usually her good mood would return, at least for a while.

🕸 When my daughter was little, I would tell her how sad her clothing felt when she threw her things on the floor as if she didn't care about them. I told her how much her shoes like to be together after she takes them off, and how her coats like to be with the other coats. Now, as a teenager, she says that she still uses this trick to get herself in the mood to pick up her things when she feels too lazy to do so.

One of the most successful techniques for teaching children not to be bothered by external annoyances is the following:

> One of my children delighted in teasing his younger brother with punches and pokes, as well as by making faces at him. It was driving the younger one up the wall, and he was constantly running to me complaining tearfully. The next time this happened, I called the two of them to me. I told them that I had purchased some stickers and that each time the older one made a face or provoked the younger one, that the latter would earn a sticker. I then told the older one to make one of his famous faces. Suddenly, the younger one was *asking* for those faces which, a few minutes earlier, had been producing such an explosive reaction. And the older one, deprived of the satisfaction of being able to provoke his younger brother to hysteria, tried to make faces, but you could tell that his heart just wasn't in it. He did make two scary faces which "won" the younger one two stickers, but he had lost his sense of power for the moment and became interested in other things. Since then, I have used this trick to break up many squabbles. Once, the younger one was driving the older one crazy by calling him, "Liar." So I told the younger one that each time he used that word, the older one would earn a dime. The older one got two dimes. I haven't heard the word for two years since!

The above example shows how we can demonstrate to our children that they can often keep themselves from being upset by external events by keeping their minds focused on higher goals. For very young children, stickers or points on a chart may serve that purpose. As they get older, you can have them think of more spiritual rewards such as *ahavath Yisroel* and *shalom*.

Using Puppets Creatively

You might try having puppets help your children become more cooperative and expressive. For example:

* Wash the child's face after meals with a washable puppet if he balks at having his face washed with a regular washcloth.

* Have an order come from the puppet instead of you, such as, "It's time to wash hands." "Time for pajamas." The puppet can tell the child where each thing belongs: "Scrap paper in the waste-paper basket, soap in the soap dish, Lego in the red basket."

* Stroke a distressed child with a puppet. He may be more willing to take that kind of touch than your own.
* Let the puppet brush the child's teeth.
* Let the puppet share feelings which may reflect what the child is feeling: angry, jealous, sad, disappointed, frustrated, etc.

Stories to Instill Good Character Traits

Tell your children inspiring stories of our ancestors and how they overcame great difficulties and maintained their love, faith and perseverance. You can also make up your own stories to fit a particular child's present problems. The following examples can be embellished and altered with appropriate names of your own children.

1. For the Whiner: "Let's Find a Solution"

Once upon a time, there was a family with many children. They decided to go to Haifa for Purim. So they packed all of their food and diapers and everything else they needed for the trip. [Depending on the amount of time you have, you can make this very elaborate or simple. For example, you can add grandparents, chickens, goats and be detailed about the food which you take.] They had just started out when suddenly there was a flat tire. Everyone started to moan and complain. "We'll never get there. Our trip is ruined." Everyone except four-year-old Chaim, who said, "It doesn't help to kvetch and cry. We have to find a solution." And so he did. He walked to the nearest gas station and got an attendant to help his father fix the car. They had gone for a little while when suddenly the battery went dead. Again, everyone started to moan and complain — everyone except little Chaim. He said, "It doesn't help to kvetch and cry. We have to find a solution." He stuck out his thumb and flagged down a bus. They all piled in. They had gone a little way when there was suddenly a big hissing noise from the bus's radiator and then the bus went dead. All the people were again very upset. Everyone was afraid that they wouldn't get to the Megilla-reading in time — everyone, that is, except Chaim. He said, "We have to have faith! Don't be discouraged. It doesn't help to cry and groan. We have to find a solution." And, sure enough, he did. Just then, there was a car hauling a boat. Chaim again stuck out his thumb and asked the driver if they could get into the boat. The man agreed. And they were on their way. Sure enough, they got to Haifa in time for the Megilla-reading, thanks to Chaim, who always focused on solutions.

After a few days of telling this story to your whiner, you can then remind him when he whines, "Remember? It doesn't help to moan and cry. Let's think of a solution." [If you want to make the story longer, you can also have the goat jump out of the bus, or have someone get sick, etc. This will add spice and drama and give you a few more opportunities to remind them to look for solutions.]

2. To Build Trust: "You Have to Do What's Right, Even If No One Is Looking"

There once was a king who had a son whom he loved very much. The prince was a very good child and always did what the father wanted. However, the king often wondered to himself, "Maybe he's being so good because my advisors or I are around him all the time. What would happen if no one was around? Would he still be so good? He decided to tempt his son. He contacted a group of boys in his son's class and told them that he wanted them to tempt his son to do bad things and that he would pay them handsomely if they succeeded. Each day, the king told them what to do. For example, one day the group went out to buy ice cream. When they walked out, one of the boys said, "Let's throw these ice cream wrappers on the floor. No one will see." But the prince said, "Even if no one is looking, it's wrong to throw garbage around. We'll find a garbage can and put the wrappers inside." Another day, the boys told the prince, "Let's go tease the animals in the zoo. No one will see." The prince was horrified. "Oh no," he said. "We have to be kind to all living creatures. As we are kind to others, God will be kind to us." Each evening, the group of boys went back to report to the king and get new orders. In the end, the king was convinced that his son was truly a fine person who could be trusted to do what was right even if no one else was around. He gave the boys their reward and at the celebration which followed, he told them that they hadn't failed after all. They had really succeeded!

3. To Build a Positive Attitude: "Look at the Positive"

Avi was often sad. It seemed that things just didn't go right for him. He felt that he was unlucky because his best friend had a new bike and he didn't. Also, he wasn't the best in his class. Other boys learned better and faster. He was quite miserable and grumpy, that is, until he met Mr. Simcha. When Mr. Simcha met Avi, he saw right away what the problem was. He told Avi that in order to be cheerful, one must know which thoughts to think and to choose them carefully and to find things which make one feel productive and useful. Otherwise, he told Avi, you turn into a real grouch. Mr. Simcha demonstrated this in many ways. For example, one day Mr. Simcha fell down and twisted his ankle. Avi felt very sad for him. But Mr. Simcha said, "No, no, Avi, don't pity me. Sure, it hurts me when I walk and I can't do some of the things I am used to. But look at the bright side. I didn't break it! And this is the first time I've ever sprained my ankle. It's a new experience. So now I'll know how other people feel when they have trouble getting around. I'll be more sympathetic about their pain because of this experience. And look at all the things that are working just fine, my eyes, my ears, my arms! *Baruch Hashem* I have so much to be thankful for. Plus, I'm happy that I can give you the opportunity to help me, because I know that that will make you feel good!" Avi was amazed that Mr. Simcha could be so cheerful even though he was in pain.

Another time, Avi was busy sawing a new piece of wood. He got so carried away that he didn't realize that he had made a gouge in Mr. Simcha's table. Avi felt so bad that he started to cry. But Mr. Simcha said, "Avi, you have to save your tears for the really important things in life, not trivialities like this piece of wood!" But Avi still felt bad and said, "Mr. Simcha! I'm such a failure! I can't do anything right. I bet you are so angry with me!" "Not at all, Avi," said Mr. Simcha. "You are much more important than the table! I'd rather have the whole table be destroyed than hurt your feelings. Let this be a *kaparah* —

Hashem let the table get hurt instead of me or you! We'll turn this loss into a gain. I can teach you about giving the benefit of the doubt. You didn't do it on purpose. You were just so absorbed in your work that you didn't realize what was happening. Anyway, mistakes are meant to teach us something. Now I have the chance to show you how to fix a table! Avi, I love building things and I want to pass this information on to you. How would I have that opportunity if we didn't have any accidents? So I'm glad this happened! And it's important for me to know that you think you are a failure when something goes wrong! That's one attitude which is bound to make you feel bad. We have to work on that one! In my book, the only failure is the person who doesn't care about people. You're not a failure. You are human. You make mistakes just like everyone else. But you have a heart, Avi. You care. And that's what really counts in life."

Once, Avi came sadly to Mr. Simcha to show him a poor grade he had received on a test. "That hurts," said Mr. Simcha, sympathetically. It's not a triviality to you because you take your learning seriously, and that's a good sign. But don't think that that mark you got is a reflection of what you are. You are still Hashem's most beloved of all creations. Hashem gives every person some special gift to give the world. You might not be the world's greatest genius, but together, we're going to discover just what your gifts are.

Little by little, Avi's attitude toward himself and life changed. He wasn't so glum anymore. He often had a smile on his face. He began to be the one who would "look for the good" whenever anything went wrong. He told Mr. Simcha that he just didn't know how to thank him for all that he had learned. Mr. Simcha smiled happily and said, "Just pass it on, Avi. Find someone to teach these lessons to. That will be my biggest reward."

Using Presuppositions

Another important tool for gaining cooperation and instilling positive feelings in your children is to use presuppositions. These are statements which presuppose that the child already has the ability, the inclination or the solution to do what you want. For example:

* "Tell me what you can do to solve this problem." (You presuppose that the child has a solution.)

* "Let me know when you want to talk about what happened. It can be in a few minutes, if you like." (You presuppose that the child does want to talk about the situation.)

* "Tell me two things that you like about your sister." (You presuppose that he can think of two things, hopefully!)

* "Tell me what you can do to make sure that what happened does not happen again." (You presuppose that he knows that he did something wrong and has the intelligence to think of how to prevent it from happening in the future.)

Similarly, you can give suggestions which assume that the child will soon want to carry out your desires:

* "Watch the egg timer. As soon as the sand has gone down, you will jump up and get your pajamas/come to dinner/go to the market for me, etc."

* "As you sit there eating, you will begin to think about your homework and think about how good it will feel to get it over with so that you can then go out to play for the rest of the afternoon and not worry about it."

* "As you sit there, the urge to help me will become stronger and stronger until you cannot resist getting out of your chair and helping me."

* "There are always two ways to look at any situation. You have told me your insecure thoughts. Now tell me another way of approaching this problem."

Note, you do not ask questions such as, "Is there anything you like about your sister?" "Do you have any solutions?" The person can simply say, "No!" With presuppositions, you want to help the other person get in touch with his own inner sources of strength, creativity, love and joy by making statements which presuppose that these resources are present and active within him.

Drills

Most schools have fire drills. The bell rings and the children file out and do various activities as if there is a real fire. It is fun because there is no tension which would exist if there were a real emergency. Yet they learn proper behavior and procedures far more quickly than if someone tried to teach them in a time of panic. The same principle applies to your children. You will not have much success in instilling positive patterns if, at seven in the morning, you are screaming at them for being slowpokes or brats. It would be far better for you to break down the procedure into steps and teach them during a quiet time later in the day. For example:

* In the afternoon, tell them to put their pajamas on (even over their clothing) and get into bed. Then, pretend to wake them up and carefully explain what you expect them to do step by step: wake up; say *modeh ani*; wash hands; pull covers up or fold them at bottom of bed; get undressed and put pajamas under pillow; get dressed quickly and come to eat, etc.

* If your children are not hanging up their coats when they come in the door, have them walk out of the door and come in and immediately hang the coats up. Do this a number of times in order to erase the old "program" which is in their minds: i.e., come in, throw coat on floor, get yelled at, then hang up coat.

* Have a "pretend meal" with paper plates and no food. After they have "finished" the meal, drill them in the proper procedure which is fitting for their age group.

* If you have a child who is hitting a lot, drill him on how to react nonviolently. Tell him that you are going to do something deliberately to annoy him, such as giving him a light tap or taking away a toy. Then have him practice not hitting back, but perhaps stating, "I don't like what you are doing. Don't do it again." "I am SOOOOOO frustrated, I could scream!" The more he is able to express himself in words, the less likely he is to resort to violence. After such training, one mother was pleasantly shocked to have her four year old tell her (after she had *potsched* him), "Mommy, I don't like when you hit me. Talk to me!"

* To train children to come when you call, have them pretend to be very involved in a game or project. Tell them that when you say, "It is time to stop, NOW," they have to put their things away.

* Drill your children in how to express themselves to you when they are angry about something you have done. Give them words to express themselves so that they do not have to resort to whining, yelling or grimacing at you. For example, have them say out loud, "I don't like what you are doing." "I disagree with you."

* If a child is unusually reactive to others, drill him in playing, "The Palace Guards," like those of the Queen of England who are able to remain totally indifferent to any insults or provocative behavior of the tourists who walk by. They are trained to react only if there is real danger. You can have him stand up straight like a Palace Guard, and then walk by him and mention the words or make the faces which have caused him to overreact in the past. You can have a game in which the kids all line up like palace guards and you see who can keep a straight face the longest.

All drills should be practiced at least four or five times for two or three days in a row at least, to instill new behavior in their minds and muscles. With deeply-entrenched habits, you may have to practice even more.

Spiritually Uplifting Plays

A wonderful learning technique is to act out stories of our Sages. A very special one which children love is the story of Rabbi Akiva, who always said, "This also is for the best," even when his candle blew out in the darkness and his rooster and donkey were killed. In the end, he realizes that all these things occurred in order to save him from being killed by thieves. Stories of the Chofetz Chaim are also excellent for instilling good character traits. Your children will have an opportunity to put themselves into the shoes of other people and will experience what it is like to put Torah principles into practice in the midst of hardship and disappointment.

Problem Solving

One of the most important skills you can teach your children is how to solve problems in a mutually respectful manner. "Cultured" people use force only when absolutely necessary. When there are differences of opinion, point out some of the possible choices which they have. For example:

* Take turns using a toy or other item for a certain period of time. One can flip a coin to see who goes first.

* Find an alternative that pleases both parties. For example, if Chaim wants to go to the park and Meir wants to go to the museum, there may be a third alternative which would please both, or perhaps they can do both for a shorter period of time.

* Abide by the decision of a third person. They can call on a friend or an adult and abide by that person's decision.

* Giving in. Making *shalom* for the sake of the mitzvah itself. Tell them that they get a "double mitzvah" if they do so cheerfully.

Let them know that non-constructive "choices" involve trying to get one's way with a) passive aggression: sulking, pouting, brooding in silent hostility, or unnecessary delaying tactics which keep the person on the string (e.g, "We'll discuss it later.") or b) active aggression: forcing others with bullying tactics or humiliating others to give in (e.g, "You're stupid for wanting to do that." "If you really cared about me you would do whatever I want.")

Provide Alternatives

When your children are misbehaving, you often want to scream at them, "Stop that." "Go away." "Calm down!" However, the child may not be able to think of any alternatives for his nervous energy or relief from boredom. Therefore, try offering alternatives:

> ✇ My three boys were driving each other crazy one rainy vacation day. I couldn't stand the noise and kept screaming at them to be quiet, which wasn't having any effect at all. Then I thought of making play-doh. They punched, pounded and pinched that stuff for half an hour before they could quietly begin making little objects. That showed me how much they needed to have some lively motor activity before they could calm down. [Play-doh: 4 cups flour; ½ cup salt; 1 cup water to start after which you can add a few drops more as necessary; food coloring; 1 tsp. cream of tartar; 2 Tbsp. oil]

Give Analogies

Often, your children do not understand what you want or why you want it because they cannot understand your way of thinking. Therefore, find analogies which will help them understand your needs and feelings:

෯   My five year old was moving around while I was trying to braid her hair. I was getting so exasperated that I wanted to smack her hard and threaten to cut off her hair. Finally, I decided to try an analogy. I took off my watch and told her to try to put it back on me while I kept moving my hand up and down. She quickly got very frustrated. I told her that that was how I felt when I was trying to braid her hair while she moved. After that, she kept still.

෯   Before leaving for a class, my eleven year old promised to clean up the kitchen. When I came home, I expected to see it in tiptop order. Instead, I found that she hadn't done it. I was furious. I wanted to wake her up harshly and drag her out of bed to do it. But I decided to give her the benefit of the doubt and I cleaned it up myself. The next day, I used an analogy. I asked her how she would feel if I promised to take her to the shopping center to buy her a new dress in the afternoon and then, after she was all excited about it, changed my mind. I told her that that was how disappointed I felt when I came home and saw a messy kitchen. She felt really bad and promised that she would try not to let it happen again. I felt that I accomplished much more than if I had been punitive. If she does keep forgetting, then I will have to try harsher tactics, but I felt that I should at least give the analogy tactic a try.

Demonstrate Flexibility

A man should be soft like a reed, and not hard like a cedar.

(TAANITH 20a)

Therefore, the reed is privileged to be fashioned into a pen used for writing Torah scrolls. . . .

(DUTIES OF THE HEART, p.119)

Decide ahead of time what issues are worth fighting for in life. Be flexibile when there is no *halachic* issue of right and wrong or danger.

෯   I was going crazy in the mornings with a new baby and three slightly older children to dress, feed, and get off on time for the school bus. I was getting so hostile and hysterical that they often didn't get fed and would go off crying or angry, after which I would castigate myself for hours. Then I decided that for a few weeks, I would simplify my life to the extreme: store-bought cakes for the Sabbath instead of homemade ones, simple meals, and having the courage to say, "No," to outsiders' requests for involvement in committees and projects, etc. I found that it calmed me down to focus on priorities and essentials. It helped return my feeling of joy and control.

   My learning-disabled seven year old hated to say the entire blessing after bread. He would resist angrily or lie about having said it. Finally, I called his Rebbe who told me that there are many boys like him with the same problem. He told me to let him say only the first paragraph for the next six months and then to add an additional paragraph each six months. He reminded me that the important thing is for a Jew to do mitzvoth with joy.

You can never have complete control over your children's thoughts and actions. They will have cravings for certain foods, friends, articles of clothing, or activities. There are inevitable "grit-your-teeth" periods when you will have to show great tolerance and faith as they go through some difficult phase. You cannot force maturity or awareness. You cannot change their natural drives or passions. Don't panic as long as the situation is passing, not permanent. No child goes to the *chuppa* with a pacifier in his mouth or eating peanut butter three times a day. Children eventually do learn to be polite, to like a variety of foods, say their *berachoth* and *daaven* faithfully without coercion *if* they have seen adults do these activities with joy and love as they were growing up. However, do get help if a bad habit seems to be intensifying or going on for longer than normal.

Teach Your Children Non-Temperamental Language

Even before your children can understand you, you can already begin to talk to them in a way which will calm you both.

   I had a collicky baby whose cries were difficult to bear. I would sing to her my EMETT language to calm us both. Like, "Bear the discomfort and comfort will come." "It's distressing, not dangerous." "Comfort is a want, not a need." "The total view is positive." I needed to hear these words more than she!

As your children grow older, introduce EMETT language slowly, making sure not to make light of their distress when you do so.

   My son lost at a game of Candyland and was very upset. He came to me crying. First, I acknowledged his pain. Then I told him that I was going to teach him an important principle: the difference between trivialities and major disappointments. I told him that a major loss is when something could not be fixed, like a friend who is paralyzed, another who has muscular dystrophy, or the manager of the gas station across the street who lost his arm in the Yom Kippur War. Then we thought of examples of trivialities: breaking a glass, spilling juice on the floor, etc. I opened my arms wide to indicate a major loss and brought them almost together to indicate a minor one. He himself concluded that losing the game was a minor loss, even though, at the moment it happened, it seemed like a catastrophe. I hugged him and said, "You may have lost a game, but you're a winner in my eyes!"

🕸   My daughter said that she absolutely had to have a new dress for a relative's wedding, even though I had bought her one for the holidays a few months earlier. When I asked her if the dress was a *want* or a *need*, she quickly said that it was a want, after which she was able to drop her demand and her emotionalism about not being able to have one.

🕸   I made a rather unsuccessful casserole which tasted terrible. One of my kids said, "Mom, endorse yourself for effort, if not success. You had the courage to make a mistake." We all laughed, and I thanked them for tasting it at least and then asked them what they would prefer to eat instead. I was happy for the opportunity to demonstrate non-dramatic, non-emotional handling of a *triviality* to them.

🕸   My daughter was angry at me and wouldn't talk about it. I wrote her a note that I had faith in her ability to handle whatever was going on and that I loved her and would appreciate talking about what had happened. I said that the *total view* of our relationship was positive and that I was sure this was a temporary setback. That broke the ice and she came to talk to me. That night, on my pillow, I found a thank-you note from her.

🕸   When I bought our youngest son a new pair of shoes, his older brother started sulking angrily because I didn't buy any for him. When I asked if his *insecure thought* was that I didn't love him as much as his brother, he said, "Right! You don't." I then explained the difference between *fantasy* and *fact*. I told him that it is not for us to think that we know what is in other people's hearts or minds. For that, we have to ask people directly. He looked at me sheepishly and asked, "Do you love me?" I was able to reassure him that I did, and that material possessions were no proof of love.

🕸   My daughter is overweight. She asked me how she could stick to her diet. I told her that what helps me is to tell myself, "Do the thing you fear to do most and do the difficult. That will give you self-respect." That made her realize that self-control builds self-esteem.

You will soon notice that your children will give you back your own sayings.

The M & M Game

We can't eat the non-kosher M & M candies. But we have other M & M's which bring far greater sweetness into our lives. These M & M's are mitzvoth and *middoth* which we can focus on at any moment, especially important in the midst of disappointment and pain. The worst thing is to feel that our pains and losses are meaningless. With the M & M game, you teach your children that every distressing event becomes a test of our *middoth* and an opportunity for inner growth and *chesed*. You can also make up hypothetical situations and ask for their possible M & M's.

  🕮   My son felt very hurt when he lost his treasured sticker collection. First, I sympathized with his loss. Then I showed him a list of positive attitudes mentioned in chapter 6 of *Pirkei Avoth* and asked him which ones he could focus on at this time. He said he was thankful that nothing worse happened to him, and that he could be happy for the good fortune of whoever found the collection. Then he added that he was going to practice the *middah* of perseverance and look for it!

  🕮   I had promised to take my children to the zoo, but the baby got sick and we couldn't go. The kids were feeling very disappointed, so I told them to look at the list of *middoth* which I had taped to the wall and see which ones they could practice. They picked cheerfulness, resourcefulness in finding something else to do, and acceptance of Hashem's will. My youngest daughter said, "And silence not to kvetch about not being able to go!"

  🕮   My teenage daughter was going through a difficult phase and often seemed moody and depressed. I talked about *PMA's"* (positive muscular acts) to help us out of our lowered feelings. I mentioned that often, when we cheer others up, we ourselves are cheered. A friend of ours is the head of volunteers at a local hospital. I suggested that she call her and see if she could work there. She was so excited. By the end of the week, she was full of enthusiasm for her work.

You can also have a "Theme for the Week" in which you focus on a specific *middah*. One mother came home from a shopping trip before the holidays to find that her children had pasted up dozens of signs saying "PATIENCE," which is precisely what she had been lacking before.

  🕮   Before each holiday, I give extra *tzedakah* to the poor, usually in unmarked envelopes so that the people will not know where it comes from. My children and I have a lot of fun figuring out how to give this money to the recipients anonymously. One will slip an envelope into a mailbox. Another will put it through an open window at night. Or, we'll ask a neighbor to give it to the person and not mention where it came from. We all treasure this experience of manifesting what is greatest about the Jewish ethical system, i.e., *gemiluth chesidim.*

You give your children a great treasure when you teach them that giving is life's greatest joy, and that no event need seem meaningless or unfair if looked at as a test of our character and an opportunity to learn and to give.

FOUR

Understanding Your Child's Mind

One manifestation of love is the effort you make to understand how others think and feel. It is important for you to remember what life was like for you back when you were small. This helps you to empathize with what your children are going through now. It also helps you to understand your own irrational responses, for that little child which you once were exists within you now, and often influences your thoughts and actions. When you get snubbed, misunderstood, attacked or disappointed, it is not only the mature adult part of you which reacts. Part of you reacts as you did as a child. For example, when you ask your husband to help and he tells you that he's too busy, is it the child in you which responds or your rational adult? When a child refuses to come when called or eat what you serve, which part of you reacts, your inner adult or your inner child? To sympathize with and understand your child, you have to acknowledge that you, too, have an inner child who is sometimes irrational and selfish. Therefore, as you read the following, realize that this child lives within you as well.

Children Expect External Events and People to Make Them Happy

The Torah obligates a father to teach his son three things: Torah, a profession and good character traits (Rambam, *Commentary on the Mishnah, Makoth* 2:3). This is what eventually brings happiness to a person. Thus, your job is not to make your child happy, but to instill Torah values in him, which alone will help him to face life with a positive attitude.

However, a young child does not know this truth. After all, for his first few years of life, happiness does come from external sources, from the parents and siblings who feed him, play with him and stimulate him. Their presence does mean safety, security and happiness. As he grows, he still expects others to be the source of his inner feelings of happiness. When he is unhappy, he looks around to see who is to blame. And he often wants external sources to provide the solution. He is apt to see his happiness as dependent on the satisfaction of four major desires for:

* possession (toys, clothing, etc.)
* power (freedom to make their own rules and decisions)
* pampering (to be indulged and protected from all discomfort)
* pleasure (fun, excitement, variety, and stimulation)

The problem is that these desires are insatiable. No matter how much you give or where you set the limit, they are bound to want more and be upset that you don't give in to them. If you keep giving in, you encourage them to be more demanding and tyrannical about getting those demands satisfied. You have to make a firm decision as to where you want to stop. That is an individual decision, to be made jointly by you and your husband. Well-meaning friends and relatives are bound to tell you that you are either too strict or too lenient. Do what is comfortable and fitting for your own and your children's particular personalities.

It won't help to get angry at their anger about your "No's." That is the normal, natural and healthy response of a child who will inevitably test your limits to make sure that they are firm and haven't changed since yesterday! As long as you are empathetic yet decisive, they will soon get used to those limits. You can tell them that adults also have trouble with these four areas. After all,

No man dies with even half his heart's desires fulfilled.
(RASHI, MIDRASH RABBA KOHELETH 1:34)

Do try to satisfy your children's reasonable desires for clothing, stimulating toys, independence and decision-making powers and for a realistic amount of love, nurturance and enjoyable experiences. If a child gets upset about your limitations, try the following suggestions, to be used according to his age and level of understanding:

* Empathize with him: "It's really disappointing not to get what you want. I often feel the same way when I don't."
* Fantasize with him: "I bet you would like to own the entire toy store." "I bet you wish I could read to you for the whole evening every single night."
* Write down his request: Put it on a "want list" taped to the fridge. This lets him know that you take his request seriously, even though you know you cannot fulfill it.
* Have him identify whether it is reasonable or unreasonable, a want or a need.
* Distract his attention: "Let's talk about your birthday (or Chanukah celebration)." (Or, you can talk about the birthday which has just passed, if that is closer in time.) This helps him to focus on a different pleasure than the one he wants right now.
* Reassure him that you love him. "Even though I can't always give you what you want, I still love you." This helps eliminate a common insecure thought of children which is, "If Mommy/Daddy/God really loved me, they would give me everything I want and pray for."
* If his disappointment is short-lived, praise him for accepting the pain of the loss without excessive bitterness or anger. Tell him that this is a mark of maturity.
* During non-crisis times, make up stories of children who don't get what they want and have to suffer from pain and disappointment. Then ask your children, "What do you think this child has to do in order to accept the will of Hashem and not sink into anger, jealousy, hatefulness or vengefulness?"
* As they get older, remind them that the only things worth having are those things for which one has struggled. A person who does not know how to endure deprivation in order to achieve a goal is truly deprived!

> My teenage son wanted to go on a trip with friends which we couldn't afford. He was very upset. I had to bear the discomfort of his mood, but I stuck to my guns. I kept being empathetic and after a few hours, he decided that he wanted to earn money by tutoring younger children in math so that he could go on the next trip.

Children Often Do Not Understand the Impact of Their Behavior on Us

Don't assume that what is important for you is important to your children. They often have different priorities and urgencies. Thus, a child may not understand why it is so important for you that he finish his peas, stop his game, go to bed at a certain time or wear some particular item of clothing which you want but which he doesn't. He doesn't care much for clocks and schedules or what the neighbors will think. He cares about **his** stomach, **his** concerns, **his** needs. He sees his desires as being as legitimate and as urgent as yours. He may think that you are being just as inflexible, petty and mean for your lack of cooperation as you think he is for his. He also tends to see his obnoxious behavior as innocent and his mistakes as trivial. Therefore, he may not understand why you explode or feel hurt and may not **want** to understand. Therefore, you have to let your child know that you have feelings and a position of authority which must be respected no matter how he feels. Let him know, very matter-of-factly, without being hostile toward him for not automatically having this knowledge already.

Because parents usually withhold their innermost feelings of hurt and inadequacy from their children, the latter tend to think that we are far more secure, wise, insensitive and invulnerable than we really are. There you are, exploding because he doesn't like your gefilte fish. How does he know that it's really not the fish that concerns you but the fact that a microsecond before you got angry, you were thinking that you must be a real failure if you can't get him to eat your fish when your sister/neighbor/or mother-in-law never had such a problem! Therefore, take the time to let your children know that you have feelings, that you can be hurt, and that he must learn to consider the effect of his actions on others.

Parents are often surprised that children as young as one and a-half or two are responsive to such explanations. It may seem like an enormous investment of time at the moment, but you will find that these explanations ultimately save you from having to use so much force and violence. Obviously, you do not want to tell him a hundred times a day that he is hurting you. That is too guilt-provoking and would lessen the effect of your words. Save your comments for matters which affect your priorities in life.

Insecurity

Children live in a far more insecure world than we do. They are small, dependent on us and often helpless. There may be older siblings who are far more capable, teachers or adults who are insensitive and abusive to them. Because children do not readily distinguish between fantasy and reality, the monsters and ghosts which people their minds seem as real as this book in your hands. If your child had a difficult birth or your home is unusually chaotic and strife-filled, or he has suffered other traumas, his sense of insecurity will be even greater than average. Children may mask their feeling of insecurity by becoming bullies, by over-controlling themselves in a self-punishing way or by adopting various obsessive-compulsive habits (e.g., hand-washing, nose-picking, nail-biting, etc.) These are signs of internal stress which the child cannot handle positively. Do not ignore or minimize his pain. Remember, he does not have the tools to cope with his fears and feelings of inadequacy that you may have developed. He is dependent on you and your husband for his sense of security. He needs to feel loved and successful. If not, he will be scarred.

Awfulizing

Children are "natural awfulizers." The word "awful" implies danger or the threat of great loss. It doesn't take much to provoke a danger response in children, especially those who are deeply-feeling or insecure. A child is apt to attach danger to discomfort because of his vivid imagination and basic sense of helplessness. Also, because he has no sense of time, he fears that the discomfort he is experiencing at the moment will go on forever, which makes the situation seem unbearable.

Whether it's an ice cream or your attention, a child may feel that it's "awful" (i.e., dangerous) not to get it because not getting what he wants reminds him of his vulnerability and powerlessness. If, in addition, there are truly "awful" things happening around him (such as constant criticism, serious illnesses, failures in school or unpopularity with peers) he may carry this pattern of awfulization into adulthood, maintaining a state of constant anxiety in order to prepare himself mentally for what he feels are inevitable disasters lurking around every corner.

To a child, feelings reflect fact. If something feels terrible, he assumes that it must be terrible. If he feels scared, he assumes that something scary must be present. A tired child may react to almost any outside stimulus as if it is dangerous. A more deeply-feeling or insecure child will, of course, have more difficulties in this area. You may not be able to completely eradicate a natural tendency toward anxiety, but the following may help.

* Watch what you "oy vey" or awfulize about. If you react dramatically every time he spills something or makes a mistake, he will internalize the message that, "It's awful [i.e., dangerous] to make mistakes." "It's awful to be imperfect." "It's awful to be me. I have to hide my real self because the truth is that I am no good, a failure, not worthy of being loved or respected."

* Explain the "one-to-ten" scale to your children, in which "ten" is a real tragedy. Tell them that anything below six is a triviality. The next time someone explodes over muddy shoes, a broken pencil, or a less than delicious meal, say, "This is a triviality. We don't cry over trivialities." Or, ask, "On a scale of one-to-ten, where is this?" If a young child is awfulizing, ask him, "Should I call the ambulance or the police?" You can explain the "one-to-ten" scale to small children by spreading your arms wide for a "ten" or major loss and putting them close together for a trivial discomfort.

* Don't awfulize his awfulizing! Realize that he lacks tools. We can philosophize about loss. He can't. Only time will bring the maturity he needs to face disappointments with a Torah *hashkafa*.

> Before we moved, I noticed such a difference in my two girls. One was excited at the adventure. The other had endless psychosomatic illnesses and was positive that she would have no friends and would hate the new place. All I could do was help her identify all her insecure thoughts, write them down, and have her imagine positive things that would happen to replace those thoughts. Even though she is only ten, I've already decided to teach her EMETT. It made her feel better to know that she has a personality type and that she can always take the secure thought that she adjusts once she is in the midst of the difficulty.

Coping with Children's Irrationality

Many parents have unrealistic expectations that their children be rational and reasonable at all times. These are traits which come with maturity. Don't expect your children to be adults. Expect:

1. Irrationality: Do not expect to get a logical answer to questions such as, "Why did you stick your foot out when your brother walked by?" "Why haven't you gotten your shoes on when I told you ten times to do so?" "Why do you always start giggling or hitting someone just when Daddy is about to say *kiddush?*" "Why are you wearing that?" "Why are you fighting about something so stupid?" If, in response to such questions, your children look at you as though you had just spoken Japanese, expect that you have made an unreasonable request for rationality on their parts.

2. Self-preoccupation: Children are self-preoccupied with the gratification of their own needs, not yours. They tend to be self-absorbed. They are not too interested in what others want. You have to train them to care about your need for sleep, quiet, order, privacy and cooperation because such sensitivity does not come naturally. Don't take their insensitivity personally.

3. Shame resistance: Children, like adults, hate feeling ashamed of themselves. Therefore, they will often make excuses for their behavior or try to evade responsibility or awareness of it, e.g.:

* Deny the deed: "I didn't eat the frosting off the cake/didn't cheat on the test/didn't lie/didn't hit him," etc.

* Rationalize the deed: "All the other kids were doing it." "But I was hungry." "But I couldn't control myself."

* Resort to "selective amnesia": "I don't remember doing that." "I don't remember that you told me I couldn't do it."

* Reverse cause and effect or deny cause and effect: "She hit me and that's why I hit her back." (He denies that he was actually the one who hit first or took away a toy or did something else to provoke the incident in the first place.) "My teacher gave me a punishment for no reason! He just hates me, that's all. He's just prejudiced."

* Ascribe volition to objects: "The glass fell." "The juice spilled." "My jacket got lost." This is instead of the more responsible, "I broke a glass." "I spilled the juice." "I lost my jacket."

4. Willingness to give up love for power: You know that your child's most compelling desire is to feel loved by you. Why, then, does he refuse to let you cut his nails/bathe him/come when you call/or take his medicine? Why does he make faces and say that he has no strength when all you have asked is that he do some simple chore or stop fighting with a sibling when he knows how upset you get about this? Because feeling powerful is sometimes a more immediate pleasure than feeling loved!

Don't take your child's drive for power personally. To him, being "grown up" means having power. A sense of personal power is an essential quality in order to cope with life's difficulties. While this drive may sometimes be exasperating to you, it is normal and healthy. The less you "awfulize" their defiance or see it as a personal insult or threat, the more you will be able to find creative solutions which will help your children feel less helpless and, ultimately, less in need of being defiant.

The Need for Stimulation, Excitement and Variety

The nervous system hungers for stimulation. Sensations are "nourishment" for the brain just as food is nourishment for the body. Children have a natural, healthy, innate hunger for this stimulation. When they do not get it, they become fretful, distressed and anxious. A child is biologically driven to crave "sensory nourishment," and the more intelligent the child, the greater will be the desire for a great variety and intensity of such stimulation. You will notice his desire for the following:

TOUCH: He wants to touch everything in his environment and also wants to be held, cuddled, rocked, tickled and played with.
OTHER SENSES: He wants a variety of stimuli for his sense of sight, sound, smell and taste.
MUSCULAR STIMULATION: He wants to experience the sensations which arise from his muscles and joints when he wrestles, pulls, pushes, jumps, swings, runs, hops, skips, lifts, climbs and spins his body. While some of this activity may involve some degree of spontaneous impulsivity, he also needs organized sports and demands for disciplined effort. This builds self-confidence mentally as well as physically.
MENTAL STIMULATION: He wants to know and understand. He is curious. He fills his mind with dreaming, learning and fantasizing.

While every child needs experiences in all four areas, children differ in terms of the areas which are most attractive to them and the optimal level of stimulation which their particular brains find pleasant. Thus, one child loves to be held tight, tossed in the air and tickled while another does not like to be handled roughly, preferring a more gentle, soothing approach. While all children love to learn and all children love muscular activities, some are more "mental" and others more "physical." These differences are inborn. Any attempt to change these innate patterns through force will cause profound disturbance in the child since he instinctively reacts to any attempt to force him to go against his nature.

Many parents do not recognize the urgency of a child's need for stimulation, particularly the need to move, explore, touch and be touched. A child cannot say, "Mom, I'm suffering from sensory deprivation and I feel biologically compelled to ride my bike or climb a tree." Instead, he starts jumping on the bed, fighting with a sibling, whining about how awful he feels or doing something else to get your attention. Parents may condemn the child for being "wild," and become exasperated at him for not being more studious, serious and calm. They may think to themselves, *"Davka,* when I tell him to come in from outside, he doesn't listen to me! What disrespect!" "I tell him to stop jumping and *davka* he keeps it up! I'm a lousy parent if this is how he acts when I make a simple request." With such anger-provoking thoughts in mind, they may scream at or beat the child instead of providing an outlet for those energies or a soothing voice or calming touch which will help him make the transition from a stimulating activity to a non-stimulating one.

It is helpful to think that in most cases it is not lack of respect which causes your child to continue doing what makes him feel good instead of cooperating with your commands, but rather his own inner compulsion to fulfill his need for sensory stimulation. That may not be much help when you are trying to calm him down so that he can get ready for bed or come in from riding his bike to do his homework or eat dinner. You still have the frustration of having to overcome his natural urges and make him submit to your needs. However, when you realize how important stimulation is to him, you will hopefully be less angry at him and less likely to consider his behavior a deliberate insult to your authority.

Realize that the need to play is essential for children. What looks like play to you is essential developmental work for him. The result of getting the appropriate amount of stimulation is that he feels self-confident, powerful, successful and happy. He needs to dig in the sand, climb on the jungle gym and swing on the swings. This is not a waste of time. It is worth the mess and the effort to provide these activities. Children should be provided with equipment such as large tires, ropes, large pieces of foam padding, boxes and heavy objects to push, pull and lift. They need to feel that they can manipulate their environment successfully. All these activities help organize the brain and build self-confidence and stability. Improper stimulation, too chaotic and threatening or too little for the child's needs, can cause a child to become aggressive, listless, withdrawn, anxious or fidgety.

A child with an intense drive for physical stimulation will have a much harder time sitting in school or concentrating on the written word than a more easygoing type. A "cerebral" type may be threatened by more aggressive children. Don't compare types. You may be envious of your neighbor who has such studious, placid types and wish that your lively brood could be the same. But these inborn propensities cannot be changed, no matter how much you scream, beat or nag. Be accepting of your children's natures. Try to provide an environment which suits their individual needs so that they will feel good about themselves as they are.

Obviously, there are times when your children will be bored and hungry for stimulation when you cannot possibly provide it. You cannot be a full-time entertainment director. Even the most creative children will, at times, be bored and in need of gross motor activity which you cannot offer. This is a discomfort which all mothers and children must bear at times. Do the best you can under difficult circumstances. However, if you do see extremes, such as extreme lethargy or extreme hyperactivity, seek help. The average parent does not have the skills to know how to provide the proper organizing activities which will help such children's brains function more effectively.

Also realize that you yourself may suffer from lack of sensory nourishment if you are home all day in a relatively boring, unstimulating environment. Your brain sets up a distress signal because your brain cells feel starved for "food," i.e., for stimulating experiences, even if that may mean a conversation with an adult or a trip to the supermarket. If you feel cranky, restless, anxious and depressed, this may be your problem, one which is very similar to the way a child feels when bored at home or in class.

The Need To Be Touched

Touch is the universal language of love. Yet it is a need which some modern parents dismiss as unessential. Parents often pride themselves on having "good" babies, which they define as babies who make no demands on them. Many such parents avoid holding their children for fear of spoiling them. Such children do sometimes seem to be more independent and serious at an early age, which thrills the parents. What they do not realize is that such "independence" can actually be a sign of despair and lack of trust. The child has learned not to reach out to others because no one will be there. Later on, these adults have little or no ability to make truly loving commitments to others. A touch-deprived child often becomes an adult who is prone to depression and other self-destructive patterns.

In Biblical times, children were not weaned until the age of two. This implies that they received a great deal of physical cuddling and contact. This physical warmth is the foundation for good mental health and emotional intimacy. A person who is out of touch with reality has probably been literally out of touch with the people in his environment as a child.

When your infant is fretful, you may go through your list of possible causes and conclude: "He's been fed, burped, re-diapered, and dressed. He just wants attention. I won't fall for these manipulations on his part." This is a tragic attitude, for cuddling is as important to the child's emotional development as food is to his physical health. Children need to be hugged, rocked and stroked. Stroking gives him a sense of security and self-worth. Furthermore, touching has been found to enhance brain development and strengthen the immune system! Premature infants whose parents are allowed to stroke them through specially made holes in their incubators gain weight faster and are more resistant to infection than those who are not stroked. This is an important lesson for us all. A baby swing can provide a satisfying feeling of being cuddled when you are too busy to hold.

A "high need" child needs more physical reassurance than others. Such children are more anxious and more easily irritated by frustrations and discomforts. It is important to satisfy this need early in life. Otherwise, they may become adults who are so self-preoccupied in getting that attention and reassurance which they missed early in life that they cannot give to anyone else. Furthermore, you may find out around the age of five or six that your child is learning-disabled or has slight neurological weaknesses which were too subtle to be picked up by the doctor at birth. You will be very grateful that you gave him what he needed during his formative years, instead of trying to undo the damage you did by denying him attention out of fear of spoiling him. If your child had a difficult birth or if you or your husband are anxiety-prone, or there are any unusual problems in the environment, do not reject your child's need for extra reassurance. He is not trying to manipulate you. He is turning to you because he has no one else to soothe him.

A child needs love most when he is least lovable. If your child is angry, it is a sign that he is in pain. Do not withdraw from him or reject him at this time. Show him that you care. A touch-deprived child is apt to be hostile or withdrawn. Do not be the kind of parent who thinks, "Well, if he's being obnoxious, then I'm not going to be nice because then he'll be even more obnoxious. And when he's being nice, he doesn't need my attention. So I never need to pay attention to him."

Obviously, you cannot jump every time a child whimpers or hold a child every time he asks to be held. Make every attempt to satisfy his reasonable need to be held and go to him when he is in real distress. Two minutes of holding is often enough to calm a cranky child. Children want so much to be touched that they will often provoke a spanking, have accidents, or pretend to be sick in order to receive even that minimal physical contact. Therefore, schedule "holding time" when they are happy and healthy so that they do not form negative habits. If you feel that they are doing an excessive amount of whining, then tell them that you are no longer going to answer them when they screech or whine (unless, of course, they are in real distress). The next time they whine, say, "I will talk to [or hold] you as soon as you use your grown-up voice."

Sibling Rivalry: As Old as Cain and Abel

Sibling rivalry begins with the birth of the second child. Expect it. Don't think that there are "perfect" families in which sibling rivalry does not exist. It exists in all families. Don't think you have done something wrong if your children fight with each other and manifest signs of intense jealousy. Children look at love the way they look at a bag of cookies — as something which is limited and capable of being used up. They think that the more attention someone else gets, the less there is for them. It can be extremely annoying when they vie for your attention or cry bitterly because you have given something to one and not another.

It takes many years to develop a non-possessive, mature attitude toward love. Until then, expect that your children, some more than others, will fight to get the most and the best and will be angry at you if they end up with what they feel is "mere crumbs." Jealousy can cause your children to be depressed or hostile. If you get violent in return, the children will feel even less loved and more jealous. Time, and the ongoing reassurance of your love will usually heal these wounds. In the meantime, you can allow them to express their jealous feelings in words, but tell them that they must not act on them.

> ☙ I had three children in just under three years. My oldest daughter, who was not yet three, became so obnoxious that I ended up hitting her a lot and calling her names. It was all I could do to keep from telling her that I hated her. Then I went to a Rav who quoted from *Pirkei Avoth* 3:14, "Beloved is man for he is created in the image of God." He told me that this child is no less precious than a *Sefer Torah*. If there is a defect, I have to have it repaired lovingly. That image changed my whole attitude toward her.

Obviously, a child will have more problems with rivalry if there is a sibling who really is more loved than he is or is far better than he in some particular area. Also, if there is a high degree of marital disharmony, the children will fight each other for the bits of attention which are forthcoming and will fear that you feel toward them the way you feel toward your spouse.

After the birth of a child, whatever your expectations, it is likely that your children will surprise you. The oldest might be a real "mommy" or "daddy" to the next born. Older children usually feel very protective and loving toward the newborn, unless they feel that you are already so overburdened that another child means even more screaming and strife. Although about ninety percent of firstborns display some disturbance such as bed-wetting, sleep-disturbances and hostility toward either mother or baby or both, many children, especially boys and girls with strong nurturing capacities, welcome the newborn and show great warmth and protectiveness. Nevertheless, there may be little you can do to lessen their fear that there will be less love for them no matter how much you reassure them. They may test your love by withdrawing from you, hurting the baby or misbehaving when you are nursing and are unable to control them. If your home life is basically happy, see these jealous moments as normal and temporary. It is the price you pay for the joy of having children who will hopefully be less selfish when they grow up because they learned to share as children. Only time and maturity will convince them of your love. The following may be helpful:

* Make up stories about children who don't get along all the time but who love each other underneath it all and come to each other's aid in times of crisis.

* Let them know how happy you are when they **are** cooperating with each other.

* Remind children of the obligation to love each other even if they don't always like the other's behavior.

* Don't play favorites. However, when you are alone with them, tell each one how special he is to you. Mention qualities which you particularly appreciate. If you have a problematic child whom you find difficult to love, be especially attentive to his needs. Work to understand him. Awaken positive feelings in yourself toward him by showing him affection and concern even if it is not sincere initially.

* Don't compare children to each other e.g., "How come Sara is always so helpful, polite, considerate and smart while you are so impossible?"

* Reassure them that, "Mommy has love for everyone." Or, "Mommy's heart stretches. The more love she gives, the more she has to give."

* Replay conflicts and show them that they can find non-violent solutions to problems.

* Don't play favorites. Spend time with each child alone. Make appointments for games of checkers or a walk around the block.
* Before the birth of a baby, purchase a few inexpensive toys which can be taken out and unwrapped during stressful times.
* After nursing the baby, hold your other small ones for a minute or two and tell them how much you love them.

Let your children know that jealousy is a fact of life for all of us. Admit that you yourself sometimes feel jealous and let them know how you deal positively with your own feelings of jealousy when they arise, such as by trusting that Hashem gives you exactly what you need, though maybe not all you want! You can tell them that jealousy essentially stems from insecurity and fear. Work on the source of their insecurity which is their low self-esteem, rather than the jealousy itself.

Attention vs. Spoiling

Many parents are so fearful of spoiling their children that they withhold their love, physical affection and reasonable material possessions from them. They rationalize their stance by saying,

"I'm afraid that if I give an inch, they'll take a mile."
"I'm afraid that if I protect them too much, they'll be tyrannical, selfish brats all their lives, or dependent little weaklings. I want tough kids who can cope with a tough world."

There is actually some truth to these fears. There certainly are men and women who were so pampered as children that they are crippled as adults: they resent hard work, do not know how to sew, clean or do other important life tasks, and resent having to give. The simplest task seems like a difficult burden, and they constantly complain about all their discomforts.

It is not easy to strike a middle balance. No one wants children who are spoiled tyrants who think only of themselves. We want children who know how to work hard, delay gratification and be considerate of others' needs, but who are not deprived of their childhoods. In making this dream a reality, keep the following points in mind:

1. A child, by his very nature, wants to develop his potential to the utmost. He wants to feel important. Therefore, make demands which are appropriate to his age group. Let him know the thrill of working hard to achieve a goal, whether it be a new toy or a new article of clothing.

2. You cannot spoil children under a year with too much holding, except perhaps at night when they do need to learn to fall asleep by themselves. Mothers in countries who carry their children on their bodies all day and sleep with them at night are not known to have spoiled children. Spoiling comes from being over-protective, from not allowing them to be independent and self-sufficient and from overindulgence to their unreasonable demands. You don't have to worry about spoiling if you combine your giving with demands for responsible behavior.

3. A Torah-observant lifestyle makes spoiling difficult since, from an early age the child is habituated to delay gratification, to forego his own desires in order to carry out the many religious obligations and to make *chesed* a major life priority. Also, in a large family, he quickly learns that he won't always get the attention he wants and that he must share with others.

Stubbornness

Many parents use the word "stubborn" as if it were a diagnosis of what is wrong with their uncooperative child. However, the word "stubborn" does not explain a problem. It merely provides an external label, and labels have a way of becoming self-fulfilling prophecies because they guide the behavior of the one using the label as well as the one labeled. The word "stubborn" can be an anger-producing thought if it implies that your child is being deliberately disrespectful and uncooperative.

There are many reasons why a child may balk at cooperating with you, such as fatigue, fear and anxiety. In a young child, stubbornness is an important and healthy manifestation of the child's natural urge toward independence and the development of self-control and mastery of his body and environment. He is simply testing the limits. However, excessive stubbornness at this stage may be a manifestation of your failure to give clear messages about what is permissible. His oppositional stance may be a sign of confusion if you have been wishy-washy and inconsistent. Because a child's inner reality is so fluid and ever-changing, he assumes that external reality is just as flexible, and will test to see if yesterday's rights and wrongs still hold today. It makes a child feel safe to push up against the old rules and find that they are still firmly in place. ("Right, you still cannot eat in the living room, and you must wear your jacket if the temperature is under X degrees.") Therefore, although your child may seem outwardly to be fighting restrictions, it is important that you enforce reasonable limits which enhance his sense of being protected by secure boundaries.

On the other hand, if you have been excessively strict, his resistance may be a sign of tension and anxiety, as he fights to maintain his sense of integrity and power in the face of your excessive demands. Such a child is stubborn because he needs to experience *more* control over his world, not less. He may also be stubborn toward you even though the source of his anxiety is some outside force, such as an abusive teacher or domineering older sibling. Since he can't flex his muscles against them, he turns against you to experience a sense of power.

In addition, a child may become oppositional if the home environment is chaotic, in order to provide himself with an illusion of power in what, to him, is an essentially frightening and unstable world. The ability to enrage his parents can give a child a feeling of power to lessen his feeling of helplessness.

Another source of excessive opposition is found in the basically insecure, learning disabled or minimally brain-damaged child. This child feels anxious just being alive. He often does not even know where he is or who he is! He becomes easily disoriented. He tries to control those around him because he himself feels so out of control. He may cling obsessively to habits because they give him a sense of security and order. It is as though he is saying, "Everything else is so chaotic. At least I can bite my nails/pull out my hair/say 'No' to everything I'm told to do/suck my thumb, etc. These are things I can count on which give me a sense of control." Slaps, screams and nagging only make him feel in greater need of such habits. It takes great patience and a very understanding adult to avoid rejecting the child in such a state and to give him the direction and positive controls he so desperately needs.

Just because you understand what may be causing your child to be oppositional does not mean that you should let him run wild! On the contary, it means that you have to work even harder to give him clear, consistent rules and to provide security and order. He needs to be obedient and cooperative for his own self-esteem and self-protection as well as your peace of mind.

The oppositional child who is insecure will require a different approach than one who is basically self-confident and secure. The child whose inner world is in turmoil needs more structure along with greater physical attention. The confident child may need more demands placed on him in terms of performance and responsibility. If you are confused as to how to approach your child, consult more experienced mothers or an Observant child-care expert. Remember, you want to retain what is positive about the quality of stubbornness, the sense of integrity and self-protection, but eliminate the lack of consideration and selfishness involved.

The "First Child Syndrome": Pushing Independence and Success at the Price of Mental Health

Many older parents sorely regret the excessive pressure they put on their first child to be grown-up and "successful" at too early an age. All too late, they realize that they were trying to satisfy their own need for public approval and selfish comfort by being excessively harsh and making demands of their first child which the child should not have been forced to fulfill. They wanted to make their baby "tough," so they did not go to him when he cried. They wanted to show everybody how impervious they were to "manipulation," so they never gave in to even reasonable requests of the child for attention, possessions or decision-making powers. They wanted to show the world that they were more successful than others by having the smartest child on the block, the first child to be toilet trained, and the most obedient of all children. No thumb-sucking or defiance from this one!

When the second child comes along, there is even more pressure on the first to "grow up fast." The parents think they can skip over important developmental stages, particularly the stage of dependency by being harshly authoritarian. Oftentimes, these little children do appear superficially to be fulfilling their parents' wishes. They often do become toilet trained very early and maintain a serious demeanor. However, the backlash may come later as the child suddenly develops "nervous symptoms" such as nail-biting or stomach disturbances or sudden bed-wetting after having been dry for a long period. The child becomes a "nervous wreck" or an aggressive, angry bully. Only then do the parents sometimes realize that the incredible tension that had been imposed on the child too early in life has done irreparable damage.

A child who feels loved and secure will automatically develop according to his own inner timetable and will crave independence without any pushing on the parents' part. Any excessive tension which you impose can only inhibit or distort that process.

It is common for adults to impose their own standards on their first child. They simply do not realize their child's limitations. Because they are used to assuming *davka*, they think, "He wet his pants on purpose!" "He's crying just to get me upset!" "He is deliberately defying my authority by not eating!" They do not realize that a child below the age of five or six is ruled by passions and impulses, not logic.

Realistically high standards can be exciting and challenging to a child who feels he can reach those standards. You can push a child to the limits of his capacity as long as he is showing interest and having success. But if the child fears that you will reject him if he fails and that your love is conditional upon his accomplishments, he will experience an inner anxiety and tension which can be emotionally devastating. Be in touch with your child's own particular needs for nurturance, play and mastery and do not subordinate those needs to your own desire for public approval and excessive control.

Leaving Your Child

During the first few years of life, your child establishes a basic sense of trust in people if he is protected from harm and treasured as special. A good caretaker can protect him, but only a parent can make him feel cherished.

> I saw such a change in my seven month old when I stopped teaching for summer vacation and spent more time with him. He brightened up. He stopped being so sickly. He became happy and more responsive. I hadn't even realized that he had been lacking anything until I saw the change.

At the same time, we are all aware that periodic separations between children and their mothers prevent boredom and irritability. Do not feel guilty about leaving your child in the hands of a really caring mother-figure who will hold him and stimulate his mind. Being away from him for a few hours a day may improve your relationship with him and make you more appreciative if, and this is a big "if," you do not come home so harried and overwhelmed that you are too tense and busy to give him quality time.

A child under the age of five has no sense of time. When you are gone for more than a day or two, he may think that you are never coming back. When you are out of his sight, it is as if you do not exist. Therefore, try to keep your absences short.

Most children love being in play groups with others their age. They thrive on the stimulation and companionship that only a group can provide. If your child protests when you leave, stand by the door for a few minutes and note how long it takes him to stop crying. Often, his attention is diverted within a few minutes. If he cries for over an hour, he may not be ready to be left or the caretaker may not be to his liking.

Make a firm decision about leaving him with a sitter when you must. Any ambivalence on your part will be detected by him and make him more fearful and anxious. If you are an insecure mother, it may be more difficult for you to separate from him than for him to separate from you. This is another good reason for you to spend some time away from him, as he needs to be away from your anxiety and to develop his own sense of independence and self-mastery.

Body Exploration

All small children explore their bodies. The body is the child's first and foremost source of pleasure. Do not get over-anxious, hysterical or disgusted, or the child may feel compelled to turn to himself even more for the pleasure which is lacking in his outer environment. The tension, fear, confusion and shame aroused by this subject often leads to a lifelong, negative attitude towards one's body. And since the child's feeling about his body reflects his feelings about himself, he may internalize a feeling that, "If my mommy thinks that my body is bad and disgusting, then I am too."

Self-stimulation is usually a sign of boredom more than anything else. This is especially a problem with a child who has a greater hunger for muscular activity and general stimulation than other children. Distract him with a toy or a book. Keep his hands busy by giving him clay, paints, hammer and nails, or other activities which will provide that stimulation. As he gets older, provide creative outlets for his nervous energy such as sports, crafts, and music. Do not expect that studying will satisfy all his needs for sensory nourishment.

You want your child to feel positive about his body because this will help him feel good about himself as a whole. His future intimate relationships in marriage will directly reflect his feelings about himself and his experiences as a child. Any anxiety on your part will be translated by him as a sign of rejection and shamefulness. If you have problems in this area, discuss your anxiety with an Observant therapist so that you do not pass your negativity on to your child. The Jewish religion wants marital intimacy to take place in a context of joy and mutual love and respect. This cannot take place if the foundation is one of fear and shame.

Children's Sleep Problems

Second only to eating problems are problems with sleep. This is one time when you often have to let a young baby have a good cry. A ten- or fifteen-minute cry in the evening can help him release the tension of a very stimulating day. Sometimes it may take even longer for him to relax. This cry is different from his other cries. You usually notice that he seems to be "winding down" after crying for some time. However, if he seems to be getting more hysterical, then you may need to hold him. This is a tricky situation, since by going to him, he may be learning that if he just cries long enough, you will eventually come, whereas what you want him to learn is that he needs to fall asleep by himself. If you have given him plenty of attention and holding during the day, don't feel guilty about his cries.

Dr. Richard Ferber, director of the Center for Pediatric Sleep Disorders, in Boston, has written a very practical book which provides strategies to ensure good sleep habits for children. Among his very important points, he states that many parental habits may actually be interfering with their children's sleep. Because bedtime means a time of separation, the child may experience some anxiety and be frightened. Therefore, it helps to have a bedtime ritual to allow for the smooth transition from waking to sleeping. You can rock him, cuddle him, read him a story and end by holding him while you say the *Sh'ma.* Then say a firm, "Good night," and walk out. He needs to know that it is now time for him to be by himself, just as it is time for you to turn to your other interests. [Note: Some mothers, with their close, almost symbiotic relationship with their children, have more trouble separating from them than other mothers.]

However, some children put up resistance for one reason or another or awaken throughout the night. Dr. Ferber explains that one reason for this is because of improper "sleep associations." When you go to sleep, you are used to having a certain pillow, position or other associations which help you relax. We all awaken momentarily during the night and usually fall back asleep without even realizing that we have awakened if our "sleep associations" are still there. However, if the pillow is on the floor, the blanket at the bottom of the bed, or a light on which wasn't there before, we are apt to become more alert. The same thing happens to a child. He associates sleep with certain sounds, stimuli or people. If he is used to being rocked to sleep while nursing, or being sung to and having his crib shaken, then when he awakens, he wants those same conditions to be present. If they are not, then those momentary wakings which we all experience briefly become sources of anxiety and fear. He wants his bottle, his pacifier or you. He is not used to falling asleep by himself. Therefore, you must make sure that your child's sleep associations are such that they can be maintained even if you are not around. If your child has already learned the wrong "sleep associations," you can usually undo the damage within a few days by the following:

* Each night, follow a "bedtime ritual," after which you leave the child **while he is still awake.**

* If he cries, wait for five minutes before going back in the room. Then go to him, reassure him, but do not pick him up if he

cries. Leave after two or three minutes. If he cries again, then wait ten minutes this time before going back in to him and repeating the previous procedure. Next time, wait fifteen minutes before going to him if he cries. Then wait twenty minutes. Usually, the child will fall asleep by himself after the fourth or fifth time.

* If you are tempted to go in before the time is up, remind yourself that the most important thing for your child is for him to learn to fall asleep by himself and that he will eventually do so if you let him.

* Do not use the "cold turkey" approach of letting him cry it out for hours. This actually keeps the crying period to a maximum as he becomes more and more terrified at your absence. With the progressive approach, you offer him reassurance. [Most mothers find the "cold turkey" approach difficult on their nerves and impossible if there are close neighbors or other children in the same room who become hysterical at the prolonged crying.]

* If he has been using a bottle, gradually dilute the amount of milk or juice with increasing amounts of water (one ounce at a time) along with the volume in the bottle until he no longer has a bottle. He will then urinate less and will also not look frantically for the bottle when he awakens.

* If he is old enough to get out of bed and does so, close the door for one minute. Tell him that you will open it only if he gets back into his bed. Do not lock the door since this will terrify him. You want to show him that **he** has some control over the situation: i.e., that he can control whether the door is open or shut by his behavior. If he gets up, it closes. If he stays in bed, it stays open. His feeling of control calms him down by making him feel more secure.

* If you are nursing, try to put him in bed while he is still awake. If he cries, have your husband go to him rather than yourself. That way, he does not become stimulated by your presence.

As with all problems, you want to minimize your tension so that you do not arouse anxiety in the child. You want to communicate to your child that you sympathize with him and see that he is having a difficult time but that with patience, it will be solved. Give him support, not punishments. [Note: the above recommendations are for a child above the age of three to six months. A colicky or insecure child, especially one born in distress, may require even more time. No child should be left in distress for any prolonged period of time.]

It is easy to have a rather peaceful bedtime ritual with only one child. However, once you have more than one, things become far more complicated, especially if you have more than one small child in the same room keeping the others up with giggles and cries or, as they get older, with complaints, arguments or conversations.

> ✍ Last night was typical. My older boys came home from yeshivah famished, one at 6 P.M. and the other at 7 P.M. They wanted to eat right away. The baby was crying to be nursed and the two year old was squeezing her hard to get her to stop crying. My four year old had a stomachache and my seven year old was crying because he hadn't learned the multiplication table for the test the next day. I've learned that I cannot be all things to all people. I just do the best I can with the energy, creativity and time I have at the moment. I can so easily become hateful and hysterical. It takes all the spiritual tools I have to keep from going under. Mostly, I remind myself that they do not understand what I am going through because they have never been in my shoes, just like I didn't understand my mother's need for help when I was a child. I give them the benefit of the doubt to calm myself down and to be able to talk to them respectfully. Definitely a big test of my *middoth*.

No one said it was going to be easy! Nighttime is when everything that didn't hurt your children during the day begins to hurt. Everything they forgot to tell you suddenly becomes a burning topic of conversation. This is when you discover lice, undone homework, unread notices from teachers and sundry other problems. This is when it may be most difficult to control your harmful impulses. When they get cranky, whiney, stubborn, irrational, mean and aggressive, you may be sorely tempted to do the same. While there are no simple solutions, the following may help:

* Have a neighborhood teenager come in around five o'clock to bathe the younger ones and read to them.
* Have an older child perform your bedtime ritual with a younger one.
* Make sure meals are prepared for the ones who come home famished in the evening, even if you have to make them in the morning.
* Turn off your phone. This is time for your children. They need your full attention.

* Play soothing music.

* Try, at least, to hold the younger ones while saying the *Sh'ma* with each one before they go to sleep.

* To give a positive end to the day, try two "games": a) The "*Baruch Hashem* Game," in which you ask the child what particular things he has to be thankful for that day, and b) The "Mitzvah Game" in which he tells you what mitzvoth he did that day. Both "games" leave the child with pleasant memories and, hopefully, will become lifelong habits.

* This is not the time to be putting yourself down with guilt-producing thoughts, such as "I can never be enough or do enough," or putting your kids down with anger-producing thoughts, such as, "They are inconsiderate, bad children." Be creative and constructive.

> 🐝 My six year old said he couldn't go to sleep because he was having scary thoughts. I kept telling him to just leave me alone and go to sleep, but he kept whining. Then I remembered the method that another mother in my group had used with her teenaged daughter, in which she compared the mind to a radio with many stations. I thought he would be too young for such a technique, but I tried it anyway. I touched the left side of his forehead, and told him that that was the station for sad thoughts, the right and said that that was the place for scary thoughts, the middle and told him that that was the place for happy thoughts. I touched the right and left sides again and had him give me a thought for each one. Then I touched the middle and we spent about five minutes talking about all the happy events we could remember from the past and all the happy things we could think about that might happen in the future. I told him that he was in control of his "radio" and could tune into whatever station he wanted. By that time he wanted to go to sleep. Over the next two days, I touched him a few times in the middle of his forehead and asked for a happy thought. By the third day, he told me, "I'm O.K. now, Mom. No more scary thoughts."

Remember, when you yourself are tired you are most apt to make mountains out of molehills and have pessimistic thoughts about yourself and your life.

Toilet Training

Toilet training, like any other skill which you want to teach your child, should be done in a relaxed manner. Any tension and anxiety on your part will delay the process. Successful training requires neurological maturity, which develops differently in different children. According to experts, the best time to begin training boys is at two years, seven months, and girls, two years, three months. However, there are many variables which can affect this recommendation.

As with feeding problems, the child resists because he feels that the parent is not interested in him as a human being with individual needs. Rather, there is an infantile power struggle taking place in which the parent wants to prove that he's more powerful than the child by making the child submit to his will. Withholding the desired "product" or releasing when not appropriate then become the only weapons the child has to assert his right to have control over his own body. One way to avoid this is to allow the child to take as much control as possible over the process. Another is to avoid thinking of yourself as a success or failure according to your child's performance.

It is important for your child to associate the potty with a pleasurable experience. If the child is tense, then his muscles will naturally tense when he is on the chair, and only after he is off will he be able to relieve himself! Your pinched, angry face or hostile words convey to the child that he is wrong and bad, which makes him more tense so that it is even harder for him to relax his muscles. He might eventually become trained, but he will do so despite your efforts, not because of them. Do whatever possible to keep yourself calm. This means not competing with neighbors whose children have been trained earlier than yours, avoiding relatives who tell you that you are doing everything wrong, and avoiding the tendency to see your competency and worth as a human being determined by how quickly you toilet train your children.

Training requires a complex set of skills, including awareness of the need to void, which some children do not develop as early as others, the ability to communicate his need to you, and the ability to wait until he gets to the potty before voiding. These are complexities to a child. To maximize success, you should completely avoid punishments, threats, spankings and scoldings. Continue training him only if he shows interest and enthusiasm for continuing. If not, go back to diapers. It is not worth your mental health or his to force him before he is ready. The added stress on him will eventually backfire somewhere.

There are excellent books on the subject which will teach you how to recognize a child's readiness to be trained and good exercises you can use. For example, at various times during the day, ask him to detect if he is "wet" or "dry." Praise him if he is dry. Don't say anything if he is wet. Or, say, "Good. I'm glad that you knew that you were wet." Once he is able to sit, make it a pleasant experience. Read to him. Give him lots to drink along with salty snacks which encourage him to drink more. Try to distract his attention so that he doesn't tense his muscles. Praise him for being able to sit quietly. Start with a minute or two and gradually increase the time. If he does not urinate, **praise him for sitting.** If he does urinate, reward him with a hug.

Toilet training is a crucial stage in the development of a child's self-image. If you recoil in horror when he has an accident or hit him, he may feel that he is bad, unworthy and incapable of being successful or of winning your love. This will only increase his tension. Make the experience a pleasurable one which will give him a feeling of self-confidence. Don't tell him that he is dirty or keep using that word in reference to what he makes. Remember, the Jewish attitude is to feel blessed that everything is in working order!

Bedwetting

According to Dr. Ferber in *Solve Your Child's Sleep Problem*, 45 percent of all children are likely to be bedwetters if one parent was, and 90 percent if both parents were bedwetters. Fifteen percent of all five year olds and five percent of all ten year olds wet their beds. About 60 percent of all bedwetters are boys. The effect of ongoing enuresis can be far-reaching because it affects the child's self-image. A bedwetter may believe that he is incapable of self-control in general and that he is shameful, immature and incompetent.

Doctors disagree as to the source of the problem. One doctor claims that eight out of nine bedwetters are allergic to some food (*Prevention*, July 1986, p. 59). However, other doctors disagree, and feel that all nighttime incontinence is mainly due to an immature bladder. Specialists can advise methods to strengthen the sphincter muscles and increase the bladder's ability to hold increasingly larger volumes of urine. Some recommend a rubber sheet and alarm system to alert the child to the fact that he is wetting. Both methods take quite a bit of persistence before success is achieved.

All theorists agree that children who are unusually stressed are more prone to bed-wetting. Excessive academic pressure, or a hostile environment at home or in school can create tension which is only released at night when the child releases control. Lack of an outlet for his physical energies during the day can also create inner tension and lack of sensitivity to bodily cues. Do not increase your child's feeling of failure and tension by scolding, shaming or punishing him for wetting. Tell him honestly, but non-dramatically, that you do not like the extra work involved in changing his bedding, but do not indict his whole character.

Do not assume that your child is doing this *davka*. **No normal child would consciously choose such a humiliating and self-punishing method of expressing anger.** Instead, assume that he has not learned self-control yet and is in a lot more pain than you are about the matter, even if he does not seem to be upset about it on the surface. As soon as he is old enough, he should take over the responsibility for laundering his bedding and putting on fresh sheets. All of this should be done without tension caused by your anger or impatience.

You may be able to prevent or diminish the problem to a certain degree by making sure that your babies and growing children get plenty of physical affection and have outlets for their energies. This trains a child to be in touch with the subtle physical cues which must be noticed in order for him to know when he needs to void. Excessive pressure to perform academically may make the child feel cut off from his body. He lives "from the neck up," because the physical realities are too painful. This is especially true if he is being hit or abused in school or at home. It is well-known that such children have a greater tendency to be incontinent.

FIVE

Respecting Your Child's Individuality

Most young parents have an image of what the "perfect child" should be like and then try to force their children into that pre-existing image. However, a child does not come to us as an empty vessel. He has natural talents and dispositions which may conflict with that image. When parents force a child to behave in ways which conflict with his innate personality, the child feels uncomfortable, bored, irritated and distressed. Obviously, we all have to do things we do not like to do at times. However, if a child never has the opportunity to experience fulfillment in accordance with his God-given talents and propensities, he cannot help but suffer profoundly.

Different Personalities

Hashem obviously meant for there to be as many differing personalities as there are people.

Just as there are no two faces exactly alike, so too are there no two people with exactly the same way of thinking.

(BERACHOTH 5:9)

Despite our differences, many of our Sages have tried to classify people according to major common characteristics. One well-known system classifies people according to the degree of air, fire, earth and water which any given person has within his nature. A variation on that theme mentioned here* is based on the notion that every human being has many emotional and intellectual

---
* Taken from *Please Understand Me.*

drives. What differentiates one person from another is a variety of factors, such as the degree of energy with which one pursues those drives, whether the person is introverted or extroverted, secure or insecure, and his cultural conditioning, intelligence level and value system.

Among the hungers which impinge on every normal person are the following: 1) hunger for independence and pleasurable action, 2) hunger for usefulness and structure, 3) hunger for knowledge, and 4) hunger for love and meaning. We all have some degree of all four. But some people are more balanced than others. Many people have innate or culturally-imposed dominances. Do not think of the following categories as exclusive. Rather, think of your child as strong in some areas, while weaker in others. Hopefully, by recognizing his nature, you can help him maintain a proper balance, or "middle path" recommended by the Rambam (see *Hilchoth Deoth* 1:4) and keep him from going to harmful extremes.

1. Need for Autonomy, Action and Mastery Over Objects in the Environment (AMO)

A child who is dominant in this area is usually good-natured, optimistic, exuberant and somewhat insubordinate, for he relates to others on an equal, fraternal level. He takes great joy in life. His desire for excitement often causes him to get into messes and trouble rather easily. His possessions may be in a jumble because he is so busy doing other things that it is difficult for him to take time out to hang, fold, put away and organize his belongings, even though, in a spurt of orderliness, he can do so very nicely. Most of the time, his attitude is, "Why should I waste my time doing these tedious chores when I could be doing more important things like having fun?!" Yet, if you can make the activity fun, he'll do it willingly.

If a child has a strong drive in this direction, he will tend not to think too much of the past or the future, but will live in the moment and delight in being able to do things spontaneously. One of his greatest pleasures is in creating commotions because he loves excitement. He may jump from one thing to another because his main interest is action. Yet, if he is excited about a project, he will exhibit tremendous stamina and endurance, persevering in an activity with excited concentration and determination. These children have great resilience and can bounce back from a physical or psychological blow with even greater strength and determination.

The strong-willed, dominant AMO does not like to prepare or plan in advance. He loves to do things impulsively. He gets easily excited and can be difficult to calm down. He should not be called "hyperactive" if he sleeps well and is able to concentrate for long periods on things which interest him. He is simply exuberant and needs time alone, space to be by himself and training in how to relax himself in order to be able to wind himself down.

The action-oriented (AMO) child can have great difficulty in school since he tends to become lethargic and sleepy when he is not active. It is difficult for him to concentrate when he is in the position of being a passive vessel. You may wonder, "Won't he ever grow up and be serious?" But he cannot wait to be done with what, to him, is often a boring and restrictive classroom atmosphere and to get on with the "really important" things in life. In school, he may dream of some action-filled fantasy instead of paying attention. When he thinks about being grown-up, he dreams of doing things which involve physical action and the use of tools. These children are often labeled "underachievers," since most school systems fail to tap their potential with challenging activities.

A teacher or parent can best engage this child's cooperation by making the task fun and injecting an element of risk, competition, drama and excitement into the lesson. This child loves hands-on experiences: crafts, sports, music, carpentry, sewing, cooking, anything which involves the manipulation of tools or objects in the environment. If disciplined for being wild, he is apt to be indifferent or to run away, hoping to escape adult wrath next time by being more clever, or philosophically accepting the adult's anger as the price he must pay for his treasured freedom.

It is very tempting to use violence with AMOs because they are the most defiant. However, they are also tough and are the most apt to be violent in return and also to be most hardened to it. Learn to be strict and authoritative without violence. Obviously, this is easier said than done, since these children resist control and like a hands-off approach from parents! But you must find ways to allow him to use his energies constructively. Otherwise, you will begin to resent his existence and become abusive, which will provoke constant battles between the two of you. Don't let this happen. These children have wonderful spirits. Don't try to break them. Instead, direct their exuberant energies. Find people who can interact creatively with him. Find outlets for his great physical energies. Remember, it is not his fault that he has such a strong need to interact physically with his environment. That is a God-given temperament which must be respected and directed, not denied or squelched.

These children often respond very well to *paradoxical interventions,* in which you make statements like, "Please do **not** get up and help me," or "I'm not going to let you practice the piano more than five minutes. Even if you beg me to continue, you'll have to stop." These statements appeal to the fun-loving, independent side of the AMO so that you find that he will jump up and start helping or insist on practicing.

The strong AMO does not like to work under close supervision. He does not want external controls and may see even normal obligations and commitments as too restricting, since he hungers for freedom of movement. He is democratic and does not stand much on ceremony or rank. Since his initial response is to avoid commitments and obligations, you must patiently teach him to balance his desire for freedom with an awareness of the importance of being responsible and reliable.

The AMO, while capable of impulsive generosity at times, often has difficulty with the quality of giving, for he sees the act of giving as something which then binds him to the receiver, thus reducing his treasured freedom by creating connections, obligations and responsibilities. He may also have difficulty being compassionate, since his feeling side is often undeveloped. To maintain balance, it is important to make sure that he has opportunities to give to others and develop sensitivity to other people's pain. Endorse him when he does display such behavior.

2. Need for Duty, Obedience and Service (DOS)

As much as the AMO wants to be free, the DOS wants to be *bound* by schedules, rules and regulations, family responsibilities, and group obligations. He prides himself on being obedient and wants to be praised for being so. He says, in effect, "Tell me what to do and I'll do it, no questions asked." The way they are told to do things is *law* to them.

The child who is a dominant DOS serves because he *should*, because that is what he is *supposed* to do. Just as the dominant AMO feels compelled to be free, the DOS hungers to be of service, to carry out orders and to fulfill obligations. He likes organization and order. He loves to plan and prepare in advance. He can run a little camp for younger children at an early age, plan a big event and organize a party with aplomb. He loves ritual and routine, and easily accepts the notion of status, rank, class and position. He likes to feel that he belongs to his particular place in a hierarchy, group or organization. He enjoys history and will be interested in family trees and traditions.

The duty-oriented DOS likes the security of the same neighborhood, school system and friends and is greatly distressed by a move away from the known and the familiar. A dominant DOS child does well in a large family, and enjoys the responsibilities of taking care of others and being of service. He is usually self-assured, efficient, and decisive. He hungers to feel that he belongs. He is very concerned with what is legal, socially acceptable, right and proper. He is a saver and a conservator. His conservatism is seen in his desire to do things the way they have always been done in the past and in his resistance to innovations. The best way to get through to this child is to appeal to his sense of propriety and duty. He does not usually cause discipline problems. When he is disciplined, he wants to try even harder to please.

The DOS child enjoys learning in a step-by-step procedure and having things explained to him with clearly-defined rules and regulations. Schools were made for the dominant DOS child and he feels very much at home in school. He prides himself on being obedient and being of service and wants to be acknowledged for what he gives. He is responsible, dependable and duty-bound. Yet the DOS does not automatically feel deeply for the people whom he serves. Unless he is also a very feeling type, he can be very devoted to an ideal, a cause, or a group because he hungers to feel useful rather than because of any deep feeling for humanity.

On the other hand, if he has a strong feeling side, he will want so much to please that he may over-commit himself because he cannot say, "No." He will need help in learning how to avoid excessive responsibility for everyone's problems or being resentful that others are not as dutiful, giving and serious as he is (especially the AMOs, who get on his nerves for being silly and wild and the fourth type, the LTs for being "spacey" and disorganized).

The DOS can become so obsessed about doing what's right and doing it the right way that he loses all joy and spontaneity and makes himself and everyone around him tense. He must avoid the tendency to become a rigid, obsessive stickler for details and legalities while completely ignoring the need for flexibility or consideration of human feelings and compulsively performing ritualized movements and activities in a very anxious manner. This is partly due to the fact that, for the DOS, customs, rituals, personal habits and opinions take on the status of holy Law in his mind. This may cause him to be very intolerant, as he thinks that only he knows the *right* way to think and act, which to him means his way, according to his patterns and his traditions.

The above two down-to-earth, more rooted types are in contrast to the following more innovative, intuitive types.

3. Need for Knowledge and Intellectual Proficiency (KIP)

A child who is very dominant in this area is driven by curiosity-hunger. He has a quick grasp of abstract religious, scientific and mathematical facts very early. He is always questioning, "Why?" This is not the defiant "why" of the AMO, nor the AMO's practical desire to know how things work in order to use tools more effectively, but rather a love of theoretical information for its own sake. If you tell him not to do something, this awakens the desire to do it, as he wonders, "Now I have to find out what will happen if I take my watch apart/climb on that contraption/look in that box/turn that knob, etc." He wants to know everything there is to know, no matter how abstract or theoretical, whereas the AMO and DOS want practical information.

The dominant KIP is independent and somewhat of a nonconformist, not concerned about external appearances like the AMO and the DOS. He can also be very aloof and detached in his reactions to others. Pride and dignity are very important to him. If hit or scolded, he will retreat into himself and feel terribly wounded. He will be more responsive to well-reasoned arguments and logic than to physical force.

As he gets older, a dominant KIP may seem like an intellectual snob. The truth is that he is very intelligent and is a high achiever academically. What others do not see is the self-doubt and fear of failure which often underlie his passionate quest for knowledge, a quest which he himself knows can never be totally fulfilled since he can never possibly know all there is to know.

The dominant KIP tends to be intellectually precocious but somewhat socially retarded because he is apt to be oblivious to the reactions, feelings and needs of others. He may talk to, but not relate with, people, since he is so often lost in his world of abstractions. He may think that displays of emotion are babyish. In his presence, a person may feel that he does not really exist for the KIP. If his feeling side is weak, he will be reluctant to express affection and may not like to be touched. He may seem cold and unfeeling. Because he is so self-critical and stringent with himself, he tends to be the same with others, and can be curt, sarcastic and critical of those he considers less competent or clever or in any way beneath him.

The strong KIP tends not to be overly attracted to rituals and ceremonies. He prefers to pursue his solitary drive to find out as much as he can about his areas of greatest interest. He loves carefully-constructed philosophical abstractions, scientific facts and thinking things through logically. If he is very bright, he will be sought after for his keen insights and analyses of complex issues.

A warm-hearted KIP is caring and will want to share his ideas with others, thus making him a good teacher. The KIP not only *wants* to be intellectually proficient. He feels he *must* be competent in order to be worthy of respect. He is devastated by ridicule or criticism which imply that he is incompetent. When this happens, he projects his feelings of failure outward, becoming ruthlessly critical of those around him, implying constantly that they are incompetent. Because competency is so important, he hates to fail and may not admit to mistakes, to the point where he becomes arrogant and self-deluding. He drives himself ruthlessly toward perfection of his knowledge, not wanting to let his mind be idle for one second, to the point where he can lose touch with his own and others' feelings or practical, everyday needs.

4. Need for Love and Truth (LT)

The dominant LT is deeply-feeling, poetic, hypersensitive, intuitive, linguistically gifted, psychologically insightful and richly imaginative. LTs hunger for closeness with others and want very much to understand and be understood. They are often involved in *causes* to help others. They are also profoundly concerned about meaning, and may question you early about the meaning of life, particularly in the face of death and disaster. However, your logical answers may not satisfy them. Satisfying answers are more likely to come from intuitive leaps of mystical inspiration which offer them a grasp of ultimate meaning and oneness.

The LT is the most people-oriented of all (as opposed to tool-oriented or theory-oriented types). The LT is hypersensitive to rejection and conflict. He cannot help but feel what others are feeling. That is his nature. It does not help to tell him not to take things to heart. He cannot help but do so. He will go to great lengths to avoid conflict. He tries to make peace and becomes very disturbed when there is any negativity in his immediate environment. The dominant LT child often feels very fragile and vulnerable. He lives in a state of hyper-arousal to all that is going on inside and around him. He does not have the defensive armor of the other types. The slightest criticism or sign of rejection whether real or imagined is very painful to this deeply-feeling child. If the home atmosphere is hostile and chaotic, he is apt to become withdrawn and suffer from psychosomatic illnesses, particularly digestive disturbances. He may complain of fears and doubts no matter how much you try to please. And because he sees so many different sides to every situation, decisions may be difficult. He thrives on reassurance that he is loved and approved of, and needs physical displays of affection. He also needs help in being more objective and in finding an outlet for his rich innovative and creative longings. Once he has this outlet, he will be much happier.

The LT disdains superficiality because he hungers for profundity and meaning. He wants his conversations, the events in his life, his actions and relationships to be meaningful, not frivolous or insignificant. He enjoys giving meaning to events and *spiritualizing* even the most mundane situations. While the DOS believes that it is important to sacrifice the individual for the sake of the group or the ideal, the LT will be the one who will be concerned that the individual have the right to be heard and have his opinions respected.

Because the LT feels so deeply, he is often involved in activities geared toward relieving suffering. As a matter of fact, the LT, who suffers so deeply with so many profound emotions, eventually finds that the best relief from that internal pain is to be involved in helping others. By giving to others, LTs are able to restrain their tendency to be excessively self-preoccupied with or paralyzed by their deep feelings, a tendency which can sometimes be a burden to themselves as well as their family members.

The LT has a sense of anticipation about the future. If the child is optimistic, then his imaginings about the future will be positive. If not, he will be gloomy, insecure and anxious. Help him to develop a positive imagination by teaching him how to discipline his mind. [A good technique is mentioned at the end of the chapter on bedtime complications.]

Just as you must spend extra time *doing* with the AMO, providing outlets for the DOS to feel useful, engaging in intellectual conversations with the KIP, you will need to spend time listening to the feelings of the LT or that child will feel very alone and unloved. You will notice that your LT child will want to know all about the personal details of your life and the personal details of guests. He is not being nosey. He simply cares about people.

Be Tolerant

If you cannot *type* your child, it may be that he has a very good balance between all four areas or that his particular area of dominance has not yet come to the fore. Also, some children go through phases in which they try out another dominance to be more in tune with a certain friend or ideal they may have read about or met recently. In addition, a child needs to display each dominance at different times of the day.

These differences will inevitably affect a child in every aspect of his life: the way he thinks, feels, perceives the world and behaves. However, extremes are rare, and almost all children will display aspects of each temperament at times.

The degree to which any given child experiences these drives or hungers also affects his relation to Torah learning and religion in general. One child may be very interested in all the fine details of each and every law, while another may be more concerned about service, or the "duties of the heart." What is exciting for one may be boring for another. A teacher who gets along just fine with certain pupils may have great difficulty with others. You often find the down-to-earth, decisive, practical AMO and DOS types upset with the rather *extraterrestrial* nature of the KIPs and LTs, and vice versa. The LTs may see the AMOs as emotionally superficial and hard to reach. Each must develop tolerance for the other.

According to the statistics from *Please Understand Me*, about 38% of the American population are AMOs, 38% are DOSs, 12% are KIPs and 12% are LTs, with less than 2% being introverted LTs. This means that KIPs and LTs find fewer people like themselves with whom they feel a real affinity.

These temperaments represent needs which we all must satisfy to some extent in order to lead a balanced life. They are like different aspects of the body. The AMO is the feet, wanting to move and be free. The DOS is the hands, wanting to serve obediently and structure the environment. The KIP is the head, wanting to understand. The LT is the heart, concerned about people and hungry to find meaning through self-actualization and deep emotional relations with others. Another analogy is to think of these types as being like four wheels of a car: you need all four in order for the car to drive smoothly. Therefore, make sure that you provide ample opportunities to maintain balance. Since boys are most apt to deny their feeling side, take special care to talk to them about their feelings so that they develop sensitivity to the feelings of others. Since girls are most apt to deny their intellectual capability, they need to be encouraged to develop their minds and their feeling of power and adequacy.

Just as a child has a basic body structure which does not change much throughout life, so, too, does he have a basic personality structure. Your job is to help him remain balanced so that the parts of him which are recessive do not atrophy for lack of attention and stimulation. You want a child who can play happily and act assertively, serve willingly, think logically and feel profoundly all at the appropriate time and in the proper measure. An excess in any area will be destructive.

Also realize that you, too, have your own innate pre-dispositions which affect the kind of parenting you are able to offer your children and your ability to relate to each of them; and you may have difficulty loving a child who is very different from yourself. For example, a strong LT may feel quite overwhelmed by the energy of an AMO child. A strong KIP may not feel loving toward an AMO child who cannot share his hunger for abstract theoretical knowledge. A DOS parent may not understand why cooperation tactics are necessary, since her DOS children cooperate naturally and she demands and usually receives obedience from them with her rather stern, no-nonsense approach.

The more dominant a person is in one area, the less he may understand those who are different from himself. Each can become intolerant of the others, thinking that no one else but his own type is doing what is really important or thinking in the *right* way. An AMO mother may have tremendous stamina and not understand why an LT mother cannot manage as she does. Yet the LT mother often has more difficulty because she is more high-strung, which weakens her physically, and because she hungers for closeness with each child, a closeness which the other types will not understand or experience to the same degree and which she cannot fulfill if she has many children close together. She wants beauty, order and cleanliness, but has little patience for routine, mundane chores. She feels frustrated and overwhelmed if she is bogged down with the physical realities of child-care. She is often jealous of the energy and organizational abilities of the DOS and AMO, and does not understand why she is not like them.

It is important for you to take the time to understand the advantages and disadvantages of each type and to develop an appreciation for your own and your children's God-given natures so that you can love yourself and them as you are, not as you think you *should* be.

Appreciate Different Types of Intelligence

Another important area in which to show tolerance is toward the type of intelligence your child has. Children manifest many different types of intelligence, among which are:

1. Musical Intelligence: The ability to remember tunes and

learn how to play musical instruments quickly.

2. Kinesthetic Intelligence: Children with this are well-coordinated and move gracefully. They can assemble and disassemble complex mechanisms, master crafts quickly, and master sports with ease.

3. Spatial Intelligence: Children with this ability are excellent visualizers. They are very aware of details in their surroundings. They can make elaborate plans in their minds and have engineering and artistic talents. Physical beauty and harmony are very important for them.

4. Logical-mathematical Intelligence: This is the "*gemara* head" which is so prized. Such children are good at grasping abstractions, but their clothes may be sloppy and their rooms a mess!

5. Linguistic Intelligence: These children love stories and word games. They love to talk and write stories and poetry.

6. Psychological Intelligence: The ability to understand oneself and other people.

Thus, a child might be a mathematical genius, but he can't explain himself to others because he lacks linguistic ability or is "spacey," clumsy and sloppy because he lacks spatial intelligence or kinesthetic awareness. A child may be an excellent verbalizer but poor in spelling or math. Or, he may be a mechanical genius who cannot explain to others how he got his information or how others could do the same thing.

As you can see from this very brief summary of different types of personalities and intelligences, each child has his particular path toward inner fulfillment. The task of a parent is to encourage his child to develop his potential and be a Torah-loving Jew in harmony with his God-given, natural tendencies. By showing tolerance toward his child, a parent will most likely demonstrate to him how to manifest tolerance toward others.

SIX

Communication Tactics

The essence of good parenting is good communication. One of life's greatest pleasures is the joy of feeling understood by another. Likewise, it is painful to be misunderstood. All too often, parents assume that their children are being deliberately contrary or cruel when, in reality, the children do not understand what the parents want or do not know how to delay or gratify their own pressing needs. Instead of assuming that your children are being deliberately obstinate or defiant when they fail to cooperate, assume that they a) don't know your rules, b) forgot them, c) are so self-absorbed that they are not aware of or caring about your needs at the moment, d) don't know how to do what you want. You want to communicate the need for your children to become responsible and considerate, but to do so in a non-hostile tone of voice. The following will help you to do so:

* Describe what you want very simply: "The coat needs to be picked up." "Your hands need to be washed."

* Give information about consequences of non-cooperation: "If you leave your wet towel in that bag after swimming, it will get mildewed and smell awful and the stain will be difficult for you to remove."

* Give the child a choice: " You can either put the things back in my sewing box when you are finished, or start earning money to buy your own box and not use mine any more." "You can come in now or in five minutes. It's your choice."

* Write a note: "Please make sure to take the uneaten food out of your school bag when you come home each day."

A very sensitive, feeling-oriented mother will usually have to practice this unemotional, non-dramatic type of relating for quite some time before she feels really comfortable relating to her children in this way, especially if she and the children are used to the theatrics of a good deal of hysteria and hostility to get each other's attention or cooperation.

REACH: An Essential Communication Model

If you want your children to grow up to be your friends, who will be able to "pour out their hearts into yours ... and find loyal support ..." (*Horeb* p. 414), you must start early in life to build a strong foundation of trust and caring. When a person is in distress, he first wants to simply share his pain with you and know that you understand and care about his feelings. Only then can you help him to a greater understanding of his choices of attitude about the event. The following will help you to remember how to do this. It is called REACH:

REFLECT: Duplicate in yourself precisely what the person is feeling, no more and no less. Do not talk at this point. Instead, take a few seconds to arouse the same feeling that the other person is experiencing. It may be helpful to remember a time when you yourself were in a similar situation and felt frightened, disappointed, unloved, rejected, alone, angry, discouraged, etc. Allow your body, especially your face and eyes, to reflect back to the person that you know what he is feeling.

> *A wicked man hardens his face, but a righteous man understands.*
> (MISHLAI 21:29)

> *As in water face answers to face, so the heart of a man to a man.*
> (IBID. 27:19)

ENCOURAGE: Ask the person to tell you more about what he is feeling. Don't assume that you know why he is feeling the way he is. Show willingness to hear the particulars of the situation. Say, "Tell me more about what happened." Your task here is not to reassure, advise or give *chizuk*, but only to " ... bear the yoke with one's fellow" (*Avoth* 6:6) so that the sharing of his pain will relieve him to some degree.

ACCEPT: Accept whatever the person is feeling. Do not tell him that he shouldn't be angry, sad, upset, jealous or afraid or that it is wrong to feel these emotions. Validate that he feels hurt and that he has the right to be upset. Do not judge him or his feelings or argue back.

CHOICES AND CHANGES: If the person has not gotten the relief which he wanted from simply sharing his feelings, then this is the point where you encourage the person to look for ways to solve the problem or, if that is not possible, to adopt a positive attitude towards it. Be careful not to give advice yet or to minimize his pain. See if he can figure out his own solutions. If you jump in too quickly with advice, you might prevent him from using the painful experience to develop his own insights and gain confidence in his ability to solve his own problems. Ask, "What attitude can you adopt which will keep you from being angry or self-pitying?" "What practical measures can you take to improve the situation?" Or, "How might a different person in the same situation react in a way which would be constructive?" If you see that he is not coming up with anything, only then can you tactfully mention a choice of a different *hashkafa* or course of action.

HOLD, HUG: Honor the person for having shared his feelings with you. Show appreciation to him for having trusted you enough to have shared what is most precious to a person, i.e., his innermost feelings. You might simply say, "Thank you for sharing this with me."

Obviously, you will not always need all five steps. The REA portion speaks to the heart while the C speaks to the head. At times, you want to speak to one and not the other. You have to consider the circumstances in order to know what is appropriate. A child whose bike has just been stolen does not want a long REA. He probably wants you to say, "Oh, you must feel awful. Let's call the police right away or put up notices around the neighorhood." A child whose best friend is snubbing her may want a long REA, no C and maybe a quick H. A small child who is in distress, may only want to be told, "Ooo, I know how much that hurts," and then to be held for a few minutes. Sometimes a child doesn't even want to talk about his feelings. He only wants reassurance or problem-solving.

Use this model to improve communication with your husband

as well. Typically, women want their husbands to first be sympathetic and to give them at least a few minutes of REA when they are in distress. However, many men tend to go straight to C, giving reassurance or advice. Or, they withdraw from what they view as excessive displays of emotionalism. A woman who has been cooped up all day with a sick child needs emotional release when her husband comes home. She doesn't want to hear, "You're just feeling sorry for yourself." Or, "There you go, complaining again." Or, "You should be thankful that you have children." On the other hand, she might want her husband to say, "Oy, it must have been so difficult for you. You go to sleep for an hour and I'll watch the kids." Once you have explained REACH to him, you can then tell him what you need, depending on your mood or the situation.

> My teenage daughter came home in a bad mood because of a fight with her friend. I told her, "Why don't you call her right away and see if you can patch things up." She told me, "I know how much you want to solve the problem for me, Mom, but right now I just want a little empathy." She was right. So I said, "I'm sorry. I goofed. Let's do it again." Initially, I wasn't in touch with her pain. I didn't really hear her. I wanted to make everything all right fast and cover up her distress with a quick solution. Once I displayed empathy, she came to her own solutions.

> Whenever I would complain to my husband about something, he would give me advice or say, "Don't worry, everything will be fine," or "You're always dramatizing things." Even though his advice was often good and even though I know I have a tendency to be dramatic, his response always made me feel worse and I didn't understand why. Then I learned about REACH, and realized that I simply was not getting any REA. Once I explained this to him, he understood why I felt so invalidated and resentful. He learned to take time for the REA and, as a result, I was more willing to listen to his side of the story or his advice afterwards."

If a person has suffered a major loss, spend as much time as possible on REA. However, if a person is chronically angry or depressed, focus on C, change of attitude and action, instead of letting him go on and on with his complaints. Unfortunately, not all adults want to be reached or REACHed. However, children usually do. Obviously, just listening is not always going to bring a solution. A cranky child may need to get out of the house or pound some nails into a board!

You will not always have the "right" formula or spend the "right" amount of time on each stage for that particular event or person. People will usually let you know with a grimace or a comment which signals to you that you're on the wrong track. Either back up or go forward, but don't give up your desire to reach others, unless you see that they have no desire for communication.

Avoid Communication Roadblocks

Do not placate your fellow in the moment of his anger; do not comfort him while his dead lies before him.

(AVOTH 4:18)

When a person is feeling a strong emotion, it is very tempting to deny his pain or make him suppress it quickly with various "Communication Roadblocks" (a term used in Parent Effectiveness Training classes). When you do this, you leave the person feeling isolated, frustrated, misunderstood. Therefore, if your goal is to enable the other person to share his feelings, avoid the following:

* ADVICE-GIVING: E.g., "Don't say another word! I'm going to tell you just what to do." "Let me give you some suggestions."
* ARGUING: "But you shouldn't feel angry, sad, afraid, alone or upset." "But you know that you're all wrong."
* BLAMING: "It's all your fault." "I told you to be more careful/not to go there/to listen to me/not to do it."
* CHANGING TIME REALITY: "In ten years, you'll laugh at this." To a child: "Soon you'll be grown up." To a mother: "Soon they'll be grown up and married."
* COMMANDING: "Just do what I say and everything will be fine!" "Come on now, stiff upper lip!"
* DENYING: "It's all in your head."
* DIVERTING ATTENTION: "Let's talk about something else." "By the way, did you hear about. . ."
* GENERALIZING: "Don't feel bad. Everyone your age feels that way." "All husbands/fathers/mothers/people do that."
* MINIMIZING THE PAIN: "Don't take it seriously. It's nothing. It's nothing to get upset about." "You're getting all worked up about nothing." "Just be philosophical about this."

* MORALIZING: "Just count your blessings." "It's wrong for you to feel like you're feeling. You'll be punished for feeling like that."
* SHAMING: "How stupid of you!" "How could you have done such a thing?" "What an idiot/dope/nut/slob/brat!"
* REASSURING: "It will pass. It's just a stage." "Everything is going to be just fine." "You'll get another friend/baby/home, etc." "Lots of people recover completely."

Obviously, there is a time and place for commands, reassurance, *mussar*, advice, humor, counting one's blessings and changing time reality, etc. But **not** when the person is in need of emotional release. Always give at least a few minutes of REA to a person in real distress. It is very tempting to offer some trite response or some "pat answer" to cut him off and avoid having to take the time to experience what another person is feeling, especially if that person is a child.

> ⊗ When I first remarried, there was so much tension and jealousy between my husband's and my kids that it almost ruined the marriage. But I learned to avoid the communication roadblocks and not take their anger personally. I kept telling them that underneath anger was pain, and that I was willing to talk about the pain, but not let them hurt each other. They knew that they could be open and honest with me. That really brought us all together.

If you are not in the mood to listen, or do not have the time, say so tactfully. This is better than letting the person open himself up to you as you fidget impatiently, listen half-heartedly, or cut him off in the middle of his recital. Use "Roadblocks" when you think they will be more effective than listening, such as when children are just venting anger or feeling sorry for themselves and need to have their attention diverted or to focus on solutions.

However, don't delude yourself into thinking that children don't have *real* grown-up feelings and that, therefore, they do not need to talk about their feelings. Don't think that children are not as deeply hurt by rejection, ridicule or criticism or are not as worried and mystified about the unknown as you are. Just because children cannot verbalize their pain or curiosity does not mean that it is not there. Their anxiety may actually be more intense since they cannot yet philosophize about suffering or communicate their fears as well as you can.

A person who cannot verbalize his feelings may deny that they exist, thus becoming dishonest and self-deluding. Yet those suppressed emotions may emerge in various obnoxious habits or psychosomatic illnesses. Help your child develop a language to express his feelings. He will then have greater awareness of and sensitivity to yours and will be able to better control his impulses.

Be as Honest as Possible

Parents often think they are protecting their children by withholding necessary information. Yet that protective cocoon may do more harm than good if your child develops strong feelings of guilt, shame and fear because of misinformation or ignorance. Obviously, you should not cause your children unnecessary anxiety by giving them more information than they can handle. But neither do they have to be kept in the dark when doing so will lead to greater anxiety or shame. For example: Prepare your preteenagers in advance for the physical changes which will occur in their bodies so that they are not terrified and ashamed when these changes take place. If the child's first reaction to what are, to him, earth-shattering events is negative, the child may retain lifelong feelings of shame. The idea that you want to convey to your child is that the new, normal, healthy impulses must be directed in a kosher, self-disciplined manner.

1. Children are very intuitive. They become insecure and frightened when they experience tension in the home, especially if no one tells them what is going on or, worse, invalidates their feeling that something is wrong. If you are having financial problems, are ill, thinking of moving, feeling sad about the death or illness of someone close to you, or having marital difficulties, give children pertinent information without increasing their feeling of anxiety. Be reassuring, yet honest:

> "Yes, we are having some financial difficulties right now. We have to cut back, but we'll still have money for the essentials. Come, I'll show you the bills that we have to pay, like for electricity and gas, and compare that to the money that is coming in and you'll see for yourself."

"I don't feel well right now, but it's temporary. I'll be back to my old self soon. I know it's hard for you to see me like this, but all people have ups and downs. Don't worry. I'll come up again."

This is better than saying, "Nothing's wrong." They'll know that you're lying and will wonder why. The answer they come up with may be worse than the truth. Obviously, certain subjects cannot be discussed fully, such as in the case of marital distress or possibly frightening illnesses. However, even here their questions should be handled according to the child's age and temperament. In the case of a move, for example, it is best to wait until shortly before if the child is an anxiety-prone type who has not yet developed the inner confidence to see change as an adventure with which he can cope successfully.

Many adults can trace their earliest feelings of rejection and insecurity back to times when some trauma occurred, such as a serious illness, or a death or major move, and no one took the time to explain to them what was happening. They were left feeling anxious, angry, guilty and confused for many years. Realize that children have very vivid imaginations. When something awful happens, they are often convinced that they are to blame because they were horribly evil. Only by giving them appropriate information and allowing them to share their feelings with you can you prevent lifelong feelings of excessive shame and guilt.

2. Prepare children for upcoming events. Whether it is the first day of school, a trip to the dentist, a move or a hospital experience, you can staple some sheets of paper together to make your own little booklet which describes, page by page, what is going to happen in the next few days or weeks. You don't have to be an accomplished artist to make stick figures or cut out pictures from a magazine and paste them on the pages. Studies have shown that adults who are well-prepared for surgery in advance with slides or movies and written information as to what to expect have a faster recovery rate than those who are not prepared, because they are less anxious to begin with. All research shows that the more a person knows about a situation, the better able he is to cope with it.

3. Help your child understand his world. For example, you can draw a map of the block where you live, noting the people on it, the position of the school in relation to your home, and other landmarks of interest to him. Teach him about bugs, flowers, stars, how things grow, how to sew, cook, make minor mechanical repairs, etc.

Build a Strong Communication from Birth

It's never too early to talk to a baby. Even before the birth, you can sing to your child or say loving words to him. From birth on, it is important to talk to him and communicate your love verbally as well as physically. There are many communication activities you can perform with an infant. For example:

* Name what you are doing: "It's time for your bath. Ooohh, doesn't the water feel good!" "Now, I'm going to dry you and put your shirt on and your diaper."

* Name what he is doing: "Look, you rolled over on your tummy! Good for you!"

* Describe things in the environment: "This is Mommy's shoe. That's a chair." "Bread. Say bread."

* Sort things into categories: "These are animals and those are cars."

* Ask questions: "Where's Daddy's chair?" "Where's the garbage pail?"

Have fun communicating with him and show him your joy in doing so.

Communication and Anger

Unless there is danger, don't talk when you are angry. If you are seething with rage and must say something, take a few seconds to give the benefit of the doubt: "He has no intention to hurt me deliberately/is doing the best he can with the tools he has, forgot/couldn't control himself at the moment because he was overwhelmed with feelings, etc. Do this so that what you say will be constructive and not simply an act of venting hostility.

Anger can be a powerful motivator to change. Focus on solutions. Say, "I am in pain. I want to solve this problem. Do you? Do you care?" If the other person is angry, do the same, "I see that you are in pain. I want to help. Do you want to work on this problem?" Teach him how to talk when angry. For example, tell him:

> "What you just said hurt my feelings. I want to hear what you have to say, but you are not allowed to talk to your mother in an angry tone of voice."
> "I'm very upset, but I'm giving you the benefit of the doubt. Now tell me your side of the story."

> ⊛ My two year old went into my thirteen year old's bedroom when he was in school and pulled down all the books from his shelves and crumpled up some of the pages. When my son came home, he was angry at me for not watching over her more closely and at her for the mess she had made. Then I said, "Do you think we did this on purpose?" He is used to hearing that phrase. Right away, I could see him take a deep breath and calm down. He then told me, "You were probably busy in the kitchen and she was bored and wanted some excitement. She didn't know what she was doing. I guess I'll have to keep my door locked. Oy, I would have felt so bad if I had hit her like I wanted to do at first." That's when I knew that my self-control when angry had paid off and had taught them to do the same.

> ⊛ One of the things that used to make me want to scream was when all the kids would talk at once. Then I developed some images which helped them see how upset I was. I told them that when they all talk at once, I feel like a cat being chased by a bunch of big dogs. Another time, I told them that my ears were like a cup that could hold just so much water and that when they all talked at once, it just overflowed and made a big mess. Now, when I hold my hands over my ears, they quickly get the message about how I feel without my having to scream at them.

Emotional Honesty

One of the foremost signs of a dysfunctional family is the lack of emotional honesty and expression. There is a great deal of anger, but no freedom or ability to express the pain beneath the anger, find constructive solutions to problems, or any tolerance for dissent or individual differences. Although it may seem time-consuming to teach your child to express himself and sometimes inconvenient to have to listen to him, you actually save yourself great heartache later on as you see your children relating honestly and acting constructively.

When you give a name to a child's feeling, you help him understand what may be a confusing and frightening inner jumble.

Emotional honesty teaches him not to be afraid of his feelings. Therefore, give his feelings a name when you see that he is distressed. For example, "It seems to me that right now you are feeling disappointed/frustrated/bored/annoyed/worried/hurt/sad/ scared/embarrassed/helpless/ambivalent/lonely, etc. You can also let him know the name for positive emotions, such as enthusiastic/proud/happy/curious/grateful/responsible/strong/ disciplined/creative, etc.

Once a child has a name for his feelings, he is less likely to act out his pain in negative ways. For example, he can tell you, "I'm jealous of the baby," instead of hitting her. Or, "I want to hit the baby!" instead of doing so. He can say, "I'm so bored!" instead of doing something obnoxious to get your attention or provoke some excitement in his life. After being reprimanded or spoken to harshly, he can ask, "Do you still love me?" instead of assuming that you don't, and being miserable or vengeful because of his wrong assumption. Your teenager can say, "I feel like you don't care enough about me when you make the same meal day after day," instead of making angry faces and grimacing when you serve the meal. If your child is going through one of those inevitable years when he is stuck with an incompatible teacher, you should be prepared to let him express his pain every once in a while, yet without allowing him to become a walking soap opera.

Remember, it is especially important to help your male children express their feelings since they are more likely than girls to become emotionally suppressed. It is also important to be emotionally honest with him. Let him know that you also have these feelings at times and use these opportunities to teach him how to deal constructively with negative emotional states.

> ⊛ I was always on edge on Shabbath because of the fighting and bickering between my children. So, one evening, I sat them down and asked them, "When you hurt each other, do you know who gets hurt the most? Me!" That surprised them. We talked about how I felt when they bickered. I told them that they were like precious jewels, the most precious things in my life, and that when they hurt each other or got hurt, that I felt hurt as well. Over the next few days, I heard the older ones telling the others, "You hurt Mommy when you hurt him!"

Although you want your children to know that you care about their feelings, you also want to prepare them for the realities of life:

i.e., that not all people want to share their feelings and that people do not always want to listen to what they have to say. Let your child know that they must read other people's faces to know if others are interested in sharing. Don't be too available or too sympathetic at all times or you give a false picture of life. Let him know that you cannot always share or let him share with you.

Help Your Child Understand His Inner Dialogue

In addition to communication with others, your child has to know how to handle the various, often contradictory, voices within himself. A human being's emotions are like the various instruments in an orchestra. Each has a role to play. Our unpleasant emotions such as jealousy, anxiety, fear, anger and helplessness can show us where we need to make changes in our attitude or behavior. Therefore, teach your child not to be afraid to acknowledge whatever he is feeling, even though he may not always be able to give expression to those emotions to others.

When you see that your child is in a negative state, you can ask him:

"I see that you are really upset. Let your anger be like a messenger which is telling you to make certain changes in your life. So, what thoughts or actions do you need to change?"

You can also show him that one side of himself can come to the aid of another:

"I see that you are discouraged right now. But I also know that you have a part of yourself which is resourceful and can help you solve this problem. What would the resourceful side have to say to the discouraged side?"

"I can see how anxious you are about this. I have a trick for you. Close your eyes and think about the part of yourself which makes you feel strong and confident. Now, tell me what advice it is giving you."

A child also knows that he is sometimes at war within himself, between his impulse to good (*yetzer tov*) and his impulse to do evil (*yetzer hara*). There is controversy as to when to introduce this concept to children. Some children are frightened by what they picture to be a kind of "monster" or foreign power within them which cannot be controlled and which often forces them to do bad things against their will. Thus, a child may say, "I didn't do it. It was my *yetzer hara* that did."[Of course, you can then say, "In that case, I will be *potsching* your *yetzer hara* and not you!"]

One aspect of "training a child according to his individual path," (*Mishlai* 22:6) means knowing when and how to approach this concept. If done correctly, it can be very effective.

> ॐ I asked my six year old to help me, but he wouldn't budge from his chair. Then I said, "I know that your *yetzer tov* does want to cooperate and would be so happy to be able to do a mitzvah, especially *kibud ame.* I can see how excited it is and how ready it is to get you moving to help me. But there is your *yetzer hara* telling you to sit still. This is very interesting. Let's see which side is going to win. Hm...I think that the *yetzer tov* is gaining the upper hand. No, oops, now the other side is winning. I know you are strong enough to win this one! It's a fierce battle, but I think you are getting ready to defeat that old *yetzer hara.*" He was giving me a sheepish grin by this time and a few seconds later, he jumped up and did what I had asked. I praised him for winning this battle.

It is best not to be too heavy-handed about this concept. Once in a while, remind your child of his ability to control this force and his responsibility to do so. You can also let him know that the essence of the *yetzer hara* is mainly laziness and selfishness, and that this destructive force resides in every person except *tzaddikim,* regardless of age or position. We do not have to be ashamed that it exists within us, only that we sometimes do not oppose it with all our strength. [Note: If his self-esteem is poor, he may not feel he has the strength to fight this battle.]

Assertion with Empathy: "I-Message, then You-Message"

One way to remain calm in the presence of a defiant child or a critical adult is to first acknowledge and sympathize with the person's feeling and only afterwards state your own. For example:

To a critical adult: "I know how important it is for you to see the house neat and spotless at all times. I would like the same myself. However, I need a break right now. Either I'm going to have a museum here or a happy home with emotionally healthy children. I cannot have both at this point."

To a child who does not want to stop playing: "I know how hard it is to stop. I know you *'reeeally'* want to continue playing. You can either come in now, or you can come in five minutes. It's your choice, but whatever you choose you must keep your promise."

In order for these messages to work, you have to truly sympathize with the other person's feelings and let him know that you care about and validate his reality even though you may not agree with it. The other person may still balk or protest, but at least you have asserted your right to have your own needs and feelings respected. One mother reported that she spent many 2 A.M. feedings practicing being empathetic with others yet honest about her own needs and feelings. She would practice various phrases over in the dark to herself and then use them the next day with the most difficult people in her environment.

Watch Your Tone of Voice

Self-control in the midst of anger and frustration is the sign of great spiritual refinement. Thankfully, mothers have countless opportunities to refine themselves! The more important the message you want to get across to a child, the more crucial it is to have his full attention. The child cannot give you that attention if he is overwhelmed by your emotions and busy defending himself against them.

Words spoken gently by the wise are accepted.

(KOHELETH 9:17)

Many parents do not realize that you can convey a profound emotion to a child without hitting or yelling. As a matter of fact, the quieter your voice, the more likely it is that the message will sink in. You might cup your child's face in your hands or hold his shoulders as you look into his eyes and make sure that he hears what you have to say. Obviously, it is inevitable that you will have to shout at times, especially if he is in danger or being so rowdy that you simply cannot get through to him. If you have to give a sharp command such as, "Get in the house," or "Get off the couch," switch back to your normal voice after he has cooperated.

Your tone of voice influences you as well. You can calm yourself down by talking calmly even if you feel frantic or enraged. As you read this, think of a situation which gets you screaming mad. Now, tell yourself, "The more they [whatever it is that they do]... the more I will slow ... my voice ... and talk ... with ... firm intensity...." Take the time to imagine yourself actually doing this in a stressful situation right now. Whenever possible, discipline them in a matter-of-fact monotone which you have practiced in this imaginary exercise.

Be Aware of Subtle Negative Programming

Many parents are not aware of the ways that they subtly program their children to think and act destructively. For example:

> ❀ The other day, I screamed at the kids and caught myself saying, "I'm tired, that's why I have no control over myself." Then I realized that I was teaching my kids to think that when they're tired, they don't have to control themselves either. Now I'm careful not to use that expression.

> ❀ My son was getting ready for his first overnight camp experience. My oldest daughter told him, "Oy, it's so scary." I told her that she was programming negative information into him. I then told her a substitute by saying, "It's going to be a big adventure. You'll probably be a little scared and homesick, but you'll also be excited and happy and proud of yourself for having the courage to do this."

> ❀ I kept screaming at the kids, "You kids have no respect for me!" Then I realized that I was programming that into their heads! So I substituted, "You kids love me and want to cooperate, but you have to overcome your desire for comfort to do so sometimes."

Notice that you may also be programming yourself and others negatively.

> ❀ I was always telling my husband, "You never take me anywhere." Sure enough, he never took me anywhere. I had to change my tune and tell him, "I know you would love to go someplace with me." He got the message.

You may also be programming yourself negatively.

> ❀ I woke up feeling depressed and sluggish. I started complaining to myself, "Oy, my whole day is ruined. I won't be able to last. I've had it. I

just can't manage." Then I caught myself and said, "I don't want this garbage in my computer-brain." So I substituted, "Right now, I don't feel so good. It's just lowered feelings, nothing serious. I can manage. As soon as I get up and start moving, I'll feel better."

❀ My son doesn't like fish. In the past, I kept trying to force it on him, and when he refused, I'd say things like, "You're so finicky. Nothing I do pleases you. You always want to have your own way." Then I realized that I was programming him negatively. It's his right not to like fish. I didn't like certain things when I was a child and I either learned to like them later or still don't like them now. Being forced to eat those things only made me angry. It didn't teach me a thing. Yet here I was creating tension over nothing. I started to get down on myself, thinking, "I just don't know how to be a good parent. I'm such a failure. I'm a mean, terrible mother." Then I realized I was doing the same thing to myself that I do to my kids! This is a hard habit to break!

Remember, you do not want to put your children down. You want to remind them that they are God's finest creations, beings capable of the greatest moral excellence and that their misbehavior is out of character with their truest selves.

Summary of Good Communication Techniques

1. Listen. Observe your child's face and body movements as well as his words. A child may say, "Go away. I'm angry." But he may really want you to reassure and comfort him. Take the time to listen to him before you jump in with advice or shut him off with trite phrases and pat answers.

2. Make eye contact. Even if you are doing the dishes or baking bread, look at him every once in a while when he talks to you. If you want his attention, make sure you make eye contact first.

3. Make "touch contact." Touch him to let him know you care, especially after a rebuke or if he is in distress. Remember, a child needs love most when he is least lovable.

4. Validate your child's pain. Don't be afraid to let him know, "You felt really bad when the teacher put you in the corner." Or, "You felt jealous when you saw that your friend had a new pencil case, didn't you?" "You felt left out when your father took your brother and not you."

5. Don't argue with his feelings. Don't tell him that he should not be feeling jealous, sad, angry or afraid.

6. Use "I-messages," instead of condemnations. Instead of saying, "Go away you little nudnik. Can't you see I'm on the phone?" try, "I can't concentrate when grandma calls and you want to talk to me at the same time. I'd appreciate it if you would wait. You can get the timer if you want and watch the sand go down. I'll be done in about two turns of the timer."

7. Remember that your child is not always in the same reality as you are. He may have a perfectly logical reason for not wanting to get into the bathtub, not going on an errand for you or being upset about what, to you, is a very trivial matter. He may be afraid of going down the drain in the bathtub, he may be afraid of some bully on the block, or he may feel that his whole sense of honor is being threatened because he didn't win the game or get the window seat. Go down to his level and find out what's going on in his mind if possible. When he doesn't come when called, he may be in a different world. Take the time to reach him.

8. Say what you mean. Don't make empty threats that you have no intention of keeping, e.g., "I'm going to leave you in the middle of this freeway and you can walk home by yourself!" "I'm going to find another mommy to take care of you."

9. Respect his likes and dislikes. Don't force your opinions on him, except when they have to do with *halacha*.

10. Make sure he understands your instructions and has the ability to carry them out. We might think it is a simple matter to clean up a mess. But he might not know which towel or rag to use, whether or not to use soap, or which soap, and whether to use a lot of water or just a little, etc.

11. Don't lecture. People don't like being lectured to against their will. If he has done something wrong, let him know that, first of all, it is human to want to break laws, and that you understand this craving. Then find out how to give him what he wants without having to break your rules.

12. Have adequate time to talk to him about his doubts and fears, his dreams and loves.

13. Don't "pat-answer" him. You may find it very easy to be philosophical about his pain and tell him, "It will soon pass," or "It's really nothing." But your child cannot philosophize away his pain. Put yourself in his shoes and think how you would want others to respond if you were in pain. On the other hand, if he is overreacting, you might tell him a story about "Dr. Time," who heals all minor wounds.

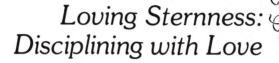

SEVEN

Loving Sternness: Disciplining with Love

Raising a child is like gardening. You have to pull the weeds lest the bad choke off the good. But you must be careful not to crush the child's emerging spirit in the process. The goal of discipline is that your child should achieve self-mastery. You cannot help him do this unless you yourself are in control. And you cannot be in control if you have a vengeance mentality which is characterized by the well-known childhood belief, "If someone hurts me, I have the right to hurt him back." Our Torah forbids vengeance (*Vayikra* 17:18) except, of course, when dealing with an enemy of the Jewish people, a category which certainly does not include our children! However, since we spent many childhood years thinking like this, it takes a very conscious effort to rid ourselves of this concept, and to remember that even if we feel hurt by what our children do or say, it does not mean that we should hurt them back.

First, Have the Proper Attitude

Ridding yourself of a vengeance mentality does not mean that you do not discipline your children. You must do so! However, you can discipline without hostility toward the child. One way to do this is to have the thought in mind, "What do I want to teach this child right now?" "What *middoth* do I want him to learn?" Or, "What is the best way of helping him change his present habit patterns?" You still must restrain a child who is out of control and rebuke a child who is old enough to understand. But you will no longer do so in fury and hatred if your sole intention is to teach him the skills and awareness which he has been lacking.

Another essential attitude to adopt in order to rid yourself of all desire to hurt your child is to think, "He is doing the best he can with the tools he has at the moment." Repeat this phrase under your breath over and over, even if you don't believe it. Say it to yourself a thousand times a day until it becomes an automatic habit to give your child the benefit of the doubt. If you are feeling violent, keep saying the words over and over so that you will not give in to destructive behavior. Then, even if your rebuke or punishment does cause him pain, the fact that you act with a loving heart will maximize the possibility of positive changes in the child instead of imbuing him with a desire for vengeance against you.

The truth is that children often do not have the tools to deal with the impulses which overwhelm them when they are tired, hungry, jealous, anxious, sad, angry, afraid or even just bored. They are not bad, but they do have some bad habits. Whether you believe it or not at the moment, tell yourself that if your child did something to cause you pain, it was not his original intention. Even if it were, this does not justify sinking to his level and hurting him back. When you stop trying to hurt your children for hurting you, you will find that you will become the strict, yet loving disciplinarian which every parent must be.

Do not underestimate the power of words in educating your children. Do not think that you have to explode violently to get your point across, for the only point you are likely to get across is that it is all right to explode.

You want your child to be moral and self-controlled, yet sensitive to the feelings of those around him. If you want responsible, loving children, you have to discipline in a responsible, loving manner. The time to discipline is not when you are furious and feeling aggressively hostile. That is when you are likely to act impulsively and irrationally.

A hot-tempered person cannot teach.

(AVOTH 2:6)

Do not have stricter standards for your children than you do for yourself or other adults. Think how you would feel if you lost your keys, spilled something on your clothing or forgot to go to the bank? Would you want to be yelled at, told what a dumb idiot you are, slapped and told that you deserve to suffer? How would you feel if you were invited out and didn't like what was being served, but were told by the host that you had to force yourself to finish everything on your plate even if it made you sick? How would you feel if you spilled something and the hostess embarrassed you in front of everyone? How would it feel to have to ask someone's permission for every little thing, and then have to wait in agonizing suspense as the person took his sweet time, completely ignoring the urgency of your needs?

When you make a mistake, lose something, feel sick, or make an error in judgment, you want forgiveness and empathy. If you deserve a rebuke, you want it to be done tactfully and in private. You do not want someone calling attention to your shortcomings night and day. You hate to be scolded and criticized. You hate to be reminded of your faults.

Yet a child is even more sensitive than an adult. He does not have an adult's wisdom or understanding. He has far fewer choices of action when he is in distress. He often forgets the rules. He does not know what to do with himself when he is bored and unhappy. When he loses something, he wants you to help him find it, not to chastise him for having lost it. If he has a tendency to be scatter-brained and disorganized, he wants helpful instructions and practice on how to be more organized. Being sent to bed without dinner or struck with a harsh smack do not help him learn skills or develop greater awareness of other people's needs.

The great test of how well you have integrated the ideals of Torah is not how you act when things are going well but how you react under stress. That is when it is most important for you to do to others what you would have them do to you. Think how you would want others to treat you, how much you want others to be forgiving and understanding, to speak respectfully, and certainly not to be punitive or indifferent when you are in distress.

It takes tremendous inner strength not to be pulled into negativity when a child misbehaves, is in a bad mood, or fails to live up to your expectations. Yet that is precisely when you make the greatest spiritual progress because that is when you have the opportunity to practice and manifest unconditional love.

Don't Discipline for Selfish Purposes

The greatest service of God lies in the purification of motive.

(STRIVE FOR TRUTH!, vol. I, p. 99)

We all have three selfish motives: for comfort, *kavod* and power over others. When you discipline for one of these selfish motives, you become insensitive to and unconcerned about your child's needs. Before you act, ask yourself, "Am I doing this for the good of the child?"

    I was about to whack my son for fidgeting and not concentrating while I was helping him with his homework. Then I thought, "Will this teach him to concentrate? Will this instill in him a love of learning?" I realized that my anger stemmed from my own feelings of helplessness and my desire for *kavod* to have a child I could brag about like other mothers, one who would catch on easily and be brilliant. I am ashamed that he is doing poorly in school, and that's why I want to hit him: as if a hit would knock some sense into him and give me a feeling of power. I wasn't really thinking about him, only about myself. Once I realized this, I became more patient and understanding.

    I was about to force my daughter to finish everything on her plate even though she insisted that she was full. At first, I told her it was for her good, so that she would learn not to be wasteful. But then I had to admit that my use of force was motivated by my own excessive desire for domination. I wasn't teaching her not to be wasteful. I was teaching her to be cruel. When I realized this, I calmed down.

    I came home from *shul* and found my twelve year old still in her bathrobe. I was furious because she knows I want her dressed nicely by the time I come home. I wanted to yell at her that she was not showing *kavod* for the Sabbath by being dressed like that. Then I thought to myself that my anger was like a fire, and one is not allowed to light a fire on the Sabbath. I want strict obedience from my children at all times and don't take the time to talk to them very often. That's the way it was in my house when I was growing up. Talking to my children about the things that bother me is new to me. But if I want to teach respect, I have to learn to practice it.

    I was frantic about making sure that my two year old was potty-trained by the time my mother visited us. The more frantic I got, the more resistant she became. Then I realized, "Who am I doing this for?" To impress my mother, certainly not for my daughter's sake. When I realized this, I stopped being so angry with her for not being trained sooner.

    My three year old didn't have a nap and was getting out of control by late afternoon. All of a sudden, he started dumping all my carefully sorted boxes of puzzles on the floor. I felt very ashamed in front of my visitors and started to go into my old pattern of condemning myself as inadequate when he misbehaved. Then I got hold of myself. I gave him a whack on the backside and told him sternly, "You cannot do that." Then I hugged him. The only way I could achieve this kind of sternness without hostility was to be aware that my sole motivation was to simply enforce reasonable limits, not to save my *kavod* in front of the guests or make him into a perfect being instantly.

🏵 My son lost his bus ticket for the third time in as many months. He has also lost other things and tends to be dreamy. I wanted to tell him that from now on, no more bus tickets. He would have to get up an hour early and walk to school. Then I thought, "What is my motivation? What am I teaching him?" With this particular child, I felt that he was sure to only be more hateful and depressed if I did this. Instead, I figured out a way for him to do certain chores to earn the money he had lost on the bus tickets. I want to teach responsibility, not vengeance.

Guidelines for Proper Punishment

Punishments can cause more damage than good if all you do is arouse anger and resentment. The following may help avoid these:

* Don't give a punishment in the heat of anger. You'll probably be excessively harsh and regret what you've said later but will feel forced to stick to your words to protect your honor.

* Make the punishment a learning experience. For example, if he has caused someone pain, let him make a gift for that person or do some act of *chesed* or write a note asking for forgiveness.

* Make the punishment fit the "crime." For example, if he left his bike out all night, don't tell him that he can't use it for the next four weeks, especially if it is his most precious possession and his main way of getting gross motor activity. That is far too harsh and you'll both suffer the entire month. If he forgot to do his homework, grounding him for two weeks will only make you both resentful of each other and you will probably not be able to hold out for the entire time.

* Don't use religious obligations as punishments. Anything which would give a child a negative feeling toward religion is a violation of Torah principles.

* If appropriate, let him decide what the punishment should be. He will then be more willing to abide by it.

* Don't make the punishment last too long. A three-minute

wait in the corner is usually long enough to calm a rowdy child of three or four. An older child may need a half hour or even less.

* Don't deprive the child of food as a punishment. This touches on his basic survival needs and will arouse great anxiety about that subject along with great hostility toward you.

* Have the punishment fit the child. You should have different expectations and demands of a very exuberant AMO (See chapter 5) than from a shy, retreating type. An impulsive child has far more difficulty controlling himself and you may have to overlook some of his failures so that you are not on his back the entire day. Let him scrub the floor or clean the yard as a useful "punishment." A three year old who bites may receive one kind of punishment if she is basically a secure child, and another if she is basically insecure.

* Every once in a while, surprise your child and tell him that you are not going to punish him because you realize that he is having a difficult time right now and didn't mean to misbehave.

* Let the punishment diminish, but not totally eliminate, some reward. For example, if you have promised to take them to the amusement park and they are all excited, but then start squabbling, don't say, "The whole trip is off." Perhaps they can have one ride or one treat less. If you have been giving a child tokens for certain behavior, which are to be exchanged for some needed item, don't tell him that you are taking away all his tokens when he misbehaves. Reduce the tokens by one. Make sure that he ends up with something.

* Instead of punishing, let the child "replay the scene" and do it right. For example:

> ⊗ My son barged in the door from school and when he saw that dinner wasn't ready, talked to me angrily. In a firm but calm voice, I said that he was not allowed to talk to me in this way. I told him that when he comes home, he should first greet me pleasantly and then, if he is upset, he can tell me what he wants in a respectful manner. I told him to go outside and come back in and practice what I had told him, which he did.

Instead of using humiliating scoldings, insults, threats and the withdrawal of privileges, first take the time to teach the child how to do things right the next time, to find positive outlets for energies or how to cope with emotions or impulses which were so strong that he failed to exercise control.

Hitting Is Powerful Medicine: Use It Sparingly

No parent will deny the usefulness of a well-placed whack at the right time and place. But many parents do not take enough time to find other means of gaining cooperation. Although a smack on the backside of a young child may be necessary at times to keep him from harming himself or others, words should be the preferred choice to convey the depth of your feelings whenever possible. Most older parents who hit a great deal are very regretful that they alienated and damaged their children with such violence. Most authorities agree that a child under the age of three can be spanked occasionally, but that this should be followed with a hug and with an explanation as to why this was done. Remember, a child is more sensitive to rejection than an adult, and must be reassured of your love following a punishment if you want to prevent a backlash of defiance and disobedience. The children of many great Sages, such as the Chofetz Chaim, said that they were never beaten by their parents. A stern look would suffice.

We are all aware of the famous statement, "Spare the rod and spoil the child" (*Mishlai* 13:24). However, along with firmness, it is important to remember that one must discipline without a trace of anger and use only a light touch if physical force is needed:

If you hit a child, it should be only with a light string.

> (HILCHOTH TALMUD TORAH 2:B, YOREH DEAH 245:1,
> KITZUR SHULCHAN ARUCH 165:13, BAVA BATRA 101a)

An angry person is as one who worships idols.

> (SHABBATH 105b)

A furious person . . . has no heart and his judgment vanishes.

> (PATH OF THE JUST, p. 161)

A person loses his wisdom when he is angry.

> (PESACHIM 66b)

Our Sages . . . warned against anger even for the sake of a mitzvah, even in a teacher's relationship with his student and in a father's with his son. This is not to say that the offenders should not be reprimanded. They certainly should be! But without anger, with no other purpose than their being set on the right path. Any anger shown should be anger of the face and not anger of the heart.

> (IBID., p. 165)

Rabbi Eliyahu Lopian wrote that his son once did something so improper that he forced himself to wait two full weeks before rebuking him to ensure that he would not have a trace of anger in himself when he did so (*Lev Eliyahu*, vol. 22, pp. 26-27). The Rambam recommends that if anger is necessary to arouse fear in the child, the parent should, " ... make a show of anger ... but in reality, his mind should be composed ... and he should not really feel it [the anger]" (*Hilchoth Deoth* 2:3). This can be referred to as *clean anger.* You may need to yell or show the child how upset you are about his behavior, but you do not feel hostile toward **him.**

If you do yell, yell something positive! For example, "You are wonderful children! You can't do such things!" "I love you! Now, out of here!" Reminding yourself of such positive feelings will reduce the chances of you becoming violent.

Violence is like a drug. It may be necessary at times. However, it is very easy to keep losing control and become addicted to hitting as a means of gaining cooperation. As with a drug, the parents may get pleasure from seeing others submit so quickly to their will, which is easy if the child is small. Then, whenever the child acts up, they think that force will again work to bring them that same satisfaction. However, as the children grow older, the parents need to use more and more of the drug (i.e., force) to get cooperation. In the meantime, the children become more alienated and damaged. In the end, the drug does not work at all. It only does increasing damage. Violence is ultimately ineffective and self-defeating.

Many people recall these incidents with such pain in their hearts that it is as if the event had taken place just yesterday:

> *In his late eighties, Rabbi Ya'akov Kaminetsky, z.l., said that he never forgot the shame of being slapped at the age of five by his teacher because he was late to cheder. He had been on his way to school when a man rushed up to him and told him that the mohel for the* brith *which was about to take place had failed to show up and would the boy please find another. The child did so and then rushed to school. When he finally got to his classroom and told the teacher why he was late, the Rebbe said he was lying and hit him. Rabbi Kaminetsky said that he never forgot the pain and humiliation of that incident for his whole life.*
>
> (EREV SHABBATH, March, 1986)

*Unless the child knows that you love him at the time of discipline,
then your discipline will arouse hatred, resentment, self-denigration
and vengeful thoughts.*

(SCHAR V'HA'ANASHA B'CHINUCH, p. 6)

The excessive use of force conveys many unwanted messages to
the child, such as:

"You are bad. You are unworthy of love and respect."
"It is all right to be violent toward those weaker than yourself."
"Your feelings and needs are not important."
"You are incapable of controlling yourself. Others have to do it
for you."

The effects of these messages are many:

* If the child thinks of himself as bad, he has no choice but to
live up to that label and act bad. Also, his feeling of shame makes
him feel that he is not worthy of being loved. He fails to establish
close ties with others.

* He learns to bully others, such as siblings and peers, in order
to get what he wants. He thinks this behavior is permissible since
the adults whom he is supposed to respect indulge in this behavior.

* He takes pleasure in hurting others.

* He becomes emotionally cold, anesthetizing himself in order
not to feel the pain of feeling unloved. This self-numbing often
becomes a lifelong pattern, causing coldness and the inability to
care.

* He learns to lie to get his way. Children will somehow get
what they hunger for, with or without parental approval. Going
behind the parents' backs increases disrespect for the parent and
disobedience on the child's part. (See Rashi, *Devarim* 6:5, on the
importance of obedience from love, since the one who serves out of
fear feels burdened and tries to escape.)

* He may become obsessively stringent about unimportant
details in a way which is self-punishing and punishing to others to
make himself feel superior and overcome deep feelings of shame.
Or he may become compulsive about doing certain non-essential
tasks and rituals to give himself a feeling of control.

* He becomes depressed as he despairs of ever being good

enough to win his parent's love. The anger he feels toward the parent is turned against himself in self-destructive behavior: carelessness, laziness, sloppy appearance, lack of concern over goals, dependency, self-criticism, etc.

* He may become chronically angry and tense and suffer from a variety of psychosomatic illnesses. Chronic violence produces what can be called "The Katyusha Rocket Syndrome." Before the 1982 war in Lebanon, Russian-made katyusha rockets rained down frequently on the small town of Kiryat Shmoneh in northern Israel, causing great anxiety to the population. Psychologists found that the anxiety level actually went **up** when there were no explosions. When there were, people at least had something on which to focus their fears. But when all was quiet, they did not know who or what would be hit next and were more anxious as they tried to go about their normal lives, not knowing when they would have to run for the air-raid shelters. A parent who "explodes" often does the same thing to his child. When he is being hit, the child feels pain. But not being hit also is painful, as he feels great tension and anxiety, wondering in suspense when the next "rocket" will hit. The result is both physical and mental damage.

* Because his earliest relationships with those closest to him were painful, he comes to believe that to be close to someone means to be hurt. Therefore, he maintains distance by being critical of others, by being depressed and withdrawn, or adopting other unpleasant behaviors.

The above should not frighten you into being an unassertive parent! These points are only meant to prevent excessive, unnecessary and chronic use of violence. An occasional whack is not going to have any detrimental effect on a child if your relationship is basically loving. It may actually be the best thing in some circumstances. However, if you are doing a lot of hitting, you should run, not walk, to your nearest Observant therapist or Rav. Do not reassure yourself with phrases such as, "It's my child's fate to have a mother who hits. If Hashem gave him the problem, He must have given him the tools to deal with it." "Hashem wouldn't give a child anything more than what he could deal with." "There's nothing I can do. At least he has a loving teacher who will make up for my mistakes." "All that matters is that he studies Torah. That will make up for everything." "They're little. It won't bother them. They won't remember." Such phrases can easily become excuses for laziness and passivity in the face of danger. Nothing makes up for feeling unloved by one's parents. The most powerful determiner of a child's *middoth* is how he sees his parents and teachers acting. Make a firm stance against violence at home and at school.

Avoid Excessive Shame When Rebuking

Although it is not a mitzvah to criticize, it *is* a mitzvah to rebuke (*Vayikra* 19:17). The difference is mainly in whether or not you have the other person's feelings and welfare in mind at the time.

We are prohibited from intentionally hurting other people's feelings (*Vayikra* 25:17). Our forefathers rebuked their sons only on their deathbeds. Rashi says that this was in order to avoid the temptation to shame their children and alienate them thereby (Rashi, *Devarim* 1:3). Rashi comments that before the age of sixteen (some say eighteen) a child does not know how to accept rebuke without becoming defensive and even hostile (*Kiddushin* 30a). Because a child does not separate himself from his actions, he thinks that to do bad is to be bad. Carelessly given rebuke can have a devastating effect, making him feel unloved and inadequate. Thus, our Sages were extremely strict about the importance of taking people's feelings into consideration before rebuking, for,

> *Shame is the greatest pain.*
>
> (SHABBATH 50b)

One reason we cover the *challoth* on Shabbath is so as not to "shame" them by saying *kiddush* first. If we are so considerate of these loaves of bread, how much more so should we be considerate of our children's feelings! If a child has misbehaved, use some face-saving comment before your rebuke (for **your** sake as well as his) such as: "I'm sure you did not intend to. . . " or "You are usually so cooperative. I assume that you forgot. . . . "

I remember once being saved from great shame when I had lost something of value and my father, Sol Dann *z.l.* said, "Let it be *rebbe gelt.*" When I asked what that was, he told me, "That's when you lose money, but you learn something from the experience. The money is your teacher, so all is not lost." Whether it is a new pair of shoes which felt great in the store but are too tight when you get them home or a burnt meal which has to be thrown out, don't emotionalize the loss. Chalk it up to *rebbe gelt.* Or, tell yourself and your children that you have a *shalom fund.* This is money which is lost but which you refuse to get upset about for the sake of your inner *shalom.*

Use the "sandwich theory" of rebuke implied in the Torah when a person is told to first rid himself of hatred, then to rebuke, then to show love (*Vayikra* 17:18-19). Apply love first and afterward. Let the rebuke be the "peanut butter." The deep feeling of pain and love you feel for the child, which he sees on your anguished face, or in your actual tears, will be far more effective than a tight, angry face. To rid yourself of hatred, practice the method of Hillel:

> *The attribute of Hillel the Elder ... transcends all of the others, for he took offense at nothing and [therefore] felt not even a stirring of anger.*
>
> (PATH OF THE JUST, p. 165)

Learning how not to take offense is one of the most important skills a human being can acquire. Train yourself not to think, "*Davka,* he's doing it deliberately!" That thought will anger you automatically. You do not know for certain what is in anyone's heart or mind unless they tell you so specifically, your children included. Certain so-called educators will say that the goal of children's misbehavior is always to manipulate the parents or take vengeance on them. While this may at times be true, it is just as often not the case. Furthermore, this is not a Jewish way of thinking, which stresses giving the benefit of the doubt. You do not know if that child tried to control himself but failed, is coming down with an illness, is out of his mind with hunger, boredom, feelings of rejection or fatigue. It is best to see his misbehavior as a cry for help, for strict discipline or loving reassurance. Children are complex beings. You never know for certain why they do things. With this humble realization in mind, you will be more likely to avoid taking offense and will, therefore, be more likely to be able to give them what they need.

    ✻ My eight year old made a *chutzpadik* remark to me. In the past, I might have slapped. But this time, I looked at him very sternly and asked, "I am Hashem's most precious of all creations, and this is how you talk to me? And you, the most precious of all Hashem's creations? This is how you talk?" That was enough to get through to him.

Make sure that when you rebuke, you do not cause a more serious transgression than what your child did in the first place. He may have broken a glass, lost his jacket or torn his pants. If you become hysterical and enraged about such trivialities, it becomes obvious to him that things have greater value to you than people.

The Most Effective Form of Rebuke

It is important to tell people, your children included, when their behavior bothers you. The worst thing you can do is judge yourself or others as failures, for then you are too full of anger or shame to respond constructively. If you stifle your feelings, one of two things is likely to happen: a) You'll explode in a moment of weakness, and then you'll want to crush the other person with the weight of all your unexpressed hurts, or b) The relationship will grow cold as the wall of unspoken hostility grows thicker and higher. However, try thinking of rebuke as a form of "surgery." If you must perform it, prepare yourself and the "patient" in advance, and make sure to use "healing" tactics afterwards.

Your purpose in giving rebuke should be to awaken greater awareness on the other person's part. If you do so in the proper manner, you actually become closer, rather than more distant, as is the case with carelessly given criticism. Properly given rebuke instills in your child a greater respect for you since you care enough to exhibit such self-discipline in a moment of stress. This increases the possibility that he will want to please you in the future. Before rebuking, you must make sure to:

1. Have no hatred, grudge-bearing or vengeance in your heart (*Vayikra* 19:17-18).
2. Rebuke in private.
3. Speak gently and lovingly.
4. Have only the other person's good in mind at the time (*Hilchoth Deoth* 6:7).

With an older child or adult, it is a good idea to preface a rebuke by saying, "I have something to talk to you about concerning our relationship. Do you have time right now?" By getting the person's agreement to talk, you will usually lessen his defensiveness. This also reminds you that it is very important not to rebuke whenever you feel like it, but to first practice self-discipline and be sensitive to the other person's feelings. A most effective form of rebuke is called, "The One-Minute Rebuke"* which has two parts.

Part I: Stating Your Displeasure (30 seconds)

1. As soon as possible after the child has done something wrong, **state specifically what it was that you did not like.** For example: "You left the dishes on the table." "You went out without telling me where you were going." "You hit your brother."

2. **Tell the child exactly how you felt about what he did.** For example, "I was very disappointed when I saw that you didn't keep your contract to clean up after eating." "I get so worried when I don't know where you are." "I am terrified that you are going to really hurt him and we're going to have to go to the emergency room again like we did last week." Let your voice match the measure of pain which you really feel about the event.

3. **Silence.** Be silent for about ten seconds to give the child an opportunity to feel how painful this is to you. Some children do *tshuvah* in seconds, as you can see from their look of true remorse or tears. Others may take longer. Do not let the child talk or defend himself at this point. These ten seconds may be difficult for you both, seeming to last for an eternity, but they are essential in order to let the impact of his actions sink into the child's consciousness.

Part II: Healing the Relationship (30 seconds)

4. **Touch** the child to let him know that you care, that you still love him even though he hurt you.

5. **Elevate and Reassure.** Tell him that you love him even though you do not always like his behavior. Elevate him with words such as, "You usually do not act like this. I know you can do better." Or,

---

* Adapted from *The One Minute Mother*.

the famous, *"Es pash nisht,"* i.e., "This is not fitting for you."

6. **Hug** him or in some other way show him that the rebuke is over and that you harbor no ill will. This is your *"kadima* signal" to go on with your lives.

This kind of rebuke is successful because:

* It allows you to express your feelings so that you do not build up a wall of resentment between you and the child.

* The child learns that hurt feelings can be expressed without destroying relationships. You demonstrate to the child how to express pain without hostility.

* You help the child save face by reassuring him of your love, by avoiding name-calling, and by making the "incision" (i.e., the rebuke) as quick and painless as possible.

* You yourself are forced to think rationally and constructively. As you try to get your message into the thirty seconds, you are forced to avoid excessive emotionalism and condemnations.

* You have the opportunity to demonstrate physical affection toward the child, which may have been lacking in your relationship. If the child does not like to be touched, at least you can express positive feelings.

* You end on a positive note. You have avoided all condemnations. You have expressed your pain as well as your love. You have used the rebuke as an opportunity to elevate your child.

Rabbi Yisroel Salanter advised educators that the way to reach people is to instill in them elevated feelings about themselves. Rabbi Noson Finkel ... praised his pupils profusely. A teacher who tends to lower the self-esteem and confidence of his students should either change this tendency or change professions. One of the most important lessons an educator can convey to students is that they have inherent worth and should strive to utilize their potential. To increase self-esteem ... have them become aware of [their] strengths and resources.

(GATEWAY TO HAPPINESS, p. 133)

Try the one-minute rebuke with adults when appropriate. You may be able to improve your relationship with your husband, in particular, by giving these clear, non-hysterical messages. The important thing is to mention the undesirable behavior as soon as possible, before you have worked yourself up into a fury, yet not until you have calmed yourself down by preparing yourself to go through the steps in a disciplined manner.

The first time you tell your spouse or child that you are upset about some act, you might not get immediate change. Repeat the rebuke. Practice the rebuke ahead of time while doing the dishes or nursing the baby. If you still get no response, you may need other tactics.

>   I kept telling my husband I wanted to spend more time with him in the evenings. But he kept coming home late and often would not even tell me that he would not be on time for dinner. I got more and more furious as my one-minute rebukes were not being heard. I felt he didn't care about me. Finally, we made a date to go out and I asked him for his side of the story. It turned out that he wants to feel free and independent and does not want to spend time talking about feelings because it makes him uncomfortable, and he does not see this as important in his life. I felt very upset and alone, but at least got him to admit that he owed me the courtesy of letting me know where he would be. I am no longer pressuring him to share, and little by little, he seems to be more willing to do so. It was very important to use the one-minute rebuke to avoid condemning him and getting hysterical. That is when I became more realistic and accepting.

>   I kept telling my children how upset I was about the mess in their rooms, but my rebuke fell on deaf ears. Then I realized that I had to get out the charts and train them to be orderly in a more systematic manner.

The tendency to criticize and rebuke children throughout the day is very strong in many parents. After all, we see their deficiencies so clearly and want so much for them to be positive reflections of us. If this is your tendency, consider the following:

A pious man ... passed by the carcass of a dog that gave forth an offensive odor. His disciples said to him, 'How dreadfully does this carcass smell!' He said to them, 'How white are its teeth!' The pupils then regretted the disparaging remark they had made. ... If it is reprehensible to make a disparaging remark concerning a dead dog, how much more is it to do so concerning a living human being. ... The object of this pious teacher was to instruct his pupils not to accustom their tongues to speak evil, so that self-restraint should become natural to them and they should accustom their tongues to speak good of others so that this too would become a fixed and natural habit.

(DUTIES OF THE HEART, vol. II, p. 99)

This lesson should be followed when speaking to your children, or speaking to them of others, including other Jewish sects and non-Jews as well.

When Your Child Talks Back in Anger

At some time, almost every mother will experience the pain of having a child say, "I hate you," or make some other angry, disrespectful remark. In a child under the age of four, assume that he does not realize the true impact of his words. He simply has no other way to vent his pain and frustration. In an older child, such an expression is a sign of very deep pain. Try the following:

* Say, "I want to know what displeases you and will be happy to hear, but you are not allowed to talk to me in an angry tone of voice. Tell me what you want to say, but say it respectfully."

* Walk away after telling him, "Come and talk to me when you are ready to speak with respect."

* It is very effective to "replay the scene" immediately by having the child go out of the room and come back in again, this time stating his desire respectfully. A young child does not know how to convey his disappointment or difference of opinion in words. You have to teach him. For example, tell him, "It is fine if you tell me, 'Mom, I disagree with you,' in a respectful tone of voice. You don't have to get angry with me to get your point across."

* Tell him that beneath anger lies pain. Say, "You must be in a lot of pain. I want to know what's going on." Restrain your impulse to be defensive, argue back or give advice. Listen! Afterwards, tell him how he could have spoken respectfully from the beginning.

Tantrums

A tantrum is a dramatic overreaction to frustration and an attempt to manipulate others. Few childhood acts are as embarrassing and nerve-racking as tantrums. When a child has one, don't blind yourself with condemnations of him or yourself. Focus on solutions. Consider your options: 1) Divert his attention, 2) Ignore him, 3) Hold him firmly so that he cannot damage anyone or anything, 4) Remove him to another room and leave him there until he has calmed down. Depending on the age of the child and the circumstances, one of these methods may or may not work.

The one thing which you do not want to do is to give in to his demands, for this will reinforce in his mind the idea that tantrums are the best way to get what he wants. If the desire to give in to him is strong, remind yourself that it is in his best interest that you do not do so because you are setting him up for bigger tantrums in the future which will eventually have to be dealt with more harshly. The child is putting on a show. You have to avoid being an involved audience. Once he gets the message that his dramatic displays of distress will not be rewarded, he will soon stop.

> My daughter would have a tantrum if I didn't get her the sweets she wanted when we went shopping. I would give in because I didn't want to make a scene. But then, one day, in the supermarket, she started screaming and I had the courage to just walk out, leaving behind me a basketful of groceries. That was it. No more tantrums.

> My two year old had a tantrum because the red pair of pants which he adores were in the wash and he refused to wear anything else. He kept screaming that he wanted the pants and I kept telling him that they were in the washing machine. My logic was of no use to him. He kept screaming. Finally, I just ignored him. Every once in a while, I would go over to him and tell him that I was sorry he was making himself so miserable. I called a friend who kept me calm by reassuring me that what he **wanted** was for me to give in. But what he **needed** was for me to stand firm. Forty-five minutes later, it was over and it never happened again.

> When my son had a tantrum, I turned on the tape recorder and recorded his screams. Then I played it back to him. He yelled at me, "Stop! It hurts!" I told him that that is exactly how I feel about his screeching. By the time we were talking, he had stopped being so upset.

Reassure yourself that the energy generated by a tantrum will soon be harnessed toward positive goals. See this passion as a sign of a child with a strong will and great persistence. (Obviously, however, if the tantrums are a daily affair, something is seriously wrong. You need help.)

Fighting

There they go again! Taunting, tormenting, teasing, poking, provoking and squabbling. It is painful to see your own flesh and blood carrying on in such a primitive manner. You see the worst in them: vengefulness, selfishness and cruelty. You are likely to have insecure thoughts such as: "They're going to kill each other." "The bully will be a lifelong tyrant." "The weak one will be a lifelong *nebbuch.*" Any thought of danger, whether real or imagined, provokes a "stress response": adrenaline shoots into your bloodstream, stimulating your heart, muscles and lungs and mobilizing you for action; digestion slows down; your heart pounds; your whole nervous system goes into a state of hyper-arousal. If there is actual danger, this is an appropriate, life-protecting response which should provoke you to take action. However, if you constantly panic over every minor squabble, then you are keeping yourself unnecessarily stressed. This not only taxes your immune system, making you more susceptible to physical ills, it also keeps you from responding effectively both to real danger and to trivial discomforts.

To calm yourself down, realize that all children fight at times and that it is distressing, but not usually dangerous. Fighting is an important life skill. We all need to know how to be assertive, how to stand up for our rights and combat evil, both within ourselves as well as in the outer environment. You would not want passive, devitalized children who were so timid and anxiety-ridden that they were unable to protect themselves from danger or take the initiative in life. Your task is to encourage the positive, protective aspects of this *middah* while curbing the cruelty and excessive desire to dominate.

AMO children (see chapter 5), in particular, enjoy making a commotion. They are natural little soldiers and love the excitement generated by a battle. They are more impulsive and live for the moment, not thinking about the consequences of their actions or the effect on others. They need positive outlets for their high energy level. If you are a dominant LT, you will be more affected by their conflicts, since you are more sensitive and have a strong need for harmony. You will have to be flexible in order to adapt to their needs as well as very firm in making sure that they learn to discipline themselves. Don't compare your children to strong DOS or KIP types. Yours have different needs and drives.

> I used to panic when my children fought. I hated them and hated myself. I felt like such a failure. I wanted to give up and run away. I'd condemn myself for being too wishy-washy, for not being more

"together," for not having given them the security, the firm limits or the consistency which I know children need. Then I would lose control and scream and hit. It took quite some time to learn how to eliminate my condemnations and then how to respond constructively.

Realize that having power is one of life's pleasures. The ability to dominate, manipulate and control others is a strong lust in some people, some more so than others. If you have a strong "shock response" to their fighting, they feel even more pleasure at having the power to make you so upset.

You cannot eliminate fighting completely, but you can try the following to reduce the intensity and duration of their fights:

1. Ignore them. As long as there is no danger to life or property, let them solve their own fights. They will eventually stop bothering you if they know in advance that you are going to tell them, "Kids, I trust that you have the ability to work things out yourself." While you are "ignoring them," you might take the following secure thoughts: "They are within the normal range of childish behavior. My response is average also." "I can bear this discomfort." "I endorse myself for not having condemnations or fearful prognostications." "I trust that they will grow up to be models of Torah values since that is what we stress most at home." Then remind yourself of times when they were cooperative and how much you enjoyed seeing them work together on a project. Keep these images in mind to remind you that the "total view" of them is positive.

2. Try a *paradoxical intervention.* This means that you tell the children to keep doing whatever it is that bothers you! Tell them, "Oh, good, you're arguing again. Please go on." While this may work better with certain other bad habits, it may have enough surprise value that they are stunned by your request and stop. Be careful about using the *paradoxical intervention.* It may backfire. On the other hand, it may be very effective.

3. Take assertive action. For example, stop the car if they are fighting. Take away the toy over which they are fighting until they make *shalom.* Send them to separate corners.

4. Since boredom is a major cause for fighting, have "emergency rations" available, such as clay, paints, and inexpensive toys which you have wrapped ahead of time for such inevitable times.

5. Remind your children often, Hashem especially loves the

person who does not return an insult with an insult or a hurt with a hurt. These are the people who have the greatest *zechuth* (*Rosh Hashanah* 17a).

It is this author's opinion that parents should interfere if children are calling each other names or being violent. They should be reminded of their Torah obligations and, if possible, given the opportunity to try role-playing so that they can find constructive means of solving disputes.

There are many who will say, "Never interfere when children fight." This is fine if the children are more or less evenly matched. But it is very wrong if the older one is a domineering tyrant and bully! It is your responsibility to protect your children, from themselves as well as from each other. If left to their own devices, the older ones may develop a lifelong tendency to tyrannize others and the younger ones may be internalizing the feeling that they are weak and helpless and must always give in to the bullies of the world.

If your marital situation is an unhappy one, expect that you will see more fighting among your children, as they are acting out their anxiety and mirroring back to you the lack of mutual respect which usually accompanies marital conflicts. They feel more insecure than other children. Fighting makes them feel less vulnerable by providing an illusion of power and strength to cover their innermost feelings of shame, sadness, impotence and fear. You cannot give your children what you do not have. And if you do not have *shalom bayith*, the children are handicapped to some degree. Try to give them as much love and reassurance as you can, but expect that they will act out their insecurities in non-constructive ways.

Lying and Stealing

Most young children lie and steal at times and such behavior is usually not a cause for alarm. However, even if he has taken only a very small amount of money and you don't really think much of the event yourself, you should make a big thing of it in front of your child, talking to him in a very serious tone of voice about what he has done and showing great pain even if you do not really feel it, until you see that he makes some gesture of *tshuvah*, such as crying or saying how bad he feels about the incident. You should start off such a session by sympathizing with the child's desire for the forbidden object which is something we can all identify with. This lets him know that you do understand him. Then remind him that he must nevertheless discipline himself and not act on impulse.

While a one-time lapse can be considered "passing, not permanent," and need not be blown out of proportion, chronic lying and stealing are signs of serious disturbance which indicate a desperate need for family therapy. Your child behaves badly because he feels he is bad. Most child therapists see stealing in children as a symbolic way of stealing love. Were you too busy to give him the attention he needed when he was younger? Are you a working mother who just has not had time to develop in him a sense of connectedness to you or give him proper guidance? Is your husband aloof, critical or physically violent? Or, he may be failing in school, which is disastrous to a child since he usually has no other outlets to make himself feel successful. He needs two things from you: to help him control his impulses and help him feel loved and successful. Encouragement from teachers is essential. Talk to them about his need for extra reassurance and support. In most cases, stealing indicates a disturbance in the father-child relationship which manifests itself as an attack on all authority figures. The father's cooperation is essential in order for progress to be made.

> ❀ We do not believe in watching television. I found out that my daughter was sneaking out to a friend's house to watch. I confronted her with the facts and told her that I understood her desire to watch, but that I couldn't allow it to continue. We talked about projects she could do so that she wouldn't be so bored, and she decided to sign up for afternoon art and music classes.

> ❀ My nine year old stole from a local store. His father was in the habit of giving him a good beating whenever he did something wrong. This time, I begged him to come with me to a child therapist. He refused and said it was all my fault. Finally, I was able to get my son's teacher to convince him to go. We have a long way to go to undo a lot of damage, but at least we have started the process.

Major Disciplinary Mistakes

Even the best of parents are likely to make some of these common mistakes in discipline. Being aware of them may help you avoid them most of the time. Remember, your goal is not to arouse anger, but rather remorse and a desire to change.

* *Thinking davka.* When you think that your child has deliberately done something to hurt you for no reason, you anger yourself and are more prone to violence. We are required to judge others with righteousness (*Avoth* 1:6). This means that we are obligated to give others the benefit of the doubt and assume that they do what they do not because they have a deliberate intention to hurt us but because they: are testing our limits, are overtired, hungry, momentarily in the grip of laziness, are in pain, lack the awareness, skills or self-control to behave differently, have lost the battle to an irresistible impulse, forgot the rules, or are overwhelmed emotionally. Tell yourself, "He's doing the best he can," not in order to delude yourself or avoid disciplining your child, but in order that you do so without hatred and violence.

* *Withholding food as a punishment.* This is too painful and frightening for a small child. It also teaches him to hurt others by withholding what is most precious to them. As an adult, he may be the type of husband who does not talk to his wife for days at a time, or the wife who withholds affection to punish him. Remember, the anger a child feels toward a parent, which he cannot express, is displaced onto other people or onto himself, or is stored away until he can take it out on those he considers weaker than himself, such as his younger sibling.

* *Provocative threats.* "If you do that again, you'll see what I'll do." Daring a child like this only makes him curious. One three year old, when asked why he did something after the mother told him he would be punished, said, "I was curious about what you would do."

* *Comparing children.* "How come your brother is so good?" Statements of this sort do not help. They only increase feelings of competition and resentment.

* *Making father the bully.* "Wait till your father comes home and he'll really give it to you." This statement implies that you can't handle the situation. Children have short memories. By the time Daddy comes home, they may have forgotten what they did. Or, the intensity of the event may have lessened in your own eyes and you no longer want him to be harsh with them. Children

should have a good feeling about their fathers and not see them as punishing tyrants.

* *Terrifying threats.* "I'll bash your head in." "I'll send you away." "You can find a different Mommy." Children have vivid imaginations. They don't need you to add to their sense of insecurity and their most frightening insecure thought, i.e., abandonment. It also makes them feel totally unloved, which then makes them want to please you even less.

* *Name-calling.* You might get what you least want, i.e., a child who thinks, "She's right. I am that label."

* *Negative programming.* "How come you never come when I call?"

* *Punishments which last too long or which deprive him of the one thing which is most precious to him* will arouse hatred rather than awareness.

* *Guilt manipulation.* "You'll be the death of me." "You'll cry over my grave."

* *Trying to teach in the midst of a crisis.* In the midst of a crisis, use a minimum of words.

* *Refusing to give explanations.* True, sometimes you need to tell your child, "Do it because I said so." Or, "When you are a parent, you can do things your way. Until then, you must obey my wishes." However, there are plenty of times when explanations are not only justified, but will help the child carry out your desires with greater willingness, such as explaining why you have to be some place at a certain time, why you don't want him to eat so many sweets, and why certain people and activities are better than others.

* *Taking trivialities too seriously.* Save your emotionalism for important things, like relationships and life-changing events. Your excessive seriousness adds unnecessary tension, making both you and your children less efficient and less loving.

* *Punishing a child for not living up to your unrealistic demands and expectations.* Don't expect children never to fight, to be able to sit quietly for long periods of time, or to be unconcerned about possessions and pleasures. Don't expect a five year old to have a developed sense of time or a three year old to have a mature conscience.

* *Thinking that to be a good parent, you always have to be in complete control of your children.* That is an impossible goal. True

obedience is based on the spirit of self-abnegation, or *bitul.* That takes quite a few years to develop. Expect that just as adults are not always able to reach this level, neither will your children.

* *Forgetting to make simple rules, give clear directions and focus on solutions.* Simple rules such as, "Whoever has a toy in his possession has it for his own until he puts it down," can do much to avoid a tug-of-war. When referring to food, teach them, "The one you touch is the one you take." *Solutionize, don't emotionalize.*

* *Forgetting how painful it is for a child to be bored.* Your life may be full of many stresses. You may long for a moment to sit and do nothing. But normal children hate to be unstimulated for long. They become terribly distressed at not having outlets for their mental and physical hungers.

* *Being afraid to punish, or doing so in a wishy-washy manner.* A child who hurts others must know that he has done something wrong and be disciplined for it, whether by being rebuked or removed from the group for a period of time. Hurting people should be the major reason for disciplinary action. Do what you must without hostility, but with resolute firmness.

Before you punish, remind yourself that your child performs thousands of acts of self-discipline each day which you do not notice. There are thousands of times when he did come when you called, did eat the food he may not have wanted because you wanted him to, did give up some pleasurable activity to do your bidding even though it was painful for him at the time, did not bother you when you were busy, and did not fight or argue with you or his siblings. Even if you need to have a mask of anger on the outside at times, keep your heart full of love by remembering his essential goodness.

With a measure a man metes, it shall be measured to him.

(SOTAH 1:7)

Make sure that what you mete to your child is appropriate. As he grows older, he will give back to you tenfold what you gave to him, both the good and the bad.

What If You Have Already Made Mistakes?

You may have made all of the foregoing mistakes and then some! The object of that list is not to paralyze you with guilt but to motivate you to change. In the past, you may have confused *emunah* and *bitachon* with laziness and apathy as you thought to yourself, "Everything will somehow work out." Now is the time to begin the process of putting more effort into self-improvement. You may have been young, inexperienced and lacking in a supportive environment. You may have had parents, in-laws or a husband who sabotaged your best efforts by disagreeing with you in front of the children or criticizing you harshly so that you lost confidence in yourself. You may not have known how to handle your anger and violent impulses. You may have had unusually difficult children, or children who were handicapped with physical problems, so that caring for them was difficult enough without having to worry about improving your own or their *middoth*. Especially if you have a non-supportive husband, realize that you can only try your best in very difficult circumstances.

Whatever your particular situation, do not hang your head in shame. You need your time, energy and thoughts to be focused on how to improve your relationships and become a more constructive parent. If your children are older, have a heart-to-heart talk with them about the changes which you feel are necessary and how sorry you are for any mistakes you may have made. Allow hurt feelings to be expressed. These feelings will rise and fall like a wave if you simply acknowledge the pain, while avoiding insecure thoughts and condemnations. Then, *kadima*, forward! The next chapter will help you to do just that.

EIGHT

How to Identify and Challenge Your Destructive Attitudes

It is essential to identify the attitudes which have been keeping you from acting in a constructive manner. A destructive, neurotic attitude is one which makes you feel discouraged, bitter, jealous and inferior. It leads to destructive desires, which are desires that can never be satisfied, such as the desire for everyone's approval all of the time or for absolute obedience from your children at all times. Destructive desires then lead to destructive actions as you hurt yourself and others with your hostility or withdrawal from responsibilities.

An attitude is a *thought habit.* It can be as hard to break as a physical addiction. These attitudes form a mental filter through which you evaluate everything you experience and everyone with whom you come in contact, including yourself. Just as one small hand placed in front of your eyes can block out the light of the sun, so too can one erroneous belief keep you from experiencing joy and love. For example, you may have attitudes about yourself such as, "I'm a born loser." "I just can't manage." Or, "My children are basically selfish, lazy and stupid." When you adopt a negative attitude, you inevitably infect those around you with your harmful beliefs, since you cannot help but radiate negativity.

The following section will teach you how to challenge and change your erroneous beliefs. Realize that it takes time to understand and unravel the intricate web of behaviors which you may have adopted as an expression of your particular attitudinal system. Ongoing effort is necessary to internalize the changes you will soon realize are necessary in order to become more caring and disciplined.

A Disciplined Mind Leads to
Constructive Actions and Vice Versa

The gematria for *doubt* is the same as Amalek, the destroyer of Israel. Doubt is closely linked to despair. When you doubt your ability to cope or to be successful as a mother, you will find it difficult, if not impossible, to function successfully. Therefore, you must establish firmly in your mind that you are a basically loving, capable person who wants the best for her children, even though you do sometimes lose control and behave in ways which you know to be destructive. If you doubt this fundamental principle, you will not be able to guide your children properly.

Mental health, like physical health, requires constant repetition of certain specific disciplines which must be performed in order to maintain internal and external harmony. You cannot hold "open house" in your mind and entertain every passing thought any more than you would hold open house in your home and allow criminals to enter along with your friends. Thoughts must be monitored just like people, because there are "criminal attitudes" which will rob you of your self-confidence. When the following thoughts pop into your mind, spot them as destructive and substitute a positive thought as well as some small positive action to prove to yourself that you can be self-disciplined. As you go through the list, think of a positive substitute for each non-constructive attitude:

"I'm not worthwhile unless I am perfectly successful in every area which I consider important."

"I am unfit for motherhood because I have no patience."

"If my children misbehave, it means that they are failures."

"If my children misbehave, it means that I am a failure."

"Children drive you crazy."

"It is my responsibility to make my family members happy at all times."

"If I just get angry and hostile enough about my children's shortcomings, they will eventually improve and be just the way I want them to be."

"If I worry about all the terrible things that might happen, then they won't happen."

"My worth is determined by what others think of me."

"My past determines what I am; I am powerless to change."
"Only mothers who are in control of everything all the time can be considered to be good, successful mothers."
"People and events are the source of my happiness. Since I have no control over them, I have no control over whether or not I am happy or unhappy."
"I have to justify my existence by always being in motion and doing for others."
"Nobody else feels like I feel or has my problems."
"Praise spoils people."
"Attention spoils children."
"Children make you feel inadequate."
"If someone hurts me, I have the right and the duty to hurt him back."

If you have not yet come up with any good alternatives, you will by the time you finish this book! For example, instead of thinking, "Children make you feel inadequate," you will realize that children merely highlight your pre-existing weaknesses so that you can recognize where you need to work on yourself. They don't make you feel inadequate or angry. You, by your own evaluation of your performance and your unwillingness to have your shortcomings brought to light, create those feelings within yourself. After all, you could come to different conclusions, namely, "I am inexperienced, unskilled and overwhelmed at times. In time, I will gain the skills I need to manage better. And even if I don't always manage well, I am still deserving of love and respect, and can still work toward greater self-mastery. I am grateful to my children for providing endless opportunities to perform acts of *chesed* and to grow spiritually."

Meanings and Feelings

The meaning you give to any event determines the feelings you have about it. For example, to one person, a rainy day means fresh smells and happy memories of stepping in puddles. To another, rain means waiting out in the cold or having the children indoors all afternoon with nothing to do. The first person is happy about the rain because she gives it a positive meaning. The second is glum because she gives it a negative one. The same thing happens throughout the day in your own mind. You encounter numerous stressful events. It is not the events which automatically cause you to feel one way or another, but rather the meaning you give them. You can look at the dirty dishes and think, "Thank God I have dishes to wash and a home to clean," or you can think , "This mess proves that I'm inadequate. I'm nothing but a maid. No one appreciates me enough to help me." Obviously, the feelings evoked by these thoughts will be quite different. You can hear your children squabbling again and think, "It's normal. That's what all children do. I can interfere if I want and teach them some problem-solving techniques or just stay out of it." Or, you can think, "I'm a failure as a mother if I have children who act like this toward each other."

The difference between a calm, happy mother and an anxious, hysterical one is mainly in her attitude toward the very same events. The calm mother habitually tells herself, "I'll pull through this stressful event. I'm strong. It's really nothing to get upset about." On the other hand, the anxious mother habitually tells herself, "I can't stand this any more. I sense danger everywhere." "I'm going to collapse. I just can't manage. I'm a failure." Anxiety is an automatic by-product of such danger-oriented thinking. Or, you might be producing hostile feelings by thinking, "This child (or person) is hurting me deliberately. He does not respect or love me. He's going to be even more impossible to handle as time goes on."

Changing Your Automatic Response Patterns

You may not have realized it, but from the time you were born, you have been developing certain habitual response patterns toward yourself, people and life. These responses are now so automatic that they seem to be part of your very nature. This is fine if those habits are positive. But if not, you will have to put forth effort to undo the complex set of thoughts and behaviors which combine to form a bad habit, such as getting depressed or screaming. One way to do this is to be aware of the meaning which you have been giving events. By changing the meaning, you can bring about a positive emotional response instead of a negative one, or reduce the degree of emotional arousal which you might have had in the past. For example, if you are a fastidious housekeeper, you may still be annoyed by dirt, but not as upset as before. Or, you might get to the point where you do not emotionalize dirt at all, but simply clean it up calmly.

To understand how this works, you must first become aware of your particular response patterns to various "button-pushing" events. For example, you may have been telling yourself something stress-producing, when you could substitute something stress-reducing and get better results.

STRESS PRODUCING	STRESS REDUCING
a. "I can't stand mess. The sight of it drives me crazy."	a. "Oh, it's messy. *Baruch Hashem* that we have all these possessions. Dishes and messes are meant to be cleaned, not dramatized. It's not so awful, just boring. It's just work."
b. "People who don't do as I want don't love me."	b. "They do love me. But they have their own interests, dispositions and pressures at the moment."
c. "I'm just not good at anything. I'm a failure."	c. "Right now, things are not going well. But most of the time, I'm doing a pretty good job. Things will improve as I learn more skills and tactics. I'm not inferior, just inexperienced."
d. "I just can't handle children."	d. "*Baruch Hashem*, they're basically normal, lively, curious children. They are a handful, but I'm not a failure if I'm not in total control of them every single second."
e. "I'm about to have a nervous breakdown."	e. "Right now, I feel like I'm going to pieces. But I know that I will soon recover and the pieces will all get reorganized again. This situation is uncomfortable, but not

dangerous. I can trust my inner strengths to pull me through."

f. "No one else feels like this."

f. "Many other mothers feel the same way and have the same problems."

g. "I'm a terrible person."

g. "Every difficulty has the potential to bring out hidden strengths in myself. I will use this event to grow."

h. "I don't have the strength to cope with my problems."

h. "If God thought enough of me to give me this test and had faith that I could handle it, who am I to argue with Him?"

i. "My family members are exceptionally obnoxious."

i. "Right now, I feel overwhelmed by them. But that is not always the case. The total view is positive. We have wonderful, joyful moments together and times like this as well. That is normal. We'll weather this storm just like we have weathered the others."

j. "These kids will drive me nuts!"

"My children are very active. In time, their strong drives will become transmuted into a passion for Torah and mitzvoth!"

[Obviously, if there is any real danger to mental or physical well-being, as in the case of children who are truly exceptionally undisciplined or a family member who has a potentially serious illness, you will want to take immediate action and **not** want to run away from the problem with self-deluding reassurances.]

To understand yourself, you must understand what is going on in your mind. Keep a written list of your stimulus-response patterns and the negative meanings you attach to events so that you will understand your reactions. Next to the insecure thoughts, write down the positive meanings you can give those same events.

Pay special attention to the major sources of anxiety, such as health, finances, whining, disorder and discord.

No matter what the event, you have the choice to give it a positive or negative meaning. There is no greater freedom, no greater expression of your essential divine nature, than the exercise of this ability. Remember: You can have only one thought in your mind at a time. Make it a secure, strengthening thought. Insecure thoughts will arise from time to time. Challenge them. Then substitute secure, strengthening thoughts and some positive act, no matter how small (e.g., a smile or brisk walk outdoors). If they still persist to bother you obsessively, treat them as you would a phone call on Shabbath — don't answer!

  I was so upset when the cookies I had baked burned. I was really angry at myself and I was putting myself down when it suddenly occurred to me that I could use this event positively. My two oldest girls were in the living room and smelled the burnt cookies. They ran in to find out what had happened. I thought this would be a great opportunity to teach them how to deal with failure. "Well, girls," I said, "I goofed. It's not awful, just distressing. I'm throwing these away and I'm going to start all over again." If nothing else, the experience served as a model for them not to "awfulize" their mistakes.

  Each day when my three younger children came home for lunch, all at the same time, I felt overwhelmed. They'd be grumpy or wild. Sometimes they wouldn't eat what I had made, or they'd run away and come back fifteen minutes later and ask me to reheat the meal. I'd get frantic and angry. Then I decided to change my attitude. Before they came home, I closed my eyes and said over and over to myself, "The noisier and more demanding they are, the more patient and unperturbed I will be. The more hectic the environment, the more aware I will be of how relaxing it is to be non-judgmental." It works most of the time for me to simply remain detached, yet loving, until they get over the difficult transition from school to home.

  I used to look at my childhood and think how deprived I was and how damaging it was to have grown up in such a critical environment. I was always telling myself that I could never repair the damage it had caused. Then I realized that I no longer wanted this thought in my mind. So I began to tell myself that the fact that I had survived these events and was still basically a loving person meant that I must have great inner strength. My childhood taught me what not to do with my own children. I started to see myself as a strong, survivor type instead of a weakling and a victim.

⊛ My kids came home from the park absolutely filthy. I groaned, "Now look at all the work I have to do! Look at them!" My mother smiled and said, " A dirty child is the sign of a child who's probably been having fun. Be happy they've been having a good time!" My entire emotional state became positive in an instant by giving dirt a different meaning. The same thing happened when my son emptied out a drawer. She said, "He must be so intelligent. Look how curious he is." (Provided by my mother, Anne Dann Luborsky)

⊛ I was one of those mothers who always felt inadequate if my children were unhappy. But I reinterpreted this. If I had to say, "no," and they were upset, I simply told myself that this was because they were young and still thought that happiness was the result of getting everything they wanted in life. I now see a crisis as an opportunity to wean them and myself as well away from this idea and to strengthen their ability to cope with disappointment and loss. To find the source of joy from within ourselves, especially from giving to others, is a great *berachah.*

A person feels deprived only if he gives a negative meaning to not getting what he wants. If he learns to be strengthened by disappointments, he will no longer suffer from self-pity.

It takes practice to learn to substitute secure, constructive thoughts for your insecure ones. It helps to share your insecure thoughts with others and to then practice the substitution process out loud.

The Major Categories of Stress-Producing Thoughts

Anxiety-provoking thoughts usually fall into one of eight categories which all start with "E" so that you can memorize them easily and refer to them whenever you are upset. These are "mental saboteurs" which will rob you of *menuchath hanefesh.*

Exceptionality: Thinking that you, your children or your spouse are the worst. Thinking that other people do not have your problems, feelings, reactions, etc. Counter thought: "Many other people experience the same difficulties."

Unrealistic expectations: Thinking that life should go smoothly, that people should all be at a higher level of spirituality and maturity, that whatever happens should seem "fair" and logical in your eyes, that people should always be communicative, co-operative, self-controlled and considerate. Counter thought: "I have to accept life and people as they are, not as I want them to be. I do not have the Godly wisdom to know the ultimate reason and purpose of seemingly unfair events. I can only know that everything is purposeful and meaningful in the overall divine plan of the universe." "It does not help me to be upset about other people's imperfections. We are all imperfect. All we can do is work on ourselves. It will not help me to be angry at those who have no desire to do so."

Exaggeration: Thinking that minor discomforts are awful. Also, using "always" and "never" when they really don't apply, as in: "My kids **never** listen to me." "I'm **always** tired." "He **never** helps." Counter thought: "I'm being excessively dramatic and over-emotionalizing this event." Excessive emotionalism usually comes because you have a feeling that there is some danger attached to the event. If danger to mental or physical well-being is a reality, you have a right to feel very anxious and upset. When you find yourself overreacting to an event, ask yourself, "Is there any danger here to my marriage, my children, myself? Is this going to lead to some major, life-changing event?" If not, you may be dramatizing the event unnecessarily.

Extrapolation into the future: Thinking that things can only get worse or that you are going to collapse or go crazy some day. Thinking that you've ruined things forever. Counter thought: "I am not a prophet. I have to have the humility to know that I don't know. I will gain in strength, courage and awareness as I get older." "I have the ability to stop obsessive thoughts by diverting my attention and moving my muscles in a healthy way."

Excessive responsibility: Thinking that everything is your fault and that you should have more control over people and events than is reasonable. Counter thought: "God has His own timetable for people's growth." "I am not responsible for other people's happiness. I can just do my best to please. If that's not good enough for them, it is not my fault if they are unhappy. I cannot be all things to all people." "I am responsible for training my children to follow Torah and have good *middoth*. I can provide the right atmosphere and the information, but I cannot force people to change." "It is good for my children to see that they have the inner resources to cope with discomfort and loss and not fall apart." "It is good for them to get themselves up on time, to face difficulties which they can handle successfully at their age and be given age-appropriate responsibilities. I have to let go so that they can grow."

Evasion of responsibility: Thinking that you do not have the physical strength or the mental awareness or courage to improve yourself or correct situations which can be corrected. You might be saying, "Let others do it," or, "I'm sure things will work out on their own as long as I have faith." Counter thought: Effort is up to man; success is up to God. Even if all my efforts are only a drop in the bucket and even if they have no effect, I have to put forth that effort to bring greater health, joy and love into the world."

Erroneous conclusions, assumptions and beliefs: Thinking that you know why events happen or what is in other people's hearts or minds. For example, "He did that because he doesn't love me." Also, making erroneous connections, as in: "The fact that I don't do well at X means that I am a total failure." Or, "The fact that I have this problem is proof that God does not love me." Counter thought: "I am worthwhile even if I'm not perfect." "I do not know why things happen. Hashem has done this for my ultimate benefit." "Other people's negative judgments of me are not reflective of absolute truth."

Eclipsing (or discounting) the good: When things don't go well, you wipe out all the good in that person or in yourself. E.g., "See what I/he just did? Now I see the truth and it's all negative!" Counter thought: "Every human being has both bad and good. No one is perfect. I remember many good things that this person (or I) did. Just because I don't see the goodness now does not mean that it's not there." "The total view of this person is positive."

The next time you are upset, go through these eight Es. You may find that your emotional charge suddenly fades, like a burst balloon, as soon as you identify which ones have been keeping you in a negative emotional state.

Feelings and Opinions: Fantasy or Fact?

It is not always simple to determine what meaning to give an event. Often, people will disagree with your perceptions or beliefs:

> ॐ I have an eight-year-old, learning-disabled child. I had the feeling that something was wrong when he was just four. But everyone told me I

was being silly and getting worked up over nothing. It wasn't until he was seven that we discovered that he had a severe perceptual problem and could have benefitted greatly if I had taken him for therapy sooner. Unfortunately, I was ashamed to do so because people made me feel like an overprotective, anxious mother.

    ❦   I have a neighbor who tells me that pacifiers are disgusting and that they make children dependent and disturbed. All I can do is remind her that that is an opinion, not an objective fact.

    ❦   One of my middle children is very independent and defiant. I am convinced that she is basically well-adjusted and will be just fine. But one of my in-laws keeps telling me that she is severely disturbed. I often have very pleasant moments with this child and she can be very helpful. To me the total view is positive.

If you are unsure as to what is "just a stage," as opposed to what is an indication of a serious problem, check with an expert. It is self-deluding to "think positively" and shrug off danger signals, even if they are very subtle.

It is also harmful to allow other people's hysteria or negativity to work you up unnecessarily. Certainly, you should take other people's suggestions and advice into consideration. However, realize that many people assume that their customs, preferences, opinions and hunches are law and reflective of absolute truth and will try to impose them on you. If possible, express your right to your own opinion. If your response causes them to be defensive and hostile, you may have to reassure yourself that you are following your best judgment and that you do not need approval from these people.

    ❦   My mother-in-law told me that my baby looked anemic. I was about to get defensive when I changed tactics and told her that I would ask the doctor for a blood test. That calmed us both down. It turned out that she was right.

    ❦   I had the feeling that my husband was upset with me because he had been so quiet lately. I asked him directly, "Is it a fantasy or a fact that you are angry with me?" He said that it was fantasy. He reassured me that it's the difficulties in the school where he teaches that have been concerning him.

    ❦   I had the feeling that a neighbor was angry with me. Sure enough, when I asked her, she told me that I had done something which hurt her feelings. I hadn't even been aware that the incident had any significance to her. In this case, my feelings were facts and I'm glad that we were able to clear things up.

🕸 I had been deprived of sleep for a few nights and kept telling myself that I wouldn't be able to function. Then I realized that the fact was that I was doing a pretty good job under the circumstances. It was an erroneous belief, not a fact, that was upsetting me. I **am** able to function with discomfort despite my former beliefs.

Total View and Part Acts

There are two seemingly contradictory tools which can be used to get you through a difficult period. One is "total view." This is when you tell yourself that the general view of the child is very positive. Therefore, you can overlook or calmly confront minor distresses or temporary phases. You know that it will pass eventually, and you keep your mind focused on the near future, when you are certain that the problem will be over. For example, "Right now, he's quite kvetchy, but usually he's a happy child." Things might be bad at this moment, but you know that the total view is positive.

The other tool is "part acts." When you feel overwhelmed by a situation or are in great pain, either physical or emotional, your words of reassurance may have no calming effect. In these cases, take each minute, hour or day one at a time, endorsing yourself for getting through the distress and focusing on whatever positive thoughts or actions you are able to take. For example, "When my son was in the hospital, I didn't know what would be. I just told myself to get through one hour at a time and not think of the future." "I felt awful. I didn't know how I would get ready for the three-day holiday. Then I told myself to do something, anything, just to get started and not to think about the holiday as a whole. I decided to start peeling potatoes and that act led to other positive actions." "We were snowed in for two days and the kids had 'cabin fever.' We were all going a little bonkers. I told myself to take one hour at a time and hope for the best."

A national group dealing with patients and their relatives who are suffering from terminal illnesses is called One Day at a Time. They try to get the most out of every moment. That is the best we can do at times.

Acceptance Reduces the Pain

Natural childbirth classes aim to instill a very important principle in the minds of their participants: namely, that you intensify pain if you resist it or are in fear of it. Therefore, instructors provide information about what to expect, and teach women to relax into the pain by having positive, secure thoughts instead of fighting the pain. A good labor coach might say something like this:

"Breathe into the contraction. Breathe. Don't fight it. Welcome it. That's it. Good . . . breathe . . . breathe. See, you did it! Beautiful. There's another one. Let's do it again. Breathe. Don't tighten. Relax. You're doing beautifully. Soon you'll have your baby in your arms. You're doing very well. O.K., there's another one. Look in my eyes. Let's breathe together. You're doing beautifully. Everything is happening exactly as Hashem wants. Good. Good. Go ahead. Squeeze my hand. I'm here. Don't be afraid. Don't tighten. Wonderful! See, you did it!"

Note that the good birth coach is encouraging and supportive so that the laboring woman maintains a positive outlook. This is the atmosphere which you want to create as you face the inevitable "contractions" during the course of an ordinary day: sleepless nights, sibling rivalry, illnesses, misbehavior, financial problems, marital disagreements, etc. The only problem is that now there is no one to hold your hand and remind you in a soothing voice that there is meaning and purpose to these events and that it's all happening exactly as Hashem wants. This is something you must remind yourself of throughout the day.

Unfortunately, all too often, when a mother is upset about something or notices that her child has misbehaved, she forgets that these events are tests of her *middoth,* and that it is Hashem's way of showing her where she needs to improve as well as an opportunity to demonstrate Torah principles to her family members. Instead, she feels attacked, discouraged or resentful. In response to her negativity, her children adopt the same *fight or flight* response typical of all living things who want to protect themselves from harm by either attacking back or escaping in panic. In this tense atmosphere, no one is able to use the event as a learning experience.

There are only two ways of facing stress: constructive and non-constructive. There are two non-constructive, or resisting attitudes:

1. **Fearful escape:** Withdrawal from responsibilities, being depressed, self-pitying and apathetic.
2. **Angry attack:** Using excessive force. Being hateful, vengeful, impatient, critical and cruel.

There are also two constructive responses:

1. **Passive acceptance:** Diverting attention from what is beyond one's control, non-hostile detachment, non-involvement with a spirit of love, joy, humor and forgiveness, etc.
2. **Active confrontation:** Assertive control over what can be realistically controlled and constructive action so that you correct the situation with vigor and zeal, yet in a civilized manner.

The amount of pain we feel about an event is proportionate to our resistance to it. Obviously, if you are very happy about an event, you don't feel any pain over it, or you are willing to bear some pain because you know there will be a positive outcome. It is only when you are resistant to a certain person being the way he is or resistant to an event that has occurred that you get upset and do not want something to be the way it is.

One way for you to reduce the pain you experience over these situations is to be aware of their positive meaning. For example, realize that each stressful event is a learning experience, that you are going to learn something about yourself and others, or that the situation will give you an opportunity to demonstrate positive *middoth* or create some positive change in your life. In this way, you "give birth" to something positive despite the pain you have been through.

As resistance (or *temper*) is lessened, objectivity and insight increase. You can then look more logically at the situation and figure out if a critical remark or squabbling is a minor nuisance to be shrugged off, a sign of the need for a major change in your relationship or symptomatic of a serious disturbance in the other person. Realize that it is often difficult to know when to take assertive action and when to surrender and accept a situation as unchangeable. Only trial and error and time will provide that information.

Obviously, the greater the loss in terms of emotional, physical, intellectual or spiritual fulfillment, the more difficult it may be to reach a state of true acceptance, since new attachments, support systems and fulfillments must be established to replace old ones. It is important to accept the grief which accompanies any loss. This is an essential stage in the achievement of full *emunah* and acceptance.

"I Will Things To Be the Way They Are"

One way to achieve this level of acceptance is to practice the great principle:

Do His will as if it were thy will... Nullify thy will before His will....

(AVOTH 2:4)

When you confront an unpleasant situation, you can tell yourself, "My personal desire [which can be referred to as *ratzon tachton*] is that this not be happening to me. However, my Godly desire [or *ratzon elyon*] wills that this happen because that is the will of Hashem." As you recognize the gap between your two "wills," you will be able to mediate between them so that you will eventually be able to subordinate your personal will to that of your Godly will. The result will be a feeling of inner harmony and an increased ability to assert yourself with calm self-assurance.

> When my husband was away, I was invited for dinner with my four young children. We started late and the kids were very cranky. The two oldest were bickering about everything and the two little ones were fretful. I started to feel resentful of them and mortified in front of my hosts. Then I thought to myself, "I don't want this to be happening, at least not with my *ratzon tachton*. However, since this is what is happening, I **will** that it be like this." As soon as I thought these words to myself, I stopped being so emotional and resistant and calmed down. I said to my hostess, "Things just aren't working out. The children are so cranky and need to be put to sleep right away. I'm very grateful for your hospitality, but I think it would be best for us to go." She was very understanding. She gave us some food and helped me get home, and I was able to leave without the shameful condemnations which I would have heaped upon myself previously.

֍   I was rushing off to my teaching job when I realized that one of my children was still in bed and whining. I went to him and saw that he had a fever and that I would have to stay home. As I went about getting a substitute and calling a doctor, I forced myself to think the words, "**I will** that this be happening since this is what Hashem wants." This thought kept me calm and after a while, I really did feel a true, heartfelt acceptance of the situation.

֍   The deal we had made on an apartment fell through. I felt crushed at first. In order to lessen my anger at the people involved, I kept telling myself that, "**I will** it to be according to Hashem's will." Sure, it felt like a lie at first, but as I kept saying the words, I really did accept that what had happened was in Hashem's hands, not ours, and that it must be accepted, not resisted. Resistance wouldn't have done me any good anyway.

֍   I desperately needed to rest and asked my husband to keep the kids quiet while I napped for a short time. As soon as I fell asleep, two of them barged into the room, wanting me to settle an argument. I was ready to throttle them. But I lied to myself to keep calm and said, "**I will** that it be like this," even though I was full of anger toward them, hostility toward my husband and self-pity. Nevertheless, I kept saying the words to keep myself from screaming hysterically. I waited until the words became a reality and then talked to my husband and children very sternly about my need to rest. I'm sure that because I didn't attack them viciously, they accepted my words and then kept quiet while I went back to sleep.

Remember, acceptance does not mean apathy or complacency.

֍   I have a tendency to be scatterbrained and disorganized. That was the label I had as a child and I just accepted that this is the way I am. But now I tell myself that even if Hashem gave me this predisposition, it is up to me to do my utmost to work at overcoming it.

֍   A family member left the bathroom a mess. When I saw it, I had an initial response of anger. Then I said to myself, "**I will** it to be this way, that this happened so that I can work on my *middoth* and my way of relating to people. That calmed me down so that I could go and confront this person honestly but without hostility. I even had some humor by that time which helped greatly so that the person went immediately to straighten things out.

֍   It was close to Shabbath, and I wanted to make an extra cake, but my one year old was clinging to my leg like a heavy barnacle so that I could hardly move from the stove to the fridge. I was gritting my teeth and ready to scream when I thought sarcastically to myself, "**I will** that this be happening." Sure, I didn't feel it at first, but the words calmed me down and in a few seconds, I was able to look down at my baby and realize that it was more important for me to hold him for a few minutes than for me to bake an extra cake. We don't need all that extra sugar anyway!

It does not matter whether you are dealing with a critical in-law, an oppositional child or even major aches and pains. The principle is the same: Will that the person or event be the way it is. Then do whatever you can do to improve it.

Realize that this process takes time. Your initial response to a loss (whether material, physical or emotional, as in the loss of respect or the loss of a relationship) may be shock, guilt, anxiety, anger, resentment, jealousy, shame or simply sadness. Allow for the natural expression of your feelings, either internally or to an understanding outside source. Do not hide your true feelings from yourself even if you must mask them for the sake of your own or others' best interests. Do not feel upset that there is a gap between your two wills.

> ⊛ My youngest was five months old and I was just starting to get back to my old self after a difficult pregnancy, when I found out I was pregnant. At first, I just cried in disbelief and anxiety. I didn't feel I could handle it all, especially since I had been wanting to give my older children more attention with their homework and to do things with them that we hadn't been able to do when I was pregnant. Now it was all down the drain. It took a few months for me to become truly accepting of the situation and be really happy about it. At first I had felt ashamed of my feelings, but my Rebbetzin assured me that I was normal, and that not every woman feels the same about every pregnancy. She helped me to get in touch with my sense of inner strength and was a wonderful source of support. She never put me down for expressing my deepest feelings. She just heard me out. In the end, by repeating my assertion of faith, I did become truly accepting.

> ⊛ My husband had invited his Rav for dinner. I figured that I would make things easy on myself by making one big casserole and putting everything inside, instead of fussing with a number of dishes. Just as I went to the door to greet them, my two year old pulled on the tablecloth and the casserole dish went crashing to the floor, splintering into a zillion pieces. Putting on a smile, I said, "I **will** that it be like this since that is Hashem's will," and calmly cleaned it all up after which I made a tuna fish salad. What a change from the past when the inner theatrics and feelings of shame and inferiority would have led to some kind of display of excessive emotionalism toward someone at some point.

Objectivity: A Major Tool for the Achievement of Inner Calm and Loving Relationships

Another important tool for achieving a calmer approach to stress is to recognize that there are events which call for a strong emotional response and those which do not. To help you distinguish between the two and reduce excessive emotionalism, you can adopt the "Oh ..." response. ("Oh ... " stands for objectivity, and the dots stand for patience as you strive to maintain your neutrality and rationality.) The Ba'al Shem Tov described this response when he spoke of the meaning of Hillel's statement, "What is hateful to you do not do to your fellow" (*Shabbath* 3la). He said that we should not allow ourselves to have a negative response to other people's shortcomings. Rather,

> ... let your love for him be so great until it covers his flaw and do not permit it to move from intellectual awareness to a negative emotional feeling.

(KUNTRES AHAVAS YISROEL, p.7.)

This means that you still notice events or behaviors which bother you [you can hardly keep from doing so!] but you avoid making blanket condemnations about the people involved. Rather, you simply observe. You place a kind of "barrier" between your head and your heart so that you observe what is happening but do not become so emotionally overwrought that you cease to act constructively.

It takes a lot of practice and discipline to get used to this "Oh ..." response. When you do, you will find that you are far more accepting of people as they are, far more tolerant and understanding. Start by making some neutral observations in your immediate environment. For example, "The table is hard." "The sky is cloudy." "The chair is blue." "The ice is cold." Note how it feels to make these observations. The next step is to maintain this feeling of neutral detachment as you notice or think about people's shortcomings. For example: "He is being hard-headed." "I'm feeling blue right now." "She is in a nasty mood." "She is usually quite cold to me." Just notice, like a newspaper reporter or a doctor might notice an event or a defect. The next step is to translate this into your daily life:

"Oh, he wet the bed." Stop all thoughts and condemnations. "Oh, his dirty socks are in the middle of the floor." Stop. "Oh, she was supposed to be here an hour ago." Stop.

Instead of focusing on condemnations, complaints and romantic demands that life and people be other than what they are, you can now focus on solutions:

> ❀ I came home from shopping and saw that the kids had left the kitchen a mess. I thought, "Oh ... the kitchen is a mess." Then I simply told them calmly to clean up. What a change from the past when I would have been full of condemnations toward them and myself and would have screamed at them with such hostility.

> ❀ I woke up feeling lethargic and despondent. I didn't know if I was coming down with something or just had a case of the blahs. In any event, I told myself, "Oh . . . I'm feeling a little out of sorts." No condemnations and self-pity. I didn't fight the reality. I simply got up and started moving, keeping my thoughts secure and my muscles active. I figured that time would tell if something was really wrong or I was simply a having a temporary case of the blues.

> ❀ I asked my husband to help and he said he couldn't. I could feel rage welling up in my heart and brain. I didn't know whether to cry in desperation or scream at him in fury. I knew I had to stop myself from doing or saying something destructive. With that "Oh," I felt like I was holding back an ocean of condemnations and disappointments. But those few seconds were enough to calm me down so that I could talk rationally to him and keep myself from drowning in anger and discouragement.

> ❀ My kids were fighting ... again! I was about to hit them angrily when I thought to myself, "Oh ... they're fighting. I have to either detach from the situation or calmly separate them." In the past, I would have been full of condemnations and hostility. *Baruch Hashem* I'm gaining more control over myself. It feels great!

Obviously, if there is real danger to your own or someone else's mental or physical well-being or a major loss, you would not be expected to be unemotionally objective. However, you may be able to use the "Oh ..." response on the minor trivialities surrounding the major event, such as people who don't say the right thing or offer help, the minor discomforts of travel or poor food, or minor aches and pains.

Acknowledge any pain you feel as the result of other people's shortcomings while you figure out if there is anything practical which you can do to help the person or if you must simply remain silently accepting.

> ⚘ My mother was angry because I let my five year old go out to play before she had finished everything on her plate. My mother told me that I was spoiling her and that I should always force her to finish anything she started. I thought to myself, "Oh ... [it was more like an "oy"] she is being critical again...." I tried to think of whether I should try to explain to her that my children's mental health is more important than the half-eaten sandwich or if I should just thank her for her advice, and remain silent. I decided on the latter since I felt that anything I said would be misunderstood and might hurt her. Her disapproval and criticism hurt. But I understand that in her world there is only one way to do things and that is her way. She would not be able to hear me at this point.

> ⚘ I have a tendency to be quite critical, so it was no surprise to me when my oldest started demonstrating the same behavior. I thought, "Oh ... we have this problem in our family of excessive criticism. We have to do something." I called a family conference and told them, "From now on, what comes out of our mouths is going to be as *glatt kosher* as what goes in." I took out a little cup, one for each of us and put ten dimes in it. I told them that whoever "talked *traife*" would "lose" a coin to *tzedakah* (which of course was not really a loss but an ultimate gain to us all). Whatever they had by the end of the week would be theirs. We had a great time with this project and we were all more careful of how we talked to each other. Little by little, I'm learning to look at our shortcomings with an eye to solving problems instead of stewing in resentment about them.

> ⚘ My washing machine suddenly started spewing water all over the floor. In the past, I would have panicked and called my husband to come right home from his kollel. This time, I thought, "Oh ... the machine is broken. I'll take the laundry to a neighbor after calling the repairman." No heavy theatrics as in the past. Now, I realize I simply have to deal with life's discomforts realistically instead of dramatically.

It is unfortunate that people don't see the tremendous inner struggle and self-discipline which it takes to employ the "Oh ..." response. However, what they *will* notice is that you are calmer and happier, that you have let go of your excessive desire for control and domination, and that you are more loving and functional.

If you are feeling panicky or overwhelmed, it is likely that you are suffering from a number of insecure or weakening thoughts all at the same time. For example, "If I give in, she will turn out to be a spoiled brat, thinking that she can whine for everything to get her way." "If I do not give in, she will whine for hours and ruin my day." "If I do not give in, she will grow up feeling deprived and unloved." Furthermore, the child is most likely having the insecure thought, "Mommy does not love me, or else she would give me what I want RIGHT NOW." To deal with the latter, tell the child, "Look into my eyes. Do you see even a tiny spark of love in there?" Then stare at the child for a minute or two. Inevitably, he will start smiling shortly. In an older child, talk about the meaning of love and challenge his belief that love means getting everything you want. Discuss examples of situations in which loving someone requires withholding attention or material objects as well as situations in which love means being generous.

As for yourself, try not to be too calculating or you will end up afraid to give your child even reasonable amounts of attention and material things. Do not make an issue of right and wrong over every minor act of giving, as some parents do. As long as you make reasonable demands on your children to be responsible and considerate in return, they will not grow up to be spoiled. Rather, they are likely to emulate your quality of generosity and loving-kindness.

No matter what the situation, anxiety is aroused by insecure thoughts and condemnations. Become aware of both. Think of the fear and trembling which we are supposed to experience on Judgment Day. That is the inevitable effect of being judged or threatened. Drop your fearful extrapolations and your condemnations and you will automatically calm down.

Learning To Recognize and Avoid Temper

Temper, as defined in EMETT terms, is an inappropriate response to a person or event. A person is not considered to be "in temper" if his response is fitting. For example, a small child might need a slap on the backside if he is touching something dangerous or being very rowdy. However, it would be inappropriate to slap an older child for not concentrating on his homework when he is tired. Anxiety when someone is seriously ill is appropriate, but a paralyzing feeling of anxiety before guests arrive is excessive. Temper "walks" on two legs: a) insecure thoughts, including condemnations of yourself and others and fearful predictions of future disasters, and b) giving in to harmful impulses, whether it be grimacing angrily when a child spills something or screaming at your husband because he got the wrong item at the store. It takes time to uncover the often hidden threats which hold temper together, particularly the "Eight Enemies of Mental Health," discussed earlier. One should be especially heedful of the following thoughts.

A. Extrapolations

Parents, and many outsiders as well, have a tendency to predict how children will turn out on the basis of insufficient data. During a difficult birth, a mother may already be told, "He's a stubborn little thing, isn't he!" Although it is true that certain basic inherent traits (such as aggression or timidity) do tend to be carried into adult life, most traits are subject to change. Remind yourself (and let others know as well!) that we are not prophets or fortune-tellers and that negative labels can easily become self-fulfilling prophecies. Unless the child is really showing exceptionally unusual behavior, do not extrapolate negatively into the future by thinking thoughts such as the following:

"My four year old is whining. He's sure to be a lifelong kvetch."

"My nine year old can't keep her room in order. No one will want to marry her! She'll have a miserable life. Her husband will hate her!"

"My six year old is so bossy. She'll make her husband miserable."

"My baby is so attached to his pacifier. He'll be dependent and passive as an adult."

"My twelve year old is so clothes conscious. She'll be materialistic and unspiritual her whole life."

"My eight year old isn't catching on to math. He's going to be a failure as an adult."

B. Exceptionality

The opposite of exceptional is average, or "normal range." For the sake of your inner peace and mental health, assume that your aches and pains, emotional distresses, financial problems, marital difficulties, thoughts, feelings, impulses and children's behavior are shared by some, if not most other parents. This is a calming thought because it suggests that if others can manage with the same difficulties, so can you!

> ⊛ My son hates his new school. It calms me to remind myself that this is an average response when a family moves to a new location and that, in all likelihood, he will adjust eventually. All I can do is remain reassuring and understanding as he goes through this adjustment. His situation, painful though it may be, is not exceptional, nor is his response. This thought makes it easier for us to bear the discomfort of his adjustment.

> ⊛ I'm usually very nervous the day before a holiday and not as much in control of myself as I would like to be. I used to think that all other mothers were very organized and calm. Then I started asking them how they felt and I found that almost everybody is at least a little anxious. That made me realize that I am average. If they can cope with the pressures, so can I.

If you do have exceptional problems, you probably need outside help in order to acquire the skills and insight needed to cope successfully Be honest! See a Rav or a therapist if you are not functioning as you should or have some unusual difficulty in your life. While you should not avoid your obligations, you also have to be realistic about what you can handle.

The Fear of Disapproval

> *... whole-hearted devotion to God ... means that in every act, public and private, the aim ... should be service of God for His ... sake, to please Him only, without thought of winning the approval of human beings.*
> (DUTIES OF THE HEART, vol. II, p. ll)

We should all strive to do the best we can not to hurt other people's feelings and to bring joy to them. It is a wonderful feeling to know that you are loved and approved of by others, and that you are a successful wife, mother and homemaker. However, there is a point at which this desire to please becomes a harmful compulsion to gain approval at the expense of one's health, one's inner peace, and sometimes one's family life.

> ❀ My varicose veins were killing me. All I wanted to do was to keep my feet up and rest. But just then guests arrived unexpectedly. I should have told them that I wasn't feeling well. Instead, even though I knew that I might be up the entire night in pain, I stood on my feet for the next two hours making a big meal and cleaning up.

> ❀ My in-laws are due to arrive in a few days. I'm so tense from worrying about what they'll think of me that I'm a nervous wreck, screaming at the kids all the time and hitting them if they drop so much as a crumb on the floor.

A "neurotic" need is one that can never be satisfied. The desire to have approval 100 percent of the time, from 100 percent of the people in your environment, is impossible to fulfill. You are bound to fail someone at some time. Disapproval may reduce you to old childhood patterns such as sulking in self-pity, withdrawing in terror, or becoming hostile and condemnatory in return.

It is inevitable that people are going to think that you are too fat or too thin, too indulgent of your children or too strict, too messy or too much of a perfectionist, too affectionate or too cold, that you are nursing your baby for too long, or not long enough, and so on. New mothers are common targets for criticism and extensive advice, whether they want it or not. Some of the advice is helpful. At other times, the advice is an attempt to dominate you in the guise of being "helpful." This latter type can completely undermine your attempts to feel confident about yourself as a mother. Yet, the fear that others will tell you that you are stupid, selfish, uncaring or lazy may make you extremely tense and may keep you from asking for the help, attention, respect or non-interference you need:

> ❀ I'd like to go to a class one night a week, but I'm afraid the baby will wake up while I'm away and my husband will think I'm an uncaring mother for leaving.

> ❀ I'd like to go away with my husband for two days, but I'm afraid my in-laws will think I'm selfish for wanting to be away from the kids and alone with him.

> ❀ I didn't want my parents to interfere in a certain matter between my husband and myself, but I was afraid to tell them. As a result, my husband was angry with me. I always want to please both sides and make everyone love me. As a result, I fail to be assertive about my needs or honest about my feelings.

❀ I had no strength to clean the dishes one night. I needed to sleep so badly. But I stayed up and did them for fear my husband would think I was lazy.

It is important to give up the unrealistic demand that everyone love and understand you all of the time. When you do so, you become less concerned about their judgments. This frees you to be more accepting of them as well as of yourself, and more capable of coping with inevitable disapproval.

Realize that not all people are interested in or have a deep capacity for communication and closeness. Some people are by nature very impersonal and emotionally detached. Some are so wounded from their own childhoods that they fear making emotional attachments. Just as you would not be angry with a retarded person who could not learn well or a color-blind person who could not see certain colors, so too is it futile to be angry with people who cannot maintain close, caring relationships. All you can do is express your desire to be understood, appreciated and treated with respect and create an atmosphere of love and trust so that the other side will respond positively if they are capable of doing so. But you cannot force it.

You can learn to cope with disapproval from non-significant people in your life just the way you handle other disappointments — by reminding yourself that it is distressing, but not dangerous to be disliked, snubbed and criticized, that it is a temporary discomfort, that you are still a worthwhile human being with much to contribute, and that other people's opinions do not reflect your true worth. However, being rejected and criticized by a significant person in your life leaves scars and is very stressful.

Whoever the source of disapproval may be, it is important for you not to lose respect for yourself. If you are the type of parent who is reading a book of this nature, then you are basically a conscientious, caring person, no matter what others think of you! The fact that they do not love you is due to an incapacity on **their** part, not yours. Loving people will love you even if you fail or make mistakes. Unloving people will not love you no matter how hard you try to please them. Mourn your loss, but do not let self-pity or hatred keep you from going on with your life and being as loving and constructive as possible.

Prepare yourself for inevitable disapproval by doing the following exercise:

Close your eyes. See yourself in the presence of a disapproving person, such as a doctor, neighbor or family member. Note your tendency to tense up with anger and shame. Now you will break that seemingly automatic response. Think of disapproval as a cue which reminds you to be assertive about how you want others to treat you. In your mind, see yourself talking to the person with calm confidence. If that is inappropriate, see yourself being silently forgiving and going on with your life despite the pain. Enjoy the challenging task of maintaining your self-worth in the midst of disapproval.

Have Realistic Standards

Don't expect to always know what to do. The typical mother thinks that mothering comes "naturally," and that she should always know what to do. When she doesn't have a quick solution, she thinks something is wrong with her. "After all," she reasons, "Other mothers always have the right answers. If I don't, I must be inadequate." The fact is that there is no "right" answer for every problem. And there are no parents who always have the answers. Although there are general principles, such as avoiding excessive permissiveness or harshness, there is often no objective right or wrong in situations. At times, we all wonder:

"Should I let them work it out by themselves or should I interfere?"
"Should I give him a pacifier or will it cause more problems in the long run?"
"Should I force her to pick up her toys when she's so tired and irrational or just let it go this time?"
"Should I call the doctor about this fever or am I over-reacting?"
"Should I confront my critical in-law or remain silent?"
"Should I hold her now, or will that make her even more demanding?"

Give yourself permission to be imperfect, to make mistakes, to not know. Although some mothers do seem more self-assured and confident, no one always knows what to do or does what is appropriate all the time. It is an erroneous assumption to think that you always have to know what to do. As a matter of fact, it is a good idea, once in a while, to let your children know, "I made a mistake." "I just don't know what to do about this problem." This lets them know that it is all right not to have all the answers and to make mistakes. This is the best way to demonstrate the importance of being honest and human.

Don't expect to always have everything under control. There are moments when you won't be able to manage. Everything falls apart. You are overwhelmed. You don't know where to start: fix a meal, do the laundry, play with the baby, rest, clean the kitchen? There is simply too much to do in too little time with too little sleep and too little energy. As long as the "total view" is positive, and you don't feel this way most of the time, then accept this as a very normal and temporary occurrence. There are other things you can do when feeling overwhelmed:

* Put the word "CHOICES" over your sink. Let it be a reminder that no matter what is going on externally, you always have a choice of attitude: e.g., to work things up or work them down, to be grateful or bitter, to think securely or insecurely.

* Do not fight the panicky feelings and sensations. Feelings have a natural rhythm. They do not last for long. Like physical pain, emotional pain rises like a wave, then falls and fades away **if** you avoid condemnations and insecure thoughts of danger. [Of course, if danger is a possibility, you *should* feel some protective anxiety in order to motivate you to move!]

* Keep things simple. Do only what is absolutely necessary. Cakes are unnecessary luxuries. Do you really need that kugel? Do not do extra cleaning, but try to keep things orderly since this helps calm you down.

* Remind yourself that it's temporary. Traffic jams eventually clear, including internal ones.

* Don't let false pride keep you from getting help.

Full Faith May Not Be Instantaneous or Complete

You don't have to really believe your secure thoughts in order to think them. A secure thought may be like a tiny flame in a huge darkness. Keep saying it over and over again until it becomes more of a reality.

> I have a handicapped child who is partially blind. When people stare at him and comment on his thick glasses, I know that it makes him uncomfortable. I have learned that it helps when I praise him for his ability to bear the discomfort of their remarks. I feel so badly for him sometimes, but I take the secure thought that he will be psychologically healthy because he has wonderful qualities, such as a very loving heart and a positive attitude toward life and people. I feel that we have all been strengthened and made more sensitive because of his handicap.

> It was *erev Pesach* when my daughter discovered she had lice. I thought to myself, "This is too much! I can't take this!" I kept myself from getting hysterical by forcing myself to take the secure thought that everything would get done eventually. It was a tiny secure thought which did not completely dissolve my panic, but it helped calm me down a bit. Getting out the lice at least gave me a chance to sit for a few minutes before I started to re-wash all the linen.

> My son's *Bar Mitzvah* is in two months. I'm sometimes in a panic about all the preparations. But what's worse is his mood. He seems so sullen and anxious. He's very insecure about it all. I keep blaming myself for his insecurity because he was our first and we were so tough on him. He just never could live up to our expectations. All I can do now is be thankful that I no longer snap impatiently at him. I have learned to be less critical. I take the secure thought that we can have an average *Bar Mitzvah* and that he will gain confidence as time goes on, now that I know how to give him positive reinforcement and restrain my impulse to criticize. These secure thoughts take the edge off my fears.

> When our fourth child was born, my oldest daughter, aged nine, suddenly started doing the most outrageous things. For example, she stole money from my husband's wallet. She lied to us. She misbehaved in school. She had temper tantrums, during which she threatened to run away from home or kill herself, God forbid! We were at our wits' ends. Then I decided that I would spend a month giving her special attention. Despite the financial hardship and extra work, I decided to give her piano lessons. I also gave her a full hour of my undivided attention when the baby was asleep by having the other two go out with a baby sitter. During our hour, I shopped with her, did homework or helped her with her piano lessons in a very positive manner, with all kinds of incentives and little rewards. We are in the middle of the month now and I can see changes already. I reassure myself that because we have a strong Torah environment, a happy marriage, and a basically happy relationship from the past, this is a temporary stage which will pass if I take the right action. I don't know what will be in the future. All I can do is keep my thoughts secure.

NINE

*Set a Goal and Gain Control**

You may agree intellectually with many of the ideas in this book and want very much to try some of the suggestions. Yet when it comes to putting them into practice, you may find yourself reverting to old, non-constructive habits. Caught up in the drama, tension and stress of everyday life, you feel so overwhelmed, enraged or impotent that your resolutions to behave more sanely are forgotten. Therefore, it is important to understand the mechanics of change: how to initiate it and how to maintain the gains, however small, that you achieve.

The human mind is very much like a computer. Whatever has been programmed into it is what is going to become manifest when your "buttons" get pushed. If you have no past experience in dealing successfully with certain situations, you have nothing positive to fall back on when these stressful events hit. Books and other people's advice do not provide the **experiential** changes in your brain cells which will make positive behaviors occur more frequently or rapidly. Furthermore, you may have adopted many negative responses to certain events which already make your non-constructive response seem familiar, comfortable and inevitable. Think of how many times you tell yourself, "I can't stand X." How is it that every time X occurs (e.g., whining, squabbling, fighting, disorder, dirt) or X walks into the room, you have the same upsetting response? Because you have practiced it over and over and over again! To overcome that response, you are going to have

------

*This expression was coined by EMETT member, Aviva Stanislawski.

to do the same thing: practice substituting a positive thought or act and practice it over and over and over again, hundreds of thousands of times.

For every thought you think or every move you make, a neuron chain is formed in your brain. These chains have the ability to attract similar thoughts and movements. That is why hitting, screaming, criticizing, obsessive cleaning or indulging in self-pitying thoughts seem to come more easily as time goes on. However, only man has the capability to willingly change those old patterns by establishing new ones. In doing so, you must avoid the pitfalls of unrealistically high goals and subsequent discouragement. You must appreciate your smallest successes, your "baby steps" toward improvement, and avoid the temptation to give up when you have failures and set-backs.

Beginning the Process of Change

The most important step in the process of change is to set a goal for yourself. Without goals, you are more easily upset, and often feel overwhelmed, exhausted, despondent and angry. Yet once you have a direction in life and have made a firm decision to focus only on your priorities, your mind and body feel invigorated, for you now have direction, purpose and meaning.

However, achieving a goal also requires sacrifice of something. In Hebrew, the word *sacrifice* is *l'hakreev*, which means *to come closer*, and whose original purpose was to come closer to God. Be aware that whenever you go forward, you also lose something. For example, if you go on a diet, you must sacrifice fattening foods. If you exercise, you give up the comfort of sitting at home. If you give up yelling and being hysterical, you give up the "pleasure" of being able to vent your frustrations whenever and however you feel like doing so. If you ask forgiveness of someone before Yom Kippur, you must humble yourself before that person, giving up your pride and risking rejection. You have to make sure that what you gain is worth that sacrifice.

The best way to begin is to write out one specific goal which expresses an important change that you want to take place in your life. The following formula is very effective:

1. Write down a specific goal on a piece of paper. It is very important to **state your goal as if you had already achieved it.** The reason for this is that when you begin to think of yourself as already achieving success, this activates your imagination which, in turn, establishes new neural chains in your brain, even if in reality you have not yet been successful. Make sure that you choose a goal which can be accomplished within the next few days or weeks. Don't be too grandiose or you will be setting yourself up for failure.

2. Write down at least one specific thing which you can do to help yourself reach that goal.

3. (Optional) Identify what you would be "losing" or sacrificing.

4. Write down the date by which you will achieve your goal. Sign your name below.

5. Review your goal at least once a day. You can tape it to your fridge or put it some other place where you will see it often.

Your goals can involve improvement in specific *middoth*, such as more patience, orderliness, truthfulness or *chesed*, or can involve changes such as losing weight, writing thank-you notes, visiting a sick friend, having less sweets in the house, etc. Keep your goals uppermost in your mind. They will add meaning and joy to your life and will be there to guide you in moments of stress and pain.

Examples

A.
  1. I will improve my relationship with my husband by having one night a month out with him alone.
  2. I will discuss this with him this evening.
  3. By this time next month, we will have had our evening out.

B.
  1. I am no longer becoming enraged when I see dirty clothes on the floor.
  2. I will provide a new laundry bin near the bathroom and have a practice drill so the children get used to immediately putting

dirty clothes in the hamper. I am doing all this with a cheerful face instead of my usual pinched one.

3. By this time tomorrow, I will have a new bin and will have had a ten-minute practice session with them.

C.

1. I am responding more assertively to X's criticism.

2. I will tell him calmly that his remarks are painful and destructive. I am feeling worthwhile and worthy of respect.

3. By this time next week, I will have calmly stated my feelings at least one time.

D.

1. Ten minutes from now, my pre-holiday "blahs" will have lessened greatly and I will start my chores with enthusiasm.

2. I will open my eyes, say my *modeh ani* again with enthusiasm, throw off the covers and spring out of bed!

3. This will happen in ten minutes ... now nine ... now eight ...

E.

1. I feel more cheerful and energetic.

2. I am going to sign up for an exercise class and will stop criticizing my family members.

3. By this time tomorrow, I will have inquired about classes and will already have counted the number of times I wanted to criticize but kept my mouth shut instead.

You will find that as you set goals, you will begin to tap heretofore hidden sources of wisdom, strength, love and joy. In addition, you will have another helping hand, for:

> *If a man consecrates himself in a small measure down below, he is sanctified much more from above.*

> (YOMA 39a)

God has granted us an infinite capacity for joy, love and understanding. The only thing preventing us from achieving that goal is our own fears and false conclusions about how we, or life, must be. No one is born feeling hateful, despondent or inferior. No one is born hating that which is right and healthy or hating certain people. We had to learn these attitudes and behaviors. And what was learned can be unlearned, by repeating certain positive imaginings and actions hundreds and thousands of times until they become part of our very nature.

Basic Relaxation Technique: P.E.P.

Once you have your goal in mind, it is essential that you constantly create a picture of yourself achieving it. Many people have wonderful goals, but cannot really imagine themselves as capable of reaching them. For example, you read stories from Torah and from the lives of our Sages which tell you how to behave, but you may be used to telling yourself, "I can't do that." Or, "That level of saintliness was for a different generation." Two powers must work together in order to achieve change: the power of the will and the power of the imagination. The latter is actually more powerful than the former in terms of initiating and maintaining change. You can *will* yourself to be thin or less critical. But if you cannot imagine yourself as being other than you are now, the power of your will is paralyzed. Together, the will and the imagination are an unbeatable team.

You can tap the power of your imagination by picturing yourself handling stressful events positively. You are capable of forming new neural chains in your brain even if you have not yet been successful in reality, but have only imagined yourself as successful in your mind. A simple exercise can greatly aid in the internalization of these goals. It is called P.E.P., for Positive, Experiential Programming. With this exercise, you first see yourself doing some constructive act and actually experience yourself behaving differently in your imagination. Your brain accepts this new "programming" as part of your experiential data. Then, when you need to use this behavior in real life, you have new information on which to rely, instead of falling back into your old non-constructive patterns.

P.E.P. starts with a relaxation exercise which simply helps you become more open to new and heretofore untried experiences. Find a comfortable place where you know you will not be disturbed for the next ten or fifteen minutes. Read the following exercise to yourself two or three times and then repeat it over in your mind as you sit or lie in a relaxed position. As you become proficient at using the long version, you will find that you begin to relax almost immediately, as soon as you begin to count.

> Close your eyes. Sit or lie comfortably. On the count of ten, be aware of your face. Scrunch up your face so that it is like a wrinkled prune. Hold it tight for the count of five. Tight ... tight ... Now let go. Relax all the muscles in your face: your forehead, behind your eyes, around your nose, mouth and ears. Breathe away any tension you feel in your face. Nine, now hunch your shoulders up to your ears. Hold ... hold ... and let go of the tension as you drop your shoulders. Eight, allow that feeling of relaxation to flow down your back, from your neck all the way down to the base of your spine. Feel the tension melting away all the way down your spinal column as your entire back becomes relaxed and free of tension. Seven, now let that relaxed feeling flow into your arms and hands. Tighten your fingers into a fist. Tighter ... tighter ... hold to the count of five and release. Breathe away all the tension. Six ... now be aware of your breath. Breathe gently. As you breathe in, think of breathing in feelings of self-appreciation and calm self-confidence. As you breathe out, feel that you are breathing out tension, anxiety and resentment. Good ... breathe in trust and breathe out mistrust. Breathe in love and breathe out hostility. Five, let this feeling of relaxation flow into your stomach, relaxing all the muscles in your stomach. Four, allow all the muscles in your intestines and pelvic area to become relaxed. Three, be aware of your legs. Tighten your leg muscles tighter ... tighter ... hold ... Now let go and feel the tension flowing out of your thighs and knees. Good. Two, let the tension flow out of your calves and right out the soles of your feet. One ... go over your entire body mentally and breathe out any tension which you may still be holding, as your body becomes even more deeply relaxed with each breath you take. Feel relaxed ... and safe ... as you become more deeply relaxed. From the comfort and security of your position, you are now ready to begin P.E.P. and to open yourself up to your own inner source of strength, wisdom, creativity and joy.

After a month or two of doing this exercise each day, you can use a short cut by simply counting from ten down to one, relaxing your body with each step, taking only a minute or two if you are rushed. You will find that just saying the number ten to yourself will already have a calming effect. You might also want to imagine a favorite scene at a beach or in a quiet garden or cozy room someplace if this helps you to relax.

Sample P.E.P. Exercises

The following sample P.E.P. exercises will help you develop and empower previously undeveloped aspects of yourself. They will help establish and then maintain an image of yourself as creative, self-disciplined and competent. Use P.E.P. before an upcoming event, to imagine yourself handling the situation with calm confidence. Use it when you know you may have to face a critical person, in order to practice being assertive or silently compassionate. If you have just exploded with hostility or hysteria, sit down for a minute or two as soon as possible and replay the scene in your mind, this time seeing yourself responding constructively. If you do not do this, then what remains in your memory is a negative image of yourself. The next time that event occurs, it will be easier to respond negatively because that is what is in your memory bank. However, if you have replayed the scene and imagined yourself responding positively, you have a greater possibility of doing so in reality, since you now have an image of yourself being disciplined.

Start with the Basic Relaxation Technique. Then, from the comfort and security of your relaxed position . . .

Imagine yourself in the kitchen before the holiday. You see yourself flustered, anxious, on edge. As you watch yourself, become aware that this "flustered self " needs certain tools which would ease the tension. Step into the scene and tell yourself what tools you need to become more calm and relaxed. . . . Take as much time as you need. Now, see yourself using these tools, handling the children and the household chores with greater cheerfulness and confidence.

Sleep deprivation: You have had a difficult night and must function with the discomfort of inadequate sleep. You are feeling confused, lethargic, jittery or sad. See the strong part of you going to the discouraged part and giving you the support and reassurance which you need to function adequately despite your lack of sleep. [Wait] Notice that with these tools, you are able to avoid screaming at the children or hitting them. You are maintaining your feelings of self-worth even though you are fatigued. Notice that you have confidence that the condition is temporary and that there will be no permanent danger to your mental or physical well-being. This thought helps you bear the discomfort of various unpleasant physical sensations. Even though your body is somewhat distressed, your mind is thinking secure thoughts. The greater the discomfort, the more you are in touch with your inner core of strength.

Painful past events: Think of a time when you were small and were in a situation where people hurt your feelings, neglected or rejected you. You felt vulnerable, ashamed and frightened. You were little then. But you are grown up now. Then you did not have the resources to protect yourself. But now you do. Go back to that scene and talk to that little child which was you. Tell her what she could do to make herself feel more secure and loved. Let that little child know that you are here for her now, here to protect and heal her with your adult skills of forgiveness, understanding, compassion and assertiveness.

A negative character trait: See yourself manifesting this trait which you so dislike about yourself. (E.g., complaining, criticizing, yelling, hitting, over-eating; being depressed, hateful, jealous, selfish, indecisive). Realize that at this moment you are stuck in a negative pattern and that you can get unstuck. Step into that scene and with the part of you which is wise, resourceful and strong-willed, tell the other part of you what it needs to do to change. Now see yourself doing those things which are necessary to become more positive and self-disciplined. See yourself using those new tools while in the midst of a stressful event.

Think of yourself in one of your *I can't-stand-it* moods, such as when you hear the children fighting, or being grouchy and whining. You are about to give in to your old harmful impulses. But suddenly, you feel a surge of strength and maturity. Instead of responding as you did in the past and condemning yourself or your children as failures, you respond to your child constructively, focusing on problem-solving and your goal of demonstrating good *middoth*.

Disappointment in a relationship: You had hoped for a deep, mutually respectful and trusting relationship with a certain person. Instead, you found that the other person was not trustworthy, or was superficial, self-centered or critical. You feel angry and bitter. Then you use your "Oh ..." response, becoming accepting of Hashem's will that you not have fulfillment right now in this area of your life, since the person remains unreachable and unreasonable despite your best efforts to have a more satisfying relationship. Despite your disappointment, you maintain your self-esteem, your joy in life and your love of people.

A major life change: See yourself handling a move to a new home, an illness, or a *simcha*, with a feeling of competency.

End with the closing statement following P.E.P.

On the count of four, you will open your eyes and will come back into this room, into this reality, with a deep feeling of relaxation, confidence and love. You feel more tolerant of yourself and those around you. You feel strengthened, for you have contacted your own inner source of wisdom, creativity and joy. You will feel invigorated, as if you just had a refreshing nap. One ... two ... three... four... Open your eyes. [It is very important to end P.E.P. with this closing statement so that you do not remain in an altered state of consciousness, feeling "spaced out."]

Break a Habit with Your Own Special Cue

You can do a "mini P.E.P." exercise for your particularly irritating events or people by breaking your past habits. For example, you might have the following automatic responses:

"Whenever my daughter whines, I tense up and want to hit her."

"Whenever I see disorder, I lash out angrily at my husband and children. I just panic."

"Whenever this particular person is around, I feel totally worthless."

"Whenever I get sick, I sink into self-pity."

You can break these negative "button-pushers" by making the very same stressful event into a cue for thinking or doing something positive. For example:

"Her whining is a cue for me to think of my Lamaze breathing, lower my shoulders and become objective and solution-oriented."

"Disorder is a cue for me to practice overcoming my tendency toward excessive emotionalism." Or, "Disorder is a cue to think of quicksand. Why? Because if you are in quicksand, there are only three things you can do. If you panic, you drown. If you give up, you drown. But if you slowly and confidently swim through it, you will be saved."

"This person's presence reminds me that my feeling of intrinsic worth is independent of what others think of me." "The more he criticizes, the more my self-esteem will rise." [Remember, if you are a deeply feeling person, do not expect to be completely unaffected by other people's negativity, especially close family members.]

"The more I sink into self-pity, the more I am reminded of my inner capacity for cheerfulness and joy. Self-pity is a cue for me to practice my *kadima* technique: i.e., as soon as I am aware that I am indulging in self-pity, it becomes a cue for me to say to myself, *kadima!* Forward! Up and out of this negativity and into a more positive, humorous, productive state."

"The greater the pain, the more I practice *emunah* and *bitachon.*"

A final one, which, strange as it sounds, really works if you think the thought often enough:

"The more nervous I become, the more I will relax."

Have fun changing your past, automatic, conditioned response. Practice becoming more free-willed and self-disciplined with these imaginative suggestions throughout the day.

🕮 I had a young woman as a Shabbath guest. I thought she would help, especially since I have a new baby and three other little ones. But she just sat around reading or wanting to talk. I thought at first that I would rather die than ask for help, but I was getting more and more furious. Then I thought to myself, "The next time I see her face, it will be a cue for me to ask for help, for *her* sake, to help her overcome her lack of awareness and selfishness, as well as to help me overcome my tendency to be an unassertive doormat." Sure enough, the next time I saw her face, the words popped out of my mouth in a friendly manner.

Order: An Important Goal

One goal which causes all mothers a certain amount of difficulty is order. If a mother tends to be disorderly, then, when children come along, the atmosphere becomes quite chaotic, as her lack of organization becomes ever more apparent and distressing to everyone, including herself. If a mother is at the opposite extreme, and is very fastidious, her desire to always have everything in order also creates stress if she constantly is expressing her annoyance and irritation over the inevitable messes children make.

Order brings peace of mind (*Imrai Binah*, p. 102). We react so strongly to disorder because the external state of our environment affects our internal state. Order should be a value, but not a compulsion. An overly meticulous mother creates as much stress as one who is disorganized and disorderly. Parents should strive for the happy medium. Family members should feel comfortable and able to express their creativity and spontaneity without fear of being screamed at; but they should also be disciplined enough to put things in their place when they have finished using them and should be respectful of others' needs.

If you often feel overwhelmed, it may be because you are too spontaneous and undisciplined. You may be leaving things for the last minute so that you often feel tremendous tension at not knowing what to serve for a meal or what to do first. Trying to think of something to serve for lunch at half past eleven when the children are coming home at twelve o'clock is very stressful, especially when you find you don't have the necessary products on the shelves or you happen to be very tired at the moment.

On the other hand, if you have a planned menu, especially one which the older children have helped create, then you are already prepared psychologically and materially for certain set activities. If

202 Raising Children to Care

you know that you bathe the children every Monday and Thursday night in the winter and every evening at six o'clock in the summer, you are geared up for that extra demand on your time and energies and can manage both more easily if you have prepared yourself mentally in advance. That is a lot less stressful than waiting until you see that they are filthy and then finding that you don't have the hot water, the energy, or the desire to bathe them. Waiting until the last minute to make such decisions often leaves you frustrated and resentful, and angry at yourself for not doing a better job. However, if you have planned ahead and then things don't work out for one reason or another, at least you know that you have tried your best.

There is no way your home can always be orderly with children around, unless you give material objects a higher priority than human relations. Expect a certain amount of disorder and dirt and tell yourself ahead of time that you will not make yourself anxious or hysterical over such situations by thinking of them as dangerous. Your job is to train your children to have a healthy attitude toward cleanliness and order, not a neurotic one. That means, they see order and cleanliness as one manifestation of self-mastery and *chesed* to others, not as a weapon to hurt and manipulate other people or punish themselves. Too many children feel that their parents care more about cleanliness than they do about them.

To maintain balance, keep your sense of humor and cheerfulness. As you work, tell your children out loud how you take pride in keeping things neat and clean. Tell them, "It's fun to get things organized " "Look, now that we've finished, doesn't it look beautiful!" "I get such pleasure when I walk into a messy kitchen and then see it become clean in just a few minutes." Let them know that they should take pleasure in the **process** of cleaning as well as in the result. For example, let a young child organize the silverware in a drawer. As he works, ask him, "Doesn't it feel good to make it organized?" When he finishes, ask him, "Don't you feel proud that it looks so nice?"

The authors of *Sidetracked Home Executive* suggest a different color index card for jobs which must be done at different intervals.

For example: Pink — daily: sinks, toilets, garbage, beds, rugs, floors, etc.

Blue — Weekly: trim nails, clean light fixtures, wash windows, scrub bathtub, etc.

Green — every other week: change sheets, pay bills, write letters, etc.

White — monthly: clean fridge, polish furniture, balance checkbook, fix photo albums, rotate toothbrushes, cut hair, etc.

Yellow — twice a year: rotate mattresses, change shelf paper, change oil in car, rotate tires, etc.

Although you do have to make an initial commitment in terms of time and energy to decide on a basic schedule, you will eventually save yourself much time and aggravation as you see that your life flows more smoothly and you feel more in control of things. For example, if you know that on the first of every month you change sheets, you will do so automatically, no matter how you feel, without wasting time and energy overcoming your inner inertia or agonizing over whether or not you really want to do it that day. In addition, just writing things down gives you a great sense of relief, even if you don't always manage to do everything on your list, because you get the feeling that it is already in the process of being taken care of. However, don't get in the habit of putting things off with the hope that somehow they will get done magically. Set aside specific times to do things, or the immediacy of the pressing needs of small children will prevent you from getting to those other essentials.

Realize that what may be a "happy medium" for you may not be so for your parents, in-laws or neighbors. Someone is bound to think that you are too orderly or not orderly enough. You and your husband (and older children) should find a reasonable level which gives you all a sense of structure and comfort. Don't think that you are being orderly to please others. This will make you resentful of them. Rather, do so to maintain your mental health which, to a very great extent, is based on being disciplined.

When you notice disorder and dirt, tell yourself, "This is distressing, but not dangerous. This room is meant to be cleaned, not emotionalized." Do not allow yourself to become theatrical about disorder. Remember, your tension about a person's mess gives them the message that they are bad for being that way. That can make them even more oppositional, or they may model themselves after you and become hysterical and hostile over trivialities while ignoring the feelings of the people involved.

Children run the gamut, from those who are naturally orderly, (about 20% of the population, according to some researchers) to the great majority who have to work at developing and maintaining this trait. Some have little sense of order and need a great deal of help developing this skill. Both extremes may be found in the same family. It can be very stressful if two opposite types of children share the same bedroom! Hopefully, they will develop tolerance and patience for each other. Don't let one get away with extreme sloppiness or the other get away with bully tactics.

Most child development experts say that the ideal age to train a child to be orderly is between three and five, when the urge to have things in their place is strongest. If you miss these years, it may be harder to inculcate this important *middah*, and they may be more resistant to the development of proper organizational habits. Teach both boys and girls to cook simple meals, sew, budget money and make minor repairs.

401 Ways To Get Your Kids To Work At Home is a delightful and informative book which will help you get organized and provide many effective ideas for teaching your children organizational skills.

If you have older children who have not learned these skills, do not suddenly crack down on them with hostility. Your angry, pinched face will not help them want to change, for all you are implying to them is that you care more about their things than you do about them. Elicit their suggestions on how to improve the situation. Use charts and simple rewards to get them excited about developing new habits. Be patient, especially if your children are older and you yourself are not a natural organizer.

TEN

For Husbands

There are two major civilizing and sensitizing forces: Torah and one's immediate family members. In particular, the way one relates to the latter is a manifestation of his true level of spirituality. Since many men are not accustomed to reading books on child-rearing and interpersonal relationships, this chapter provides a brief overview of some of the many important issues affecting parents. Hopefully, it will spark an interest in reading other portions of this book and practicing the skills necessary to deal constructively with the stresses involved in marriage and parenting.

We are told, "No man bruises a finger [on earth] without it first being decreed in heaven" (*Berachoth* 60b). The major goal of this book is to apply that principle to family life, i.e., to train yourself to regard every tantrum, every spill and mess, every uneaten bit of food, unpaid bill, hostile word or annoying habit of a family member as a divine test of your *middoth*. Eventually, you will automatically ask yourself, "Should I sacrifice the mental health of my family by exploding over the harmless trivialities which are merely disappointing and irritating, but which pose no danger to us?" With that thought in mind, the losses, annoyances and tensions which arise throughout the day will become opportunities for growth in patience and self-discipline, instead of excuses for anger and resentment. Our priority in life is our loving relationships with others. This book will help you focus on that goal.

Marriage

No matter how many children you have, you should consider your marriage as another child. It, too, needs nurturing and attention. It, too, has problems that need to be worked on. Even in the best of marriages, there are moments of disappointment and frustration. It is all too easy to let unspoken resentments fester, so that you or your wife becomes cold and indifferent or finally explodes in destructive fury as the accumulated hurts burst forth.

You cannot be a good parent to your children if you are seething in rage at your spouse. Some of that rage is bound to spill over onto the children and wreak havoc on the mental and physical health of the whole family. Also, it is important to know that children interpret their parents' unhappiness with each other as a sign that their parents are unhappy with *them*.

It is important for parents to present a united front to their children. Do not undermine each other in front of your children with criticism or ridicule. If you have major differences, discuss them in private or with a qualified outsider to spare your children the agony of your loud arguments and open hostility.

Your family members' emotional well-being, and even their physical health, to a certain degree, are tied to the strength of the love between the two of you, because that is what gives the home a feeling of stability and security. Sincere love manifests itself in giving.

The basis of the love of God is nothing but the quality of giving.
(STRIVE FOR TRUTH!, vol. I, p. 155)

Therefore, do everything you can to create an atmosphere wherein all the family members feel loved and successful. The best way to achieve this is with positive reinforcement, i.e., by praising children for the things they do right, rather than constantly mentioning the things they do wrong. That means avoiding all nonconstructive criticism and following Torah guidelines when giving rebuke, i.e., in private, with a gentle voice, and only with love in your heart. If one is unable to do this, our Sages recommend silence (Rambam, *Hilchoth Deoth*, 6:7). Regard tactless criticism as "spiritually traife." Don't allow it in your home.

The most frequently mentioned common denominator among happily married couples is their feeling that they are each other's best friend. They share common goals and values. They also feel free to share their feelings, their hopes and doubts, their worries and frustrations, without fear of ridicule or rejection. They take time to work out their differences in a mutually respectful manner and express their appreciation for one another despite those differences. This "companion" relationship is a goal which couples should strive for.

Because no two human beings view all events in exactly the same way, disagreements are inevitable. You and your wife may have differing opinions and standards concerning the upkeep of the home, how many guests to have and how often to have them, how to discipline the children, when and how to serve food and how much and of what quality it should be, how to spend your money and how much time to spend with each other, etc. If you have strong opinions about a certain issue which differ from those of your wife, it means that you do not share the same reality when it comes to that subject. You need to take the time to patiently get across to her how you feel. Do not assume that she is purposely doing what you dislike. Rather, it is human nature to oppose, ignore, or discount what is unfamiliar or unimportant to someone.

With the many pressures on you to learn Torah and earn a living, the additional demand to satisfy the emotional needs of your wife and children may seem overly burdensome or unnecessary. However, by taking even a small amount of time to practice the following positive communication techniques, you can actually save yourself a great deal of tension and turmoil in the long run. Think of the time you give your family members as a wise investment. Women with supportive husbands suffer less from depression and other nervous symptoms. Children with supportive fathers have far fewer behavioral problems.

Reassurance and Appreciation

Many men do not realize that it is common for young mothers to feel inadequate. The demands of child-rearing and homemaking are extremely stressful and sometimes truly overwhelming. Taken separately, a mother's daily activities do not seem all that difficult. After all, how much effort does it take to bake a cake or cook a meal, to mend the clothes or clean the house, to fold the laundry or care for a feverish child, to help a child with his homework or plan a social event, or to think of something stimulating to do with the children so they won't quarrel or make so much noise? However, when these tasks need to be performed quickly and simultaneously, under adverse conditions, such as a high noise level combined with lack of sleep, a mother can feel that her emotional circuits are overloaded. She may think, "I should be able to handle all of this. If I can't, then something is wrong with me." Since every thought has the magnetic power to attract thoughts of a similar nature, she may begin to dwell on all her dissatisfactions and inadequacies. This may cause her to lose control and become hysterical or hostile. The feeling of failure is the main cause of parents' hostility toward their children and toward each other.

The situation is exacerbated if there is a particularly troublesome child in the home or if the mother is an insecure person or lacks physical stamina.

Another source of stress is lack of stimulating activities. Many young mothers suffer from extreme boredom as a result of being isolated in the house, doing relatively tedious chores, day after day. They may become depressed because they have few creative outlets and only minimal social and intellectual stimulation. Words of loving appreciation may not be of much help when what she really needs is to have outside activities. Even a few hours a week away from home can brighten her spirits greatly.

You can alleviate the tension by helping with the chores, especially during a crisis, as your work and study schedule permit. Women differ greatly in the amount of help they expect and need. Find a happy medium which is mutually agreeable, and which can be renegotiated when new pressures arise.

Even more important than physical assistance is your emotional support. Remember that it is the nature of a woman to feel more vulnerable than a man. Also, most of her day is involved in giving to others. Reassurance of your love and appreciation gives her the strength to continue.

A man's self-esteem is derived mainly from his success in his studies and *parnasa*, but a woman tends to view herself primarily through her husband's eyes. One of her greatest joys is to know that she is cherished by him.

It is a woman's nature to rejoice in the grace she has found in her husband's eyes and so her eyes are raised toward him.

(CHAZON ISH)

You might think, "I've told her in the past that I love her. Isn't that enough?" Think of your words of encouragement and endearment as "spiritual nourishment." One meal a year would not sustain a physical body. Once-a-month praise does not sustain a relationship. A few simple words of encouragement when she feels discouraged or overwhelmed can lessen or eliminate her fears of failure and inadequacy. Even if you don't know what she's upset about or why she's so upset, be sympathetic! You might say something like:

> "I know you feel discouraged right now. You've had a long, hard day. I'm sure you'll be back to your old self after you've rested. I want you to know how much I appreciate all you do for us."
> "I realize that this child is acting really awful right now. But look at the total view: most of the time, she's happy and cooperative. You are such a caring mother. She's bound to turn out all right."

This is far more constructive than telling your wife impatiently, "There you go complaining again!" Or, "What's the matter with you? Mrs. So and So has fourteen children, and her house is always in perfect shape, her children are all well-mannered, she always has a smile on her face and looks wonderful. Why can't you be more like her?" [Your wife has probably asked herself that same question a million times! Don't add to her sense of inadequacy by comparing her to other women. No two women have the same skills.]

If your wife is grouchy, depressed and hostile a good part of the time, your words of reassurance may not be enough. She may need outside help. If either of you had an emotionally impoverished childhood with parents who were abusive, indifferent, or excessively critical, then you are likely to be untrusting, insecure and unreasonably demanding, and may blame each other unfairly for your own unhappiness. You both need to learn communication skills in order to build trust. Get help before the wall of hostility becomes insurmountable.

If either of you had symptoms of PSI when you were younger, this may have an effect on your ability to manage a home and interact positively with your spouse. This handicap must be taken into consideration and mentioned when speaking to your rabbi about relevant issues.

Many women think, "If only my husband knew what a little appreciation from him would do for me! I would feel like doing so much more for him if only he would reassure me of his love." However, women often do not realize that the average man has difficulty expressing his affection in words. If this is true for you, make the effort to develop the habit of praising your wife for her efforts. Regard this as one of your contributions to *shalom bayith*.

There will be times when you are both so upset about each other or about conditions in the home, that it may seem dishonest for you to say anything positive. Yet this is when those words are needed most. Find something for which to endorse your wife, even if it means thinking of something she did in the past which pleased you.

In family relations, we must often make an insincere gesture of love in order to awaken a sincere feeling of love. A loving pat on the shoulder or a kind word when we're feeling angry can banish our own negativity. It takes great self-discipline to do this, but it works. This is not dishonesty and false flattery. It is a matter of your own and your wife's mental health. Remember, "A man is molded by his actions," more than by ideas or philosophical concepts (*Sefer Hachinuch*, precept 16). Therefore, keep your words and actions positive, even if your thoughts and feelings are not. You will gain tremendously from doing so, for every act of self-restraint increases self-respect.

> 🕮 The house was a mess and the kids were making a lot of noise. I was about to scream at my wife and hit the kids. Then I thought of what my wife always says about making mental health our priority. I didn't feel like being polite or loving. But I made an insincere, positive gesture. I put on some Chassidic music instead of yelling. And instead of slapping the oldest, I took him gently by the hand and sat down to learn with him. This calmed me down and everyone else calmed down as well.

All too often, parents think nothing of fighting and criticizing each other in front of the children, and at the same time think it is immodest to express words of endearment around them. It should be the exact opposite!

Take Time to Communicate

It is essential to take time to talk about what pleases you and what you would like to change. This should be done in a non-hostile manner, not during moments of tension or crisis. It takes time to work out differences of opinion and come to mutually acceptable compromises and conclusions.

Look for opportunities to report your feelings in a neutral voice, without condemning the other person.

> ⊛ I was visiting a family and noticed that their four year old knew all the blessings over food. I felt so ashamed that our child of the same age has to be prompted each time and sometimes stubbornly refuses to say them. I was going to speak angrily to my wife about her failure to teach him properly, but then I thought about how much *I* hate to be criticized. That helped me control myself. Instead, I suggested that from now on we both say our blessings in a loud, joyful voice, with a real feeling of gratitude, so that our son would want to imitate us on his own initiative.

> ⊛ On Pesach night, I came home from the synagogue expecting every-thing to be ready for the *Seder*. I was not only famished, but also anxious to begin for the sake of the children. I was furious when I saw that the table was not yet set. I was about to storm into the kitchen and yell at my wife, but then I thought about all she had been through that day, especially with the stress of guests and being up nights with the baby. I decided not to say anything, but to simply help her get ready. The next day, when my anger had subsided, I expressed in a neutral voice my disappointment that things weren't ready on time. Instead of getting defensive and angry, which is what always happened in the past, she said that I was right and that next year, she would do everything possible to make sure that the *Seder* would begin on time.

Beneath anger is pain. Therefore, if your wife is upset, be sympathetic. Try the following: "Instead of attacking me, tell me what's hurting you." Take the time to listen. Ask her to tell you about her fears. Does she feel you don't love her? Does she feel inadequate as a mother? Is she afraid of breaking down? Find the source of her pain. Sympathize with her even if you don't agree with her.

Next, tell her: "I agree that we have a problem. Let's focus on constructive solutions. What do you think we should do?"

You can also use these questions with your children. When a child speaks angrily to you, tell him, "You're not allowed to speak disrespectfully to me. Under your anger is hurt. Tell me what's hurting you."

Obviously, a calm report of your feelings does not always get you what you want. Your wife may not have the time, interest, organizational skills, self-discipline or ability to fulfill your request. In that case, you may need to try a different approach, such as changing your attitude about the behavior so you won't be so upset about it, or using the behavior modification techniques mentioned throughout this book, which will encourage change. Whatever the outcome, acting in a mature manner demonstrates good *middoth* to your children. Before you become aggressive, try communicating. You'll be amazed at the effectiveness of simply stating your feelings sincerely and respectfully.

One small phrase can save your marriage. It is: "Tell me how you think we could improve our relationship." [Don't ask, "Is there anything I can do to improve our relationship?" Assume that there is always something!] These ten words, mentioned every few weeks, will surprise and delight your wife and will keep the inevitable hurts and disappointments from accumulating. Your sympathetic response to her comments will usually defuse any excessive emotionalism and encourage her to express complaints without anger. This tool can also work wonders with your children. (See chapter 6 for other communication tools.)

If your physical relationship with your wife is unsatisfactory, realize that the average woman needs to feel an emotional bond with her husband before she can express physical affection. (For a man, the reverse may be true.) Fatigue, shame, fear, resentment and feelings of inadequacy are major factors which create coldness and indifference toward physical relations. If you are having problems in this area, allocate time to develop the emotional intimacy which builds trust and understanding. True intimacy does not begin at night. It starts with the first words of greeting in the morning and develops throughout the day with a show of interest and concern.

Accepting, Tolerating and Understanding Differences

It is difficult to feel appreciative and loving when your expectations for physical, emotional, social, intellectual and spiritual satisfaction, as well as good cooking or an orderly home, are not being fulfilled by your partner. It is very difficult to avoid stewing in angry resentment, blaming one another for your unhappiness.

An awareness of the four major personality types mentioned earlier can help you to avoid unrealistic demands of one another and to have a greater understanding of where your differences in interests, temperament and talents lie. Every normal human being is a composite of the AMO, DOS, KIP and LT functions (see chapter 5). However, each person possesses these qualities in different proportions. An awareness of these differences will help you understand why some people are more successful at certain tasks than others, why some people are terribly bored with an activity which others enjoy, and why some people get so upset about certain issues to which others are indifferent.

The only thing we can request in our relationships with our children and mates is respect. Beyond that, we must show tolerance and flexibility.

When demands begin, love departs.
                                    (STRIVE FOR TRUTH!. vol. I, p. 132)

We must avoid demanding what others cannot give. For example, the greater the degree of LT in a person's nature, the more empathic, people-oriented, warm-hearted and emotionally expressive he will be. Others may not understand why the LT is so hypersensitive, taking everything to heart and being so wounded by criticism. Those without a high degree of AMO in their make-up may not understand the AMO need for variety, autonomy and adventure, the AMO hunger for sensory experiences, why the AMO finds it difficult to be housebound, or why he bristles at external demands and restrictions. The AMO will prefer to be involved in active pursuits with the children rather than sitting and learning quietly with them. The conservative, practical DOS spouse who has a strong need for explicit, unchanging rules and regulations may clash with those who are more concerned with other needs, such as the KIP for intellectual profundity or the LT for emotional intimacy. The KIP and LT are generally not good business people. Each may see the other as uncaring of, or oblivious to, the really essential things in life, and may see the other's desires as insatiable or unimportant.

Another major clash is between the introverted spouse who wants privacy and prefers solitary activities, and the extroverted partner who likes action and variety and enjoys having lots of people around. Any of the four types can be introverted or extroverted. Further, any of these struggles between different types of personalities can take place within the individual as well. Thus, the AMO within you may want to splurge on a purchase, while the DOS part of you wants to save. The LT part of you urges you to make a decision on the basis of feeling, while the KIP seeks a logical, analytical approach. Be prepared for different traits to appear under various circumstances. The "shadow," or undeveloped side of one's personality, may suddenly emerge, to your own and your mate's surprise.

In order to understand each other's differing needs and interests, it is important to be aware of the proportions of each function within yourself and your partner. For example, a warm-hearted, service-oriented LT-DOS combination will be very different from a strict, but kindly DOS-LT.

Skills which come easily to a person of one dominance will not come easily to someone of a different dominance. The LT may view other types as insensitive and shallow, because those types have less of a need to talk intimately and often lack the interpersonal skills needed to create and establish close emotional bonds, something which comes so naturally to the LT. Similarly, the KIP may not understand why others do not share his enthusiasm for studies, and may consider them inferior to himself. The decisive, organized DOS may not understand why another type is disorganized, when it seems so easy to be in control of oneself and one's environment and to have clear-cut concepts of right and wrong.

Do not be surprised if the non-introspective AMO and DOS dislike psychology and fail to appreciate this description of types. Don't be surprised if you hear the compassionate LT say, "Kids, I said 'no' and I mean 'no' and my word is final ... maybe.... " Or, "We never have enough time to talk." Likewise, do not be surprised if the DOS sticks to strict rules and regulations even when they may not be necessary. Expect the AMO to complain about excessive demands and restrictions and lack of excitement in life, and the KIP to have his head in a book when you would prefer him to be involved in some other activity. Also, expect that you may feel that you never completely satisfy the needs related to your dominant trait.

A person's dominant function influences his attitudes and interests. Behavior which may seem irrational and unreasonable to one partner may be perfectly understandable when seen in the light of the person's basic nature and strongest passions. Realize that what may be right for you may not be right for your partner. Do not force agreement in matters which do not involve *halacha*. There is usually no right or wrong in many of the mundane matters of family life, such as whether or not to give a child an allowance, what food to serve when, or who should manage the budget, etc. Do not impose your own customs, opinions or preferences on your partner unless she is committing a major transgression or causing danger to someone's mental or physical health.

We all need a balance between these functions in order to stay healthy. Therefore, find time to develop and give expression to all four aspects of your personality. For example, in order not to become cruel or irresponsible, the AMO needs DOS discipline, KIP logic, and LT loving-kindness. In order not to become immersed in emotionalism and imagination, the LT needs AMO action, DOS decisiveness, and KIP objectivity and logic.

There are periods of time when one trait seems more dominant than another. For example, right after giving birth, a mother may be mostly in an LT mode. After a few months, her AMO function urges her to get out again, her DOS function urges her to be of service to the community, while the KIP within her longs for learning.

It is normal to feel pained if you fail to win over a spouse of a differing dominance to your point of view. The main way to overcome that pain is to appreciate the "trade-offs" which your partner's dominance offers. Each dominance has advantages and disadvantages. The other thing you can do is to patiently take the time to understand your spouse's reality and help her understand yours. Obviously, a loving relationship requires that both partners make an effort to do so. Otherwise, you become estranged from each other. For example, you may think you are being thrifty and practical, while your partner sees you as stingy. You may think you give more than enough time for communication and help with household chores, while she feels that you hardly ever talk and that

216 Raising Children to Care

you must be forced to help. When this happens, take the time to understand what the other person is going through. The best way to do so is to make a date to talk away from home, without the interference of children. See a therapist if problems are severe.

When you do share, make sure that you distinguish between your needs and your wants. All human beings have basic needs for food and shelter. They also have meta needs, which are deep-rooted cravings for satisfactions beyond those related to basic survival, such as for creative expression, intellectual attainment, and emotional intimacy. Each personality type has his or her own meta needs. These must be weighed against people's wants for satisfactions which are not crucial for mental or physical well-being, but which would be nice to have, such as convenience, comfort, honor and total control over people's behavior. It is essential for you and your spouse to help each other satisfy your particular meta needs, for this is where true fulfillment is achieved. It is also important to be willing to compromise concerning some of your non-essential wants, such as for a spotless house and instant cooperation at all times.

An awareness of one's own dominance must never be used as an excuse for selfishness, laziness, cruelty or neglect. Our priority is to be loving human beings.

Do your best to be understanding of your partner and to satisfy your partner's reasonable needs, such as for being more orderly or more communicative, even if this does not come naturally to you. In this way, you will become a more well-balanced and highly-developed person. Differences should not be barriers between you, but should be stepping stones to greater awareness of and appreciation for human complexity and variety.

ELEVEN

For Fathers

The science of Torah . . . falls into two parts: the first aims at the knowledge of practical duties and is the science of external conduct. The second deals with the duties of the heart, namely, its feelings and thoughts, and is the science of the inward life.

(DUTIES OF THE HEART, vol. I, p. 17)

You have an obligation to teach your children the practical duties and laws of Torah. This is relatively easy compared to your other duty: to teach them to love God and their fellow man. Your relationship with your child is the model which he will copy in his future relationships. For example, if you are harshly critical of him, he too will be rejecting and critical of others. On the other hand, if you have treated him with respect, he will be able to demonstrate the most fundamental principle of Torah, which is loving-kindness toward others.

To be emotionally healthy, a child needs to be self-disciplined and to feel loved by both his parents. He feels loved when you show interest in his activities, when you are sympathetic to his feelings, when you take the time to listen to his thoughts, and when you help him feel competent and capable of successfully performing the tasks you consider important.

Nurture Your Child's Sense of Self-Worth

The foundation of mental health is a sense of self-worth. It must be nourished and protected just as one nourishes and protects a young plant. A plant which is deprived of necessary nutrients shrivels and dies, or grows crooked. The same is true of a child.

In order to have a strong sense of self-worth, children need success experiences and reassurance of your love on a continual basis. You can help him feel successful by praising him whenever he cooperates or performs a mitzvah and by engaging him in tasks which make him feel successful. When interacting with your child, have in mind the question: "Are my words and my actions going to strengthen his self-esteem or weaken it?" With this thought in mind, you will be able to discipline him strictly but lovingly, and you will also be more likely to give him the physical affection and positive reinforcement which all children love.

The most important principle in speaking to children is: What you mention, you strengthen. In other words, you reinforce whatever behavior you mention often to your children, both the good and the bad. If you constantly tell him that he is lazy, crazy, cruel, stupid, selfish, babyish, sloppy, clumsy, or untrustworthy, he will live up to those labels. Even if you are silent, but feel a lot of highly charged negativity about certain subjects, such as toilet-training, eating, cleanliness and academic success, your child will pick up on your anxiety and feel threatened. So, even if he has been uncooperative, or misbehaved in some other way, avoid negative labels. Disapprove of his behavior, but do not condemn him.

Needless to say, sarcasm and teasing are forms of psychological violence which you will take care to avoid. If you feel hostile toward a child for an extended length of time, seek outside help immediately. Lengthy disapproval is psychologically disastrous to a child.

Find ways to help your child experience himself in a positive light. For example, if he has lied to you, do not call him a liar. Express your disappointment. Then, during the next few days, prove to him that he is trustworthy by praising him for his honesty whenever he does give you an honest answer to your questions. The same principle applies when you notice that a child has done something wrong or adopted an annoying habit. If he is whining a lot, praise him when he has a happy look on his face. If he is sloppy, have him organize a shelf and praise him for his ability to do so. If he has been disrespectful, call his attention to those times when he does speak to you respectfully and praise him for doing so.

Tell him when he is being considerate, polite, clever, responsible, and patient. Then, when you do have to reprimand him, he will not be totally crushed. If your relationship is basically good, he can easily withstand an occasional blow-up on your part. If it is not, he may be devastated by your most well-meaning advice or comment.

If your child is unusually insecure, unconfident, hostile or defiant, remind yourself that the child who needs love most is often the least lovable and most obnoxious. It is absolutely essential that you, your wife, and his teachers make a concerted effort to strengthen his sense of self-respect by praising him for positive behavior and giving him extra doses of physical affection.

Avoid Excessive Criticism

Chronic criticism by parents and teachers is one of the major sources of emotional disturbance and misbehavior in children. Think of how bad you feel when you are criticized. Children are far more vulnerable and insecure. They do not have the objectivity or humility to handle criticism positively. When criticized, they feel rejected and are likely to respond with active hostility (e.g., becoming even more disobedient, angry and disrespectful) or passive aggression (e.g., becoming careless, slow-moving or withdrawn). Other stress-related symptoms which may be manifested by a child who feels rejected and inadequate are: psychosomatic illnesses, bed-wetting, sleep and eating disorders and all kinds of annoying nervous behaviors. Children are very intuitive. They know when their parents are disappointed in them, and they, in turn, become hostile toward themselves and others. Remember: condemnations cloud creativity and hinder constructive action.

A major area in which parents express their disappointment is scholastic achievement. A child feels terrible when he fails. Do not add to his shame by humiliating him even further. Look for the cause. Do not believe those who say that he is simply lazy and stubborn. This attitude is far too simplistic. Every child wants to succeed. If he is doing poorly, he may be a "late bloomer," have learning disabilities, have poor hearing or vision, have a mean teacher who frightens and shames him, or suffer from A.D.D. (Attention Deficit Disorder - see chapter 13).

Shame is the greatest pain.

(SHABBATH 50b)

You and your child's teachers should avoid punishments which only make him feel humiliated and hateful, such as sending him to a lower grade for the day or making him stand in a corner for hours. Instead, find ways to help him be more self-confident and self-disciplined. If you are feeling hostile, don't talk. If possible, walk away until you have calmed down. Words spoken with hostility cause more harm than good, even if what you have to say is true. (See Kli Yakar and Ibn Ezra, *Vayikra* 19:17.)

Be realistic about the demands you place on a child. These demands will vary from child to child, and even from moment to moment. High, realistic expectations enhance self-esteem; high, unrealistic expectations make a child feel inadequate and anxious. Firstborns are especially likely to suffer from premature parental demands for self-control, maturity, patience and academic excellence.

Thinking *Davka* Will Make You Angry

If your child does something which displeases you, do not assume that he is doing it *davka*, i.e., with deliberate intention to hurt. The thought that someone is doing something deliberately to hurt you is enraging. The best way to calm yourself down so that you can discipline with love in your heart, as our Sages prescribe, is to take a few seconds to perform the mitzvah of giving the benefit of the doubt (*Vayikra* 19:15) before you speak or act. Assume that he misbehaved because he was painfully bored, was in physical pain, was overcome by hunger or fatigue, forgot the rules, needed physical or emotional contact with you, or did not have the skills or self-control to do what you wanted. You are not yourself when you are sick, in pain, or very tired, hungry or upset, and neither is your child.

This is not to deny that children do have a deliberate intention to hurt at times. Of course they do! But you can never be sure when their goal is vengeance, and when there was an innocent reason for their lack of cooperation. The reason for giving the benefit of the doubt is to avoid making mistakes and punishing them for what you think is deliberate misbehavior when it has not been deliberate, and to calm you down so that you can react constructively instead of exploding angrily whenever they do something which annoys you.

When your child misbehaves, you might think, "A good whipping is very educational. It will teach him not to misbehave." While a smack may be appropriate at times, if it is used too often, the child becomes hardened to its effect, and even more reluctant to comply with your requests because he feels rejected and hostile. You then have to keep increasing the intensity and frequency of violence in order to get him to behave. Eventually, the child learns to be cruel and hateful, and to lie in order to avoid punishment and to get what he wants.

Be especially careful of your words and actions when you are hungry and tired, or there is extra commotion in the house, such as just before Shabbath or a holiday. This is when you are most likely to become enraged over minor trivialities. At such times, you might ask yourself, "Is it worth it to ruin my relationship with my wife and children because of the toys which haven't been picked up or the meal which did not turn out to my liking?" Take a deep breath and think about your priorities of mental health and *shalom bayith*. Then think of a useful, constructive response. It is a sign of spiritual greatness to wear the external mask of patient forebearance when you are seething inwardly over some petty disturbance. The reward for such self-discipline is an atmosphere of trust and joy in your home.

A good rule of thumb is to use as much force as necessary when dealing with one-time misbehavior, such as when the child is noisy, but to be patiently persistent and tolerant when the annoying behavior involves a personality trait or a *middah*, such as bossiness, disorganization, lack of concentration, poor manners or poor impulse control. Character development is our long-range goal. Parents who display continual, negative emotional charge toward their children are likely to reinforce the very behavior they would like to eliminate.

This book contains many alternatives to force. Try them whenever circumstances permit. This will provide a balance to the many times when you find it necessary to be stern and demanding.

Be Aware of Special Difficulties

If your child's birth was unusually stressful, or there was some traumatic event early in life (such as a death, divorce or severe illness), he may suffer from a slight neurological disturbance called

222 Raising Children to Care

Poor Sensory Integration (PSI) (see chapter 13). Between 20 and 30 percent of all children have some degree of PSI, of which 80 percent are boys. These children display a wide variety of symptoms, many of which appear only when they are under stress. They can often be very demanding, anxious, cranky, defiant, fidgety, have difficulty concentrating in school, and have difficulty getting along with others. They often have a low tolerance for frustration and become enraged quickly. Many PSI children are creative and do very well academically, though they may be clumsy and uncoordinated. Others are underachievers in school, but are well-coordinated. Each PSI child has his own particular stress-related behaviors.

Because PSI children can often be quite charming and helpful (usually when they are alone with you and there are no siblings around), it seems that they deliberately intend to destroy your sanity with their defiance, their apparent unwillingness to concentrate on their homework, or failure to carry out a simple order which you have asked them to do several times. They certainly seem to be "asking for it." And you certainly will be tempted to be violent when their behavior is provocative or potentially dangerous. You will be more compassionate if you remind yourself that your child is acting irrationally because he feels threatened and anxious when he encounters sensory deprivation (boredom) or sensory overload (too much excitement).

To awaken compassion, realize that although PSI children seem basically normal, they are suffering from a subtle neurological impairment which fills them with inner tension and turmoil, thus making it more difficult for them to control their impulses. It is precisely for this reason that they attempt to dominate and control their environment (you included), tend to explode over nothing, become easily discouraged, and have such a low threshold for stress.

The ages of four to eight are especially difficult for the parents of PSI children, since a child is primarily under the influence of his impulses until the age of seven. You must constantly remind yourself that your demonstration of self-restraint is the best way of teaching him to restrain himself. Remind him that every act of self-discipline is an act of self-respect. This attitude will help him overcome his handicap and help you deal compassionately with him.

When your child is having a PSI attack, do not take what he says or does personally. He is not his real self. The same is true when you, yourself, are overwhelmed with stress. Your behavior at that time is not indicative of your real self.

In addition to verbal reassurances of your love and physical affection, the PSI child needs organized physical activities to release nervous energy and build self-confidence. With proper guidance, recreational therapy, and a loving environment, the PSI child usually catches up with others his age and has normal self-control by the age of eight or nine. As a matter of fact, the extra attention that you have given him will actually make him more considerate and communicative. Also, according to educators, a means of earning money or an allowance are very important for children. Budgeting, saving, and earning money can give them a feeling of self-discipline and confidence. This is especially true of PSI children.

If you have any suspicion that your child has PSI, have him diagnosed by an occupational therapist who specializes in this field. Do so by the age of four or five, before his sense of inadequacy becomes deeply ingrained. Accept that you cannot always be calm and creative with the PSI child, or any other child. Be realistic about your strengths and limitations.

Toughness and Tenderness

When raising children, we need to employ a combination of toughness and tenderness. The problem is knowing how much of each to use. We all make errors in judgment, being overly strict at times or not strict enough because there are so many variables to take into consideration: the child's age, the time of day, whether or not he is hungry or tired, if he is distressed about school or social failures, PSI, and if there is a possibility that he might be coming down with an illness.

Don't withhold love for fear of spoiling your child, especially during the first few months of life, when his primary emotional need is to establish trust. If you are unsure whether you should or should not give in to a child's request (as we all are at times), it is helpful to think of Rabbi Samson Raphael Hirsch's advice to be strict only when danger to the child's mental or physical health is involved:

Be careful with the word "No." Let your child do and have whatever you can permit him, on the condition that it won't endanger his physical or moral well-being. . . .

(YESODOTH HACHINUCH, vol. 2, p. 56)

The children of affectionate, responsive parents tend to be more lively, expressive and talkative than those of authoritarian or emotionally cold parents. You might look longingly at the docile, obedient, undemanding children of a neighbor and think, "Why can't mine be like that?" Yours, however, may be healthier emotionally. Because you have been responsive to them, they do not suppress their feelings. They have more to talk about because they love you and seek to maintain a connection with you.

Love does not turn children into weaklings. On the contrary, it gives them a strong feeling of self-worth and the courage to face difficulties with self-confidence. You only have a few short years to instill in your child a feeling of intrinsic worth. Let those early years be years of responsiveness and caring on your part.

Compassion

When the young Solomon became king of Israel, God came to him in a dream and asked what he wanted. The young king said, A *lev shomeah*, an understanding heart (*Melachim* 3:9). That, more than anything, is what you want to foster in your children.

The best way to establish a relationship of honesty and trust with your child is by being compassionate, i.e., to empathize with his feelings. Before he goes to sleep, or during quiet times when you can give him your undivided attention, develop his capacity to share by asking about his studies, teachers, friends, likes and dislikes, desires and dreams.

Obviously, there are times when you will be rushed and cannot listen to him, when he needs to carry out an order swiftly and obediently, or when he is whining over nonsense and needs to be ignored or have his attention diverted. However, if he is in real distress, give him time to share his problem with you. His loss may seem trivial to you, but tragic to him. You always have the choice to respond sympathetically or suppressively.

1. Child: "I'm hungry."

Unsympathetic responses: "It's your own fault. I told you that you should have eaten breakfast this morning!" "You'll just have to wait. Leave me alone." "Stop feeling sorry for yourself. Millions of people are starving."

Sympathetic responses: "Let me give you something nutritious that won't spoil your appetite for dinner." "I know how hard it is to wait for a meal when you're hungry. I don't like being hungry either." "Let's think of something that could divert your attention until lunch time. What M & Ms can you do while you are waiting for dinner?"

2. Child: "I hate school."

Unsympathetic responses: "You must not feel that way! That's a terrible thing to say." "It's your own fault." "You'll just have to suffer." "Are you complaining again? Leave me alone!" "Everybody hates school. That's life. Now go away."

Sympathetic responses: "I feel so bad for you. Tell me about it, and we'll try to find a solution." "Is there someone in the class who is giving you problems? Are you having difficulty with a particular subject? Maybe I can help." "I remember the years when I didn't like a particular teacher. It was very hard. Let's talk about how people can live with painful situations which they have no power to change. What M & Ms can you do?"

3. Child: "I'm scared to go to the dentist."

Unsympathetic responses: "Don't be scared." "Don't be such a cry-baby." "It doesn't hurt."

Sympathetic responses: "It's all right to be scared. I get scared sometimes, too. We all have to do things we're scared to do. Don't let fear keep you from doing what you have to do. I'll be right here if you need me."

4. Child: "You never buy me anything."

Unsympathetic responses: "I should give you a good slap for being so greedy and ungrateful." "What are you talking about? You have more things than any other kid on the block." "Material things aren't important anyway."

Sympathetic responses: "Let's sit down and make a list of the things you would like. I don't have money to buy you everything, but perhaps there are one or two items which I could get for your birthday." "I know how painful it is to want something you can't have. I remember how much I wanted a bike when I was little and my parents couldn't afford it. I was so jealous. Let's talk about how to deal with feelings of jealousy, which everybody has from time to time."

5. Child: "She broke what I made!"

Unsympathetic responses: "Stop whining over nonsense!" "It wasn't important anyway."

Sympathetic response: "Oh, you worked so hard on it! I'd feel terrible if someone destroyed something that I had worked hard to make. I'm proud of you for not hurting her back. It's a big mitzvah to show such self-control and not be vengeful. Now, let's go to your sister. I want you to tell her, in whatever way you want, how bad you feel."

6. Child: "No one likes me."

Unsympathetic responses: "That's not true at all." "There you go, complaining again."

Sympathetic response: "Hm...it's very painful to feel like that. Let's talk more about this."

It is not always easy to be a good listener. Your first impulse may be to offer advice or minimize the child's pain. However, you will discover, as explained in chapter 3, that people think more clearly and constructively when they have had a chance to express their deepest feelings to someone who listens attentively and non-judgmentally. Therefore, do not be too quick to offer advice. Let your child come up with his own solutions whenever possible. By making his own decisions, he not only builds his self-confidence, but he will also be more willing to abide by the choices which he has come to on his own.

If you feel that your child is being unnecessarily dramatic, tell him, "This problem calls for a solution, not a tantrum." Then help him find a constructive solution.

If you feel hostile toward a child but need to talk to him, one way to overcome your negative feelings is to make an insincere gesture of kindness. If the relationship is a healthy one, the child will usually react quickly with a similarly positive response. The result is that the insincere gesture will awaken a sincere gesture.

A person comes to love the one to whom he gives.

(Ibid., p.130)

My teenage daughter had been acting very nasty and moody lately. I really felt like lecturing her about the importance of being respectful to us and being grateful for all that we give her. Instead, I waited for the evening, when she was studying. I pulled up a chair near her and asked if she wanted to talk. She was so surprised that she started to cry. Then I realized that it had been a long time since we had talked. I let her talk it all out and didn't offer any advice. I just sympathized with all the various problems she was having. She seemed so relieved. She was in a much better mood after that.

My ten year old was having a fit over the fact that he hadn't finished his term project. I wanted to give him a big slap for being such a big baby and crying like that. I also wanted to tell him how stupid he had been for procrastinating and how irresponsible he was for not getting it done on time. But then I realized that he already felt bad enough as it was. So I sympathized with him. I told him that he must feel so bad. Seeing me react calmly and sympathetically seemed to calm him down. He himself said that he had been irresponsible and lazy and that he had learned his lesson. I showed him how to set up a schedule for himself so that it wouldn't happen again. Then we were able to talk about possible solutions. He himself said that he would ask his teacher for an extension.

It is extremely helpful to tell your children that you are controlling your impulse to hit or yell. This not only lets them know that you, too, struggle with impulse control, but is an effective incentive for you to continue doing so at the very moment when you most feel like giving in to a harmful impulse.

This kind of compassion and self-discipline is what brings about good mental health and *shalom bayith.*

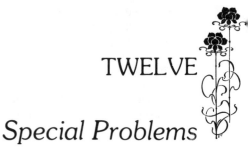

TWELVE

Special Problems

This chapter focuses on some conditions either parent may suffer from, which can impair his or her ability to deal positively with the children.

Depression

Every human being suffers from bouts of dysphoria (lowered feelings or "the blues") from time to time. Life looks bleak and dreary. You feel that you have lost touch with yourself, lost touch with your ability to love, enjoy or create. Short periods of dysphoria are normal and expected, especially if you are deprived of sleep, going through a drastic hormonal change (such as when you get pregnant, give birth or stop nursing), when you have sustained a loss, be it physical or material, or lack fulfillment in some area of your life, be it emotional, mental or spiritual.

Many people confuse dysphoria and depression. Depression is a serious condition which may require medical intervention. We all experience a few of the following symptoms at times, yet still manage to function normally. They are a sign of a serious disturbance only if the F.I.D. (frequency, intensity and duration) are high in three or more of the areas, and the symptoms persist for at least two weeks without relief.

1. Anhedonia. The inability to experience pleasure. Nothing and no one makes you happy. This is the major symptom of depression. The ability to find pleasure in life is a sign of mental health.

2. Change in eating habits. Sudden weight gain or loss.

3. Change in sleep patterns. Trouble falling asleep. Insomnia or sudden wakenings at 4 or 5 A.M. and the inability to fall back asleep again.

4. Extreme fatigue even after a good night's sleep. Tasks which used to be done automatically (such as brushing teeth or making beds) now seem enormously difficult.

5. Difficulty thinking, concentrating or making decisions. The mind feels like oatmeal.

6. Agitation. Can't sit still. Aimless, purposeless activity without accomplishing much.

7. Preoccupation with suicide or death.

8. Irritability or hysterical outbursts. More prone to anger and outbursts, more easily annoyed, and less able to control harmful impulses.

9. Discouragement and pessimism. Brooding continuously about unpleasant situations in the past, present disappointments, and possible future catastrophes. Loss of trust in yourself and others. Loss of hope that things can ever be better.

10. Self-deprecation and self-criticism. Feeling that you are less attractive, competent and worthwhile than others or than you were in the past. Feeling unworthy of being loved. Fearing that you will harm those closest to you because of your state or that they will reject you because of it.

11. Feelings of disconnection. Feeling desperately in need of support and contact with others, yet feeling that there is no hope of such connection, for you are no longer part of the reality shared by others.

12. Physical complaints for which no medical cause can be found: backaches, stomach upsets, chronic headaches and other aches and pains which are unresponsive to change in diet or other therapeutic interventions.

Do not use the word *depression* carelessly, for you can infect yourself with negativity just by telling yourself all the time that you are depressed. If you are really losing control, you need to see an expert. However, be aware that some mothers *want* to be depressed in order to have an excuse to avoid facing certain difficulties, or because they think that only by getting sick will they get the rest and the attention which they so desperately want. These "rewards" greatly hinder the chances for recovery.

While medication can be somewhat successful in the short run in alleviating the symptoms of depression, they can also mask the underlying causes, which often have to do with some great frustration, lack of fulfillment or poor mental attitude.

If you suffered from depression as a teenager or your mother or father did, you may have a biological predisposition toward depression which can be managed quite well with nutritional supplements, physical exercise and the right mental outlook.

Depression is a form of mourning. Ask yourself what it is that you have lost. A sense of identity? Freedom? Love? Adequacy? What pleasures did you once have that you are now missing? Find out how you can regain a lost sense of joy in life.

Very few therapists understand the extent to which female depression has to do with *powerlessness*. A gregarious woman who is isolated in her home, doing routine, boring chores all day, with no meaningful goals or outlets for her creative talents, emotional needs, or intellectual yearnings, is bound to feel "down." After all, the cortex *does* undergo deterioration when it is not stimulated. A bright woman who suddenly feels that she is going through early senility and that her brain has turned to mush because she cannot concentrate for more than thirty seconds or is functioning at a very low level, cannot help but fear that this might be a permanent condition! Other mothers may reassure her that this is a temporary symptom of fatigue and overwork, but she will not believe them until she experiences her ability to regain her lost sense of joy, power, identity and creativity. This is why mere talk-therapy will not, in and of itself, provide a solution. Recovery comes *only* when a woman regains a sense of adequacy and finds fulfilling release for her innermost yearnings and talents. When you think of the word *depression*, a light should go on in your head which says *power*, a sense of power which can only come from disciplining your mind and body.

Techniques for Coping with Dysphoria and Anxiety

  * Engage in *vigorous* exercise even if you don't feel like it. Exercise calms the entire nervous system, of which the brain is a part. When you are tense, there is reduced flow of oxygen to the brain, which can make you confused and fearful. When you exer-

cise, increased blood flow brings increased oxygen to all parts of your body. In addition, there is an output of endorphins, which are mood-elevating and pain-relieving chemicals produced naturally in the body. There is also an increase in norephinephrine, which reduces anxiety and depression.

* Exercise also has other benefits, such as a) an increased sense of power and mastery at having succeeded in a difficult task, b) a feeling of progress and improvement, and c) the establishment of positive, healthy habits instead of unhealthy ones. All of these benefits increase self-confidence, thereby decreasing anxiety.

* Keep a "Happiness Notebook" in which you write down all the positive things you do for yourself and others and the good things which happen to you. This might be as simple as the joy of seeing your children splash in puddles after a rain, restraining a desire to hit or yell, or sharing your feelings with a friend.

* Do the difficult. Command your muscles to act in opposition to your negative impulses: whisper when you feel like screaming, walk away when you feel like hitting, move when you feel apathetic or sit quietly if you feel agitated. Each evening, mentally replay the positive things you accomplished. If you did something wrong, then mentally replay the scene, but this time see yourself substituting positive resources such as creativity, compassion, flexibility, detachment, and forgiveness for your old habits.

* Drop your judgments against yourself and everyone around you. Avoid shaming and blaming. Don't feel guilty for feeling bad. We all feel this way at times. You probably got into a vicious cycle and simply don't know how to get out of it. If you knew how not to be depressed, you certainly would not be! However, don't blame your husband, either. He has his own life to live and work to do. He cannot give you goals, make you more disciplined, or help you think more positively. Nor can he satisfy what may be an immature longing for protection and emotional support. Don't blame others for your state unless they are downright abusive.

* Do not dignify your unpleasant symptoms. Use the "Oh ..." response. "Oh, I am feeling down." "Oh, this is not at all pleasant, but I will try to face it calmly, confident that the condition is temporary."

* Will it to be this way. "I don't want to be feeling like this, but since I am, I accept that I am meant to learn something from this

experience so that I will emerge from this state with greater strengths and new understanding and insight."

* Be proud of your ability to function to some degree despite your distress. Be proud that you are not allowing yourself to become completely dysfunctional, despite the downward pull of this state.

* Wear a mask of confidence and hope so that you will inspire yourself and others with a feeling that this is a temporary condition.

* Do not attach danger to your condition, unless you have become abusive or completely dysfunctional.

* Do not give in to harmful impulses, as this will lower your self-esteem and make you feel hopeless and helpless. What you need more than anything is to feel that you have inner strengths and can be disciplined. Therefore, think, speak and behave in a manner which will increase your self-esteem.

* Do not complain to your family members all the time. They will eventually get tired of hearing you and will tune you out, which will only make you angrier. If you have an understanding, supportive husband, you should discuss your fears with him, but do not overburden him with incessant recitals of your dismal state. Tell your complaints to a doctor or sympathetic friend. If your husband is not a supportive person, seek help to find out how you can face that loss without being chronically depressed about it.

* Don't think that you are exceptional. All people have bouts of dysphoria. Some people just hide it more successfully than others. Find a support group or start one yourself so that you can share your feelings with others who will understand and not condemn you and who will help you feel that you are really quite normal in having these feelings.

* Eat healthy foods. Avoid sugar and caffeine, which can give you a temporary "high" but then cause you to suffer from a prolonged "low." Furthermore, they rob you of certain vitamins and minerals which you need now more than ever. Eat plenty of salads and fresh fruit as well as brown rice and whole grains. Be good to yourself. Your body is a vessel for holiness! [You may also be suffering from food allergies which can manifest themselves in depression. Wheat, milk and sugar are prime suspects.]

* Maintain your appearance. Put on perfume and a little make-

up. Dress nicely. This will give you a psychological lift.

* If you do seek therapy, find a goal-oriented therapist who can help you develop a sense of power, organization, positiveness and purpose. Do not settle for someone who simply wants you to talk. As you know, **action** is essential.

It is important to realize that every thought we think produces an electrical charge which, in turn, causes certain hormones to be released into our bodies. Gloomy, hateful thoughts release harmful hormones which, in turn, place extra stress on the immune system. Positive, hopeful thoughts release an opposite set of hormones into the bloodstream, making us feel calm, secure and confident. Therefore, make sure that you monitor your thoughts. If you feel that you are truly endangered, get help, for that thought is meant to motivate you to take action. However, don't work yourself up unnecessarily by indulging in doom-gloom-disaster thinking, or you will find yourself in a negative spiral. If you, or either of your parents, suffered from long-term depression, you must actively work on your health, physical and mental. To start, you must act *as if* as if you are basically healthy. That effort will eventually bring about true mental health.

Postpartum Depression (PPD)

Postpartum depression is experienced to some degree by 90 percent of all mothers. It can range from mild to severe. It is partly physical, having to do with hormonal changes and the fact that few mothers get the six weeks of rest which is so important following a birth. One mother described this state as follows:

> 🏵 When I was pregnant, I felt like a queen. People treated me with special respect and consideration. I felt so happy, looking forward to the baby. About three weeks after his birth, it all fell apart. I couldn't take the baby crying and crying. I felt so inadequate. I couldn't take not sleeping and then having to function the next day. I felt so helpless, like a child. Some days I felt nothing. I was just numb. Sometimes, I didn't want to get out of bed to wash my face or diaper the baby. Other days, I had violent impulses toward the baby, myself and my husband. I felt so ashamed. I felt I had lost touch with myself and that this new part of me which had emerged would take over forever. I felt crazy. I hated myself. I wanted to run away. I thought it would never end, that I would never laugh again or feel good again.

This is a frightening state to a new mother, especially if she was euphoric after the birth and then finds herself plunged into this dismal abyss from which she fears she may never escape. Her husband may also feel frightened and rejected. He, too, may fear that she has changed forever, and that she will never get back to her old self. He may also go through a depressed period, feeling unloved, helpless and discouraged.

If you are suffering from PPD, reassure your husband that the situation is temporary. Tell him that PPD is mainly caused by a drastic hormonal shift, particularly a drop in estrogen which causes you to be weepy, irritable and to feel vulnerable and insecure. The estrogen drop can also reduce your desire for physical intimacy, which places an additional strain on your relationship. Because your husband may be frightened about what is happening to you, he may withdraw. Try not to become hostile toward him because of this. Realize that it is not easy to be with you right now, with your unhappy face and disheveled appearance. Don't make it hard for him to express his love to you by being excessively demanding or sour-faced. He will feel less threatened if you report your feelings instead of dramatizing them, and if you show love and hope to him. You, too, will be helped by such words of reassurance. Even if they are forced and insincere at first, they will affect you positively.

If at all possible, get out of the house with your husband, even if only for a short walk. During the day, make sure that you get out and mingle with people. Force yourself to do positive muscular acts (e.g., smiling, singing, exercising, etc.), for "Minds are shaped by deeds" (*Sefer Hachinuch*, precept 16). Positive actions of the muscles will help overcome the negativity in your mind.

Expect that you may have short bouts of dysphoria and be prepared with your favorite tools:

> I was nursing my baby while my older children were outside playing. I knew I had to get them in, feed them dinner and get them ready for bed, but I just sat there glumly, feeling that I had no strength. I started to cry. I felt so inadequate. I thought about all the things I wanted to do with my children and teach them, which I never got around to doing. I thought about how tense I'd been lately, especially since the children were on vacation from school, and how I still didn't know how to handle

them properly. Then I realized that I was having a bout of dysphoria. I told myself that I was exaggerating the negative and eclipsing the good, as I tend to do when I'm like this. The truth is that we've had many happy moments together and that I am not a totally inadequate mother. Also, I'm not exceptional. Other mothers often feel this way around dinner time. I let myself cry, not a self-pitying cry, but just a good, cleansing cry which made me feel better. Then I gave myself my *kadima* [forward!] command, which means to put on a smile, get myself together and start moving.

Premenstrual Syndrome (PMS)

Premenstrual tension affects almost all women. Some experience more distressing symptoms than others. PMS is a group of emotional and physical changes which begin anywhere from two to fourteen days before the onset of menstruation. The following are the main physical symptoms: weight gain, stomach bloating, breast pain, migraine attacks, muscular aches and pains, pimples, clumsiness, allergic responses, craving for sweets, increased appetite. Mental and emotional symptoms can include tension, irritability, depression, weepiness, lethargy, reduced concentration, forgetfulness, violent impulses, hostility, panic attacks, low or absent physical desire, mood swings, feeling "needy," in special need of reassurance, etc

Recent research has shown that a major cause of PMT is the lowering of GLA (gamma linoleic acid) in the premenstrual phase. There are only two completely natural products which raise the GLA level, thereby relieving the symptoms to some degree: a) Evening Primrose Oil (or Efamol) and b) Spirulina. You can take three tablets of each for the first fourteen days of your cycle every morning. Then take an extra three of each in the evening whenever you feel the pre-menstrual symptoms starting. It takes about two months of daily use before you will feel any significant change.

L-tryptophan is another natural product which can be helpful. It is useful in the promotion of sleep and to calm your nerves, especially if you are having "racing thoughts." Whatever you do or don't do, you will need to use the same suggestions mentioned in the section on relief of dysphoria to have a more positive attitude toward PMT.

The High-Strung Mother

All mothers feel nervous and overwhelmed at times. However, the high-strung mother has an especially low boiling point and tends to become anxious and panicky more quickly than others. You may be biologically predisposed to this condition because of birth trauma, such as a pitocin-induced birth or protracted labor. It may be a hereditary predisposition. Or, if you were subjected to a great deal of criticism or physical abuse as a child, or underwent other traumas, you probably will be more nervous and fearful as a mother. It will not help to constantly denigrate yourself for having this condition, nor is it wise to pretend that you don't. Rather, it should be looked at as a condition similar to diabetes, which can be well-managed if one is strict about practicing certain essential disciplines.

If you fall into this category, realize that you do have a handicap which is somewhat limiting, especially if you do not have a great deal of stamina. Nevertheless, you can lead a very fulfilling and happy life if you learn to discipline your mind and body so that you think and act constructively. In particular, you must learn to discipline your mind so that you no longer engage in danger-oriented thinking.

While we all exhibit many of the following symptoms, the F.I.D. in the high-strung mother is much greater.

* Feels anxious and endangered when there is nothing objective to feel anxious or endangered about. [Doctors refer to this condition as G.A.D., or generalized anxiety disorder.]

* Fears possible future insanity.

* Fears change. Is very anxious before an event, though usually manages to cope well when in the midst of the change itself.

* Constantly questions whether what she is doing is right or wrong on non-*halachic* matters. Very self-doubting.

* Often complains, "I'm not managing. I'm so untogether." "I can't do anything right."

* Feels unusually irritated by noise, disorder, smells, people's comments, etc.

* Often says, "I just can't think or get things done when the kids are around."

* Often feels helpless, inadequate, overwhelmed and panicky.

One of the most important disciplines for you to practice is to avoid attaching danger to your nervous symptoms or to the many minor aches and pains, frustrations, disappointments or losses which occur throughout the day. Keep telling yourself, "This is distressing, but not dangerous," and other calming tools. If your husband also suffers from this phenomenon, it is essential for him to learn these techniques for avoiding hostility and hysteria over trivialities. Realize that it will not be sufficient for you to say these phrases to yourself once or twice a week or even once or twice a day. To reverse your pattern of attaching danger to discomfort, you will have to have this "theme song" running through your mind all your waking hours. In time, you will become habituated to calming thoughts, which will, in turn, reverse your previous pattern of putting unnecessary stress on your mind and body with thoughts of danger.

The high-strung person is super-aware of her thoughts, feelings, physical sensations, impulses, moods, aches and pains. The slightest twinge may cause her to fear some terrible illness. A child who refuses to eat or has a headache may provoke a panic response. The thought of guests coming or of some upcoming event — even a pleasant one — may bring on very distressing symptoms. One reason for these symptoms is that the G.A.D. sufferer does a great deal of thinking, much of it negative, brooding about past and present as well as fearful prognostications for the future. This habit must be overcome in order to reduce the level of anxiety.

It is important for you to have realistic goals and be honest about your limitations. For example, since you are probably a deeply-feeling person, don't expect that you could be totally indifferent to other people's negativity or handle discomfort the way a more confident, self-assured and less anxiety-prone person does.

Learn to protect yourself from unnecessary stress and negativity, whether it comes from within you or from external sources. If you get to the point where you feel that you really are dysfunctional and terribly unhappy **most** of the time, do not hesitate to see a Rav about your condition, and consult an expert about how to manage it. This is not something to feel ashamed about. You did not choose this handicap. However, you do have a choice of attitude toward it.

In addition you should realize that many women are, by nature, more sensitive and intuitive than men. They need these qualities in order to pick up on the subtle cues which tell them what is going on inside their bodies, especially during such times as menstruation, pregnancy and nursing. To hear the faint cries of a child in the middle of the night or intuit the needs of a baby in distress requires a special sensitivity which would be detrimental to a man engaged in studies, hard physical labor, or competitive, achievement-oriented goals. You just have too much of a good thing!

You can train yourself to recognize when you are overstepping the boundary between necessary sensitivity and excessive, hyper-sensitivity bordering on hysteria. At that point, you can use calming techniques, such as taking ten "cleansing breaths" between counting down from ten to one, and with each breath, imagining yourself reacting calmly and confidently to the stressful situation. Or, you may have to forcefully involve yourself in attention-diverting activities which remind you of your hidden strengths and your ability to be disciplined at any given moment.

Many high-strung people are unusually creative and talented. Find a positive outlet for your energies. As for your children, realize that they, too, may suffer from a similar tendency. This makes it even more essential that you restrain your negative impulses and teach them to do the same in order to make the atmosphere as supportive, stable and joyful as possible.

Yes, you do have additional stress in your life because of your handicap. Yes, it is more difficult to have to function with a nervous system which is so easily panicked. Yes, it is more difficult for you to restrain your negative impulses since you are more easily irritated. However, such restraint is definitely possible. Just because it is harder for you to maintain inner balance and outer control, that is the very reason why every act of self-discipline strengthens you so greatly and brings such *kedushah* into the world. You will get stronger as time goes on **if** you develop a positive imagination and a passionate desire to be healthy, both mentally and physically. By confronting your handicap with a positive frame of mind and refusing to use it as an excuse to withdraw from normal activities and responsibilities, you will gain the confidence and self-esteem which you may now be lacking. A mothers' support group will help you greatly.

Nervous Stomach

Many high-strung mothers also suffer from nervous stomach, i.e., stomachaches, diarrhea, gas, etc. If you chronically suffer from this, a competent nutritionist can give many helpful suggestions to relieve your discomfort. The following are just a few of the more basic ones:

* Find out if you have any food allergies. The most common ones are to milk, eggs and wheat. These can cause poor digestion.

* Avoid coffee. It contributes to jangled nerves, reduction in vitamin B1 which is vital for tranquility, and a greater risk of stomach ulcers.

* Do not drink during meals. This dilutes the digestive enzymes in the stomach so that they may not be able to do their work properly.

*Wait four hours between meals to give your stomach a rest and your intestines a chance to do their work.

Sleep-Deprivation

Few things arouse so much frustration and resentment as loss of sleep. You walk around in a fog, barely able to concentrate. You may fear that you are on the verge of physical or mental collapse. You are anxious about the possible dire consequences of your lack of vigilance because of the everyday dangers which abound in your home. You feel that your personality has undergone a definite change for the worse. Other symptoms of sleep-deprivation are:

* slight body tremors
* increased sensitivity to pain
* deterioration in ability to perform routine tasks
* deterioration in vigilance and sense of caring
* lowering of mood, loss of joy and humor
* possible visual or tactile hallucinations (auditory ones are usually limited to the psychotic state)
* inattention, confusion, bewilderment, irrationality
* increased aggression, violence, irritability and hostility
* feelings of unreality (as though you really are not here in this world or in the same reality inhabited by other people)

What adds to the pain and frustration of this state is that those around you may not understand why you are not functioning normally and why you are so upset about something as "small" as loss of sleep!

> My last child had asthma and often had croup attacks as well. I often had to keep him upright throughout the night, near a source of steam. Many times I had to rush him to the hospital. All I could think of was sleep. I talked about my lack of sleep constantly with everybody. Often, I got "roadblocked" by people who thought I was exaggerating or who told me that I should be thankful that I have children and to stop complaining. But I felt like I was drowning in molasses. I remembered when I used to be a very active, intelligent, joyful person full of love and energy. Where was that person? I got so used to not sleeping that even when I could sleep for a short period, I couldn't relax enough to fall asleep. I was constantly alert. I felt so alone. I couldn't get organized. I felt I was losing my mind, my youth, my husband and children. Finally, a doctor suggested that I not give the baby any milk products. He put him on something called a "rotation diet" to see if he was allergic to any foods. It turned out that he was allergic to milk and some other things. After that, he got better and I got more sleep. But I still look back at that period as the most difficult in my life. The one thing I can say is that I found that I had tremendous strengths I had no idea existed in me. After all, I did manage somehow to get meals on the table and to try to be a good mother despite what I was going through. And when I finally did begin to get more sleep, I returned to my old, generally happy self.

If you are suffering from sleep-deprivation, don't deny the great discomfort which you are bearing. The following may provide some slight relief:

* Take the secure thought that people do not go crazy from lack of sleep alone.
* The normal person bounces back from a period of sleeplessness without severe repercussions once he has had adequate rest.
* Keep your mind calm even though your body is agitated. Take the secure thought that this is a temporary phase and that you will soon recover. Tell yourself, "I trust in my basic inner strengths to pull me through this discomfort." This is essential, since your thoughts when you are deprived of sleep are apt to be quite negative. You are likely to come up with gloomy conclusions concerning your mothering abilities, the state of your marriage, your children's personalities, and life in general. In particular,

don't think that now you see the "real you"! This is not the real you. You are not yourself when you are deprived of sleep. Instead of extrapolating gloomily into the future or being full of self-pity, perform the tasks which must be performed and think calming thoughts.

* Don't sabotage yourself by doing other things when you could be sleeping. Letters can wait. Meals should be kept simple. Clean only that which is essential to your own and your family's peace of mind and health. Lower your standards to a realistic level.

* Rest whenever possible. You might not get the deep, unconscious sleep which you crave. Nevertheless, your body will benefit from the rest, especially if you fall asleep even for a few minutes.

* Get help in! You need it. This is not the time to be a martyr and prove how heroic you are by doing everything yourself.

* Endorse yourself throughout the day for every positive act that you do, for every positive thought you think, and for every negative impulse you restrain. If possible, keep an "endorsement notebook" to remind you of all the positive things you do and the importance of this discipline. One mother put a dot of red nail polish on the middle of her watch crystal to remind herself to endorse every time she looked at it.

Sound-Sensitivity

Another problem which afflicts many mothers, especially those who are high-strung, is sound-sensitivity. High noise levels affect the cardiovascular system, causing heightened body arousal, nervous tension and fatigue. People often become more aggressive when subjected to prolonged loud noise.

Sounds are graded according to their decibel level. The higher the decibel, the louder the sound. A screaming baby's cries have been rated as high as 90 –115 decibels! In comparison, a washing machine is 65, a vacuum cleaner or blender is 70-85, a jack-hammer or chain saw is 100 and a jet plane at take-off is 120-140! Thus, it is no wonder that after spending hours with a colicky baby or crying youngsters, a mother is often very nervous, irrational, hostile and complaining of "battle fatigue."

⚘ I am usually a very loving, disciplined mother. But after spending two hours trying to get my screaming baby to sleep, I fell apart when my three older children got out of bed and came to tell me they didn't want to go to sleep either. I had a very violent impulse which, *baruch Hashem*, I managed to control, in part thanks to my mothers' group, which has been such a great help.

Some people are more sound-sensitive than others. If you are unusually sensitive, take precautions, such as living on a quiet street and avoiding apartments near parks or noisy neighbors. Make sure you have some quiet time each day if you have a noisy environment. During this time, it might be helpful to sleep with wax earplugs or even headphones. You will still hear some noise, but it will seem further away, so you can relax and feel safe. [An excellent array of noise reducers can be ordered from the Flents Company, POB 21009, Norwalk, CT 065852.]

Most mothers eventually build a tolerance for noise just as they learn to function with fatigue and other discomforts. However, that tolerance may be lowered with fatigue or illness. Prepare yourself mentally for noisy moments with a P.E.P. exercise. You probably have been telling yourself, "The noiser it gets, the crazier I get!" Instead, substitute the thought, "The noiser it gets, the more positive my thoughts will become. Noise will be a reminder for me to drop my shoulders, breathe calmly, and think securely. Noise is distressing, not dangerous." Repeat these thoughts to yourself hundreds of times over the next few weeks until they become a part of your consciousness. Each time the environment becomes noisy, remind yourself not to attach danger to the discomfort. Take a few minutes each day to visualize yourself staying calm in the midst of noise.

Train yourself to talk softly to your children. If you scream, they will naturally think that they have the same right. Also, they become conditioned to cooperate only when you scream.

People who are not sound-sensitive may not understand your need for a quiet environment. Or, they may say "Don't let it bother you," without realizing how jarring noise is to you. This lack of understanding can be very upsetting. Assert your right to have your needs respected, but don't burden others excessively with your handicap or use it as an excuse to be hostile and hysterical.

If You Come from a Violent Background

If your home life as a child was violent, then you now have special needs and pressures which mothers from more loving, stable backgrounds do not have. To the outside world, you may seem to be functioning quite normally. Only you may know that there is a terrifying side to your personality. You may fear that stresses at home will overtake you as they did your parents, and that you will repeat their patterns.

Others do not see the tight control you keep on yourself most of the time. They may see the tip of the iceberg when that nice façade breaks, and that violent, hysterical self suddenly emerges, seemingly from nowhere. Perhaps it is when you are awakened from a much needed nap by noisy children, when you are going through the ups and downs of a hormonal change, or when your simplest request for cooperation or aid is ignored by your husband or a child. Then you say and do the things you promised yourself you would never do. Even if you restrain yourself most of the time, you wonder if you will always be able to do so. The fact that you even imagine doing such horrible things to the children you love so much is almost as frightening as the acts themselves. Thus, you live with an added burden of shame, anxiety, fear and guilt, which causes additional stress to your already stressful life.

When you were a child, you assured yourself that when you became a mother, you would do a far better job than did your own parents. You thought you had escaped your parents. Now you find that you often do and say the very same things you found so hateful, as if they live within you. You act as your parents acted because that's how you saw your parents reacting to stress. You may feel discouraged, thinking that your efforts to change are futile, and that you will end up like them anyway, so why even try to be different?

As a child, your most essential needs for love and nurturance were never satisfied. Part of you still wants what you didn't get then. Yet here you are, forced to give and give and give to others. You may wonder how it is possible not to feel resentful and deprived. Furthermore, having felt so rejected and inadequate as a child, you now have a supersensitive internal radar system which keeps sensing rejection and inadequacy now, whether it is real or imagined.

If a child sucks his thumb, turns up his nose at your gefilte fish, or talks to you angrily, you are positive this means that you are in some way a failure and that the child does not love you. If your husband does not hang up his coat or withdraws when you ask for help, you are positive this means that he does not love you. Feeling hurt, you feel justified in hurting back in the same way the adults hurt you when you were a child. This *vengeance mentality* makes it more difficult for you to control yourself, and you lash out, causing others to fight back, which convinces you that you were right all along and that you cannot count on anyone else for anything you really need.

You struggle to create a loving atmosphere, but the memories of doors crashing, dishes breaking, cruelty, chaos, strife, fear and tension seem somehow more real, familiar and comfortable than calmness and love. You are not familiar with the skills of a more civilized world. Your own needs were neglected. You learned to suppress your deepest feelings. You are still out of touch with those needs, and the needs of your husband and children as well. You may not be able to express your desire for reassurance or help, and you may resent your children's demands for the same.

The fact that you are reading this book means that you want to change, that you want to overcome your tendency to be critical and cruel and to become more self-disciplined and loving. You can stop the cycle of abuse. But you will have to be very disciplined and, most likely, will need ongoing support, such as an EMETT or a mothers' group. The following points will help:

* Since love and joy are so intimately connected, try as much as possible to find joy in everyday events and to gain cooperation from your children with positive motivators. This is especially true concerning issues such as cleanliness, academic achievement and behavior when you are down with a minor illness. Make a firm decision not to emotionalize anything which is not a life-and-death matter.

* Since your children will probably be more anxious in reaction to your own anxieties, be extra reassuring and forgiving. Be consistently strict only about the most important rules and regula-

tions. If they are violent and aggressive, don't make these tendencies worse by being even more violent and aggressive yourself. They are trying to lessen their feelings of fear and helplessness by being excessively controlling. If the suggestions in this book do not help you deal constructively with their anger and aggression, seek help.

* Make a firm decision not to give in to violent impulses. "A man is made to walk on the path which he desires to walk" (*Makkoth* 10b). You must decide that you want to walk on a path toward mental health. To do so, you must build trust in yourself. Trust can be built only when you are in a stressful situation and discover that you **are** able to restrain your harmful impulses. If you do fail to exercise self-control at times, don't be discouraged. We all have setbacks and lapses now and then. The important thing is that you have resolved to think, say and do those things which will build your own and your children's sense of self-worth.

* Every day, spend some time visualizing stressful situations and imagining yourself responding constructively. Focus on self-mastery.

Speak to your Rav and husband about creating an environment in which you feel successful as a mother. It is when you feel like a failure that you are most apt to revert to negative habit patterns.

Think positively of yourself and your children. Know that more than anything, they want and need your love, and that more than anything, you want to be a healthy, loving, self-disciplined person.

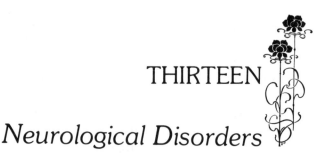

THIRTEEN

Neurological Disorders

Every parent should know something about how the brain works and how to recognize signs of dysfunction.

Poor Sensory Integration (PSI)

Approximately 20 to 30 percent of all children (80 percent of them boys) suffer from a very subtle, often undiagnosed disorder called "Poor Sensory Integration," or PSI,* which can cause a whole host of problems, from extreme aggression to inexplicable fearful anxiety. Whether mildly or severely affected, PSI children need attention, for they are the ones labeled high strung, problematic, stubborn, lazy or underachievers. Although they are often quite bright, their performance is uneven, their relationships difficult, and they do not cope well with stress or change. To understand why, it is necessary to know how the brain organizes the vast amount of information which it collects during the waking hours.

At the base of the brain is a mechanism about the size of your baby finger called the reticular activating system, or RAS for short. The RAS functions like a traffic cop, directing the flow of stimuli coming into the brain from sources such as the eyes, ears, nose, skin, organs and muscles. The RAS's job is to screen out all non-relevant stimuli and allow only the relevant stimuli to enter. For example, a child who is concentrating on a game may not hear you call, for his RAS is screening out everything except what is holding his attention at the moment. In order for you to concen-

---

* Adapted from *Sensory Integration and The Child.*

246

trate on this page, your RAS must filter out all extraneous sights, sounds, smells, thoughts or disturbances coming from your internal or external environments. When the RAS is working effectively, a person's behavior is purposeful and organized and he is likely to have a sense of well-being and self-assurance.

No one has a perfectly functioning RAS 100 percent of the time. We all get overwhelmed at times and become cranky or irrational. However, people with PSI suffer from a more intense sense of inner disorganization and external threat. The result is a whole host of nervous, "non-adaptive" behaviors, that is behavior which is not appropriate or purposeful. What may be a mild stress for the average person will often seem like a major threat to one with PSI.

Causes and Characteristics

There are a number of possible causes of PSI, such as:

1. Heredity: Parents with PSI (e.g., have learning disabilities or are anxiety-prone) are more likely to have children with the problem.
2. Birth trauma: Even very slight oxygen-deprivation or trauma caused by a pitocin-induced birth, emergency C-section, suction, post-mature baby or extra-long labor can affect the RAS, which seems to be particularly vulnerable at this time. Thus, the child may be more fussy, more reactive to irritants, and more apt to "fall apart" when stressed by hunger, fatigue or other discomforts.
3. Injury or illness which affected the brain, such as a fall or a high fever. Repeated ear infections can also affect the child's vestibular system which has to do with the sense of balance and may create a feeling of uncertainty and insecurity about himself and his world.
4. An unusually chaotic, strife-filled home environment. The child is so bombarded by sensations that his brain never learns how to organize incoming data effectively. He gets in the habit of reacting non-constructively to the "overload" by becoming aggressive or dreamy. Think of the fear and trembling of Judgment Day. That is what a child experiences when he is criticized (i.e., judged). Excessive criticism creates great inner stress, preventing maximum functioning.

The child with PSI tends to feel insecure just being alive. Therefore, in response to what he perceives as a threat, he responds with "fight or flight" behavior which may be totally inappropriate to the situation. A trained occupational therapist who specializes in sensory integration therapy can diagnose the problem quickly with a one-and-a-half to two hour test which is fun for the child and informative to the parent.

All children display the following symptoms at times. The difference between a PSI child and a normal one is only a matter of degree, or F.I.D. (frequency, intensity and duration). If you have even a slight suspicion of a problem, it is worth your while to have your child tested.

* Is exceedingly upset over minor changes or frustrations.
* Lacks initiative. Is fearful, lacking confidence and timid.
* Has superficial bravado which crumbles under stress.
* Is more territorial. Has great difficulty sharing toys.
* Hypersensitive to change, hurt and stress.
* Disorganized, scatterbrained and forgetful.
* Hard to get along with. Poor peer relations.
* Has poor handwriting: sloppy, uneven pressure, uneven spacing.
* Clumsy and accident prone. Awkward.
* Often irrational, unreasonable and unreachable.
* Uneven academic performance. Bright one day, but not the next. Catches on, then forgets a few minutes later.
* Has a poor opinion of himself: calls himself "dummy," "loser" or "crazy."
* Is called "lazy," "stubborn" or "underachieving" by teachers.
* Is a perfectionist. Must be the first, the best, the winner.
* Gives up too quickly: poor task persistence.
* Hyper: aimless, nervous movements, quick excitability.
* Hypo: dull, dreamy-eyed, slow-moving, in a stupor.
* Highly demanding, needy, and attention-getting.
* Often unhappy. Things just aren't well with him.
* As a baby, he may want to suck excessively [a valid need which should be met, as sucking soothes the RAS.]

Even if your child has only three or four of these symptoms, you have a high need level child, one who is psychologically or neuro-logically handicapped and in need of professional help. Do not try to treat or diagnose the problem yourself. The average person does not have the tools to manage this problem. Also, there are bound to be people in your environment who will deny the problem and tell you, "There's nothing wrong with that kid that a good whipping won't solve!" Or, "You're making a big thing out of nothing. He's going through a stage. Give it time and everything will be just fine."

PSI is so subtle that you might not recognize the problem early enough to take effective action, which must be around the age of four to six. After that time, the child often has such a negative image of himself that it is difficult to reverse the psychological damage which has compounded the neurological disability. Trust your "mother's intuition." It does exist! If you feel that something is wrong, seek help. You may need to go to a number of different sources since doctors, psychologists and teachers may never have even heard of PSI or know how to treat learning disabilities.

Once you understand the source of your child's problems and begin to take measures to deal with it, you will find yourself responding to him in a much more compassionate and objective manner which will improve matters immediately, even before any therapy begins. For example, because you know that this child often needs ways to release his nervousness you will be conscien-tious about seeing that he gets to jump, swing, run, swim, etc. You will go out of your way to provide him with success experiences because you know how essential it is for him to feel successful and confident. You will refrain from making him feel more anxious than he already does, since you are now aware that his nervous system is often in a state of chaos. This will also make you more compassionately stern as you help him develop self-mastery. You will not see his clumsiness, poor academic achievement, or obnox-ious behavior as a deliberate attempt to hurt you, but rather as the manifestation of a child who is struggling to organize his world, both internally and externally.

What You Can Do to Help

Unfortunately, these are the children who are most apt to get the opposite of what they need. These are the children who tend to be ridiculed, rejected, slapped, pinched and screamed at the most. Thus, what begins as a neurological problem can cause lifelong psycho-social damage. This is especially tragic since many PSI children are exceptionally bright, creative and gifted. You can help your child achieve his potential by following these guidelines, which are, incidentally, good for all children:

A. When Giving Instructions

1. Give instructions when standing next to the child. Make sure that you have his attention first by looking in his eyes directly, touching him gently, or holding him firmly.

2. Make sure that he knows what you want him to do. Do not assume that because other children his age are doing a particular task, that he should be forced to do so as well. Also, do not assume that because he could do it half an hour ago, that he can do it now. Half an hour ago, his brain may have been better organized.

3. Give instructions one at a time. If necessary, tell him, "Concentrate now on finding your shoes. Keep saying the word 'shoes' as you look for them. That will help you remember what you are supposed to be doing right now." Remember, your task is to help his brain become more efficiently organized. That will not happen if you are screaming at him, "Dummy! You scatterbrain! Why can't you ever put things in their place?" Such statements do not help him become more self-confident!

4. Give enthusiastic approval and praise when he does what you want. You don't have to go overboard, but you can say, "You see, I knew that you could find your shoes if you looked for them in an organized manner, room by room, place by place. The next thing we need to do is have a way of remembering to put them together in the same place when you take them off."

B. When Disciplining

1. Talk in a low voice.

2. Don't punish him for behavior over which he has no control, such as forgetfulness, carelessness, fearfulness, bed-wetting, etc.

3. Give the benefit of the doubt before you punish. Realize that his easily overloaded RAS may have caused him to lose control. A slap may stun him into temporary submission, but it won't help him become more organized or self-disciplined. Figure out what he

was lacking when he misbehaved and how you can give him the tools to gain greater self-mastery.

4. If you do need to be harsh, follow up immediately with some word or gesture of reassurance that you love him, but cannot allow him to be destructive.

C. Provide Organizing and Success Activities

1. Give this child opportunities to experience successful, joyful bodily sensations and experiences, such as playing with clay, riding a bike, climbing on bars, etc. Ironically, self-defense classes are especially good for impulsive children, as they learn self-discipline, greater body awareness, and self-confidence.

2. When he is hostile or anxious, find some way of reassuring him with touch. You might make a tent and let him crawl inside. Or, make him the "hot dog" between two pieces of "bread" (i.e., two thin mattresses). Then press on him firmly all over his body. Being pressed on by a heavy weight has a very soothing effect on the entire nervous system. You will find that he will calm down quickly and feel relieved by this pressure on his bones and muscles. If he is "touch-resistant," as some PSI children are, you may have to try different forms of touch to find which arouse the least defensiveness. Songs involving fingers can provide non-threatening touch experiences.

3. Provide him with opportunities to earn money, even at an early age. Earning will help him feel proud of himself and spending the money will help him with self-discipline as he decides what he can afford to buy now and what he will have to save for.

4. Read to him with your arm around him, holding him close to you. If he is young enough, find times to rock, cuddle and hug him. All children need such attention, these children more than others. This kind of touch helps the brain develop and become organized. [For the same reason, when you are pregnant, you should find time to sit and rock your baby in a rocking chair, and continue that activity whenever possible afterward.]

D. In School

Some children with PSI are super-achievers scholastically, but manifest their PSI in other ways, such as in irrational anxiety or perfectionism. Others have learning disabilities. If the latter is true, then your child needs to learn how to coordinate his body in order to effectively coordinate his brain. Therefore, organizing physical activities are essential in order to help him read, concentrate and perform well academically.

1. Computers are very effective in teaching PSI children because there are less distracting stimuli entering the child's brain at any given time. When he focuses on a screen, his mind is not distracted by what all the other children are wearing, how the teacher is moving around, and all the other sights and sounds of the classroom, as well as whatever is going on outside the classroom windows.

2. Make sure that the child's teacher is supportive and realistically demanding. You do not want the teacher to ignore your child, thinking he is a "dummy," or discourage him with work which is beyond his ability. Tell the teacher that the child has great potential, but because of a neurological problem, has difficulty sitting or focusing. Therefore, he should try to be patient and creative in order to find the right technique which will help the child learn.

3. Tell the teacher that people learn the most when they are active and happy. The more he can use games to get his ideas across, the more effective he will be. Forcing the child to read when the child cannot focus his eyes is cruel and totally ineffective. Eyes will focus when the nervous system has matured sufficiently to make this possible. Ask the teacher how he would feel if he had to read a book which was moving up and down rapidly! That may be what it is like for your child. Getting angry at him for losing his place or failing to concentrate is not going to help his eyes focus more effectively.

Coping with a PSI Child

Coping with a PSI child is not easy, especially if he is a very impulsive type. And because his handicap is invisible and not always manifest, you may think that it really does not exist. But it most certainly does. At times, you may feel that this child is ruining your marriage, your health, your sanity and the stability of your whole family. The fact is that you do have to take the time to create a more structured environment, get him to therapy, provide tutors and learning aids, and give him a great deal of love and firmness. It is not an easy task, especially if you have a number of other children. He, himself, is like an extra five! Yet the rewards of having given him this special attention early in life are great. Many mothers report that they are unusually close to these children later on in life.

    ☲ I have a son and a daughter with PSI. They could hardly ever sit still. The worst was between the ages of five and seven. The battles, the wildness, the chaos! I found that I had to be super-organized and in control, or everything would fall apart. Since organization is not one of my strong points, to say the least, I had to be very disciplined. At times, I felt that my efforts were falling on hard rocks. But little by little, I began to see great improvements. They are now both basically good kids who are creative and very helpful. They "bloomed" late and suddenly did very well in school, much to my surprise. I thank God for my mothers' support group which kept me from beating them for their obnoxious behavior. Instead, I displayed self-control and, eventually, they did too.

    ☲ I made a lot of mistakes. I didn't know how to handle my kids. Plus, my husband tends to be very critical and harsh. He thinks this PSI business is nonsense. Unfortunately, we both did a lot of criticizing and hitting. I remember thinking to myself, "I'll have another baby, and then I can escape from it all. I can close myself off in my bedroom, nurse the baby, and let it all go to pieces." I didn't want to have to deal with them. I wanted an excuse to withdraw, to not have to face their teachers or my neighbors. I just wanted to be a normal mother with normal children. I couldn't believe this was happening to me. It was all too much for me. *Baruch Hashem*, I had a neighbor whose son also had PSI and she helped me to understand the importance of taking responsibility for the problem now. She assured me that things would soon get better if I just gave this child a lot of structure and warmth and proper therapy. We made charts together and she showed me how to respond constructively when they misbehaved. It took hours and hours of her help. She taught me all the EMETT tools, and then I joined a group. It was a tremendous help.

    ☲ It was quite a learning experience for me to watch the therapist work with my daughter. She would get down on the floor with her, play games, swing her around, hug her, keep her happy the whole hour. The therapist told me that children are learning not only when they are sitting in a classroom silently and passively. As a matter of fact, "play" is important developmental work for children. One time, I tried to do homework with my daughter before a therapy session. She couldn't concentrate or read. She was hostile and aggressive. Then I took her to her session. After half an hour of "play" which was aimed at giving specific parts of her brain the stimuli which they needed, she sat down and read perfectly. If I hadn't seen it and heard it myself, I would not have believed it could be possible.

⊗ My son lost his jacket. I wanted to really rub it in and tell him over and over how much money he cost and what a scatterbrained, forgetful, careless child he was. I kept wanting to grimace every time I looked at him to remind him of what he had done. He was hanging his head in shame the whole day and looked so unhappy. Then I caught myself. "What am I doing to him? What am I trying to accomplish?" I was just being vengeful and cruel. I am ashamed to think that I can be so petty and mean, that I could want to destroy his spirit for a stupid jacket! *Baruch Hashem,* I was finally able to restrain myself. I made a forced smile and put my arm around him lovingly, even though I did not feel very loving at the time. I told him that it was a *kaparah,* and that we would put his name in all his clothes from now on. Then he started crying and told me how awful he felt. My anger had kept him from expressing his true feelings. In the end, I really felt how precious this child is to me and how much I do love him.

Attention Deficit Disorder (ADD)

You might have a bright child who does poor academically. He may be able to build the most imaginative Lego constructions, but cannot sit still in class. Or, she is a bright and communicative child who is very insightful and understanding, but she is always calling her friends to find out what the homework was. Why? The child may have ADD. The following is a partial list adapted from the *Yale Children's Inventory.* Rate the child from one (rarely) to four (very often). Then take your evaluation to your doctor or school therapist and ask for further help:

A. Inattention
* Confuses the details of games and stories.
* Needs a calm atmosphere in which to work. Easily distracted by anything in the room or on the table.
* Doesn't finish what he starts, such as book or puzzle.
* Hears, but doesn't seem to listen.
* Has difficulty concentrating unless in a one-to-one situation.
* Asks to have things repeated. Says, "What?" even though he heard.

B. Activity
* Is always on the go. Acts as if driven by a motor.
* Fidgets and squirms when forced to sit.

* Does things in a loud or noisy way.
* Must always be doing something.
* Moves around excessively during sleep. Has sleep terrors or nightmares. Has difficulty falling asleep.

C. Impulsivity
* Provokes, teases, and torments other children.
* Has trouble waiting his turn.
* Talks excessively.
* Laughs wildly. (May be the "class clown.")
* Blurts out in class; makes noises in class.
* Extremely excitable.
* Untrustworthy. Needs supervision to keep from doing harm.
* Has difficulty organizing work.
* Acts before thinking.
* Shifts randomly from one activity to another.
* Poor self-control. Overreacts with hostility or violence if teased or frustrated.

D. In School
* Complains that he cannot copy correctly from board.
* Has poor "snap memory" (as for multiplication tables).
* Poor handwriting: uneven pressure, spacing, size.
* Task impersistence: gives up too easily.
* Stubbornness: clings tenaciously to his way of spelling or doing things, even though it is wrong.
* Is anxious, dreamy and fidgety.

You know if your child is "difficult" or "problematic." The tendency may be to blame yourself and think that you have been such a terrible mother that you have caused all the child's problems. Certainly, part of the problem may be psychological. But do not cause your own feelings of shame to keep you from getting help. Do not withdraw when others tell you, "It's all your fault." Or, "There's nothing wrong." Many people know little or nothing about PSI or ADD. You need help. The earlier you get it, the better you and your child will be. Do not wait until your child is seven or eight. Seek help early.

APPENDIX A

Summary of Stress Reducers

The following is a quick guide to the major tools which you can use to calm yourself down when you are distressed. You can make a number of copies and keep them in various places in your home, as well as in your purse. In this way, you can review them when you are standing in line or grab them in desperation when you've slammed the bedroom door in a frantic attempt to get away from the demands and commotion. References to holy writings have deliberately been omitted so that these pages can be taken anywhere.

Self-Respect

* You have intrinsic worth.

* Do not let your self-esteem rise and fall with the mess in the kitchen or your children's behavior.

* If you are busy endorsing yourself, you won't have time to blame and shame yourself or others. Right now, think of five things for which you can endorse, acts which required self-sacrifice and self-discipline.

* Every act of self-restraint strengthens you.

* Other people's opinions of you do not reflect your intrinsic worth.

* Love yourself for the sake of your children as well as for your own sake. You can only love them to the extent that you love yourself.

Discomfort

* Unless you are in actual danger, assume that whatever is happening at the moment is distressing, but not catastrophic.

256

* Endorse yourself for functioning with discomfort.
* Don't attach danger to your discomfort.
* Comfort is just a want, not a need.
* Give discomfort a positive meaning — learn from it.
* Avoid: criticizing, complaining, condemning and comparing.

Secure Thoughts

* You can only have one thought at a time, a secure one or an insecure one. Make it a secure one!
* Tell yourself that you have hidden strengths, wisdom and joy.
* Look at the "total view." If it is positive, then relax!
* There can be no anxiety without a thought of danger or loss.
* Unless you have positive proof to the contrary, assume that the situation is temporary, not dangerous, and capable of being handled. Assume that you are doing at least an adequate job and that you and your children are within the normal range.
* If the "total view" of yourself, your marriage and your children is positive, then you are working yourself up unnecessarily.

Feelings

* Ask: Are my feelings based on objective facts?
* Let your feelings work for you to motivate you to change.
* Let your distressing feelings rise and fall like a wave. Don't fight them, while you think of constructive solutions. Surrender to them. Let them teach you what you need to know about necessary changes in attitude or behavior.
* Report your feelings to others without excessive theatrics.
* Don't rely on hunches, guesses or intuitive assumptions about people when you are in temper, for then you are apt to sensationalize, catastrophize and project gloomily into the future.

Children

* Your child's unhappiness is not an indictment of you.
* You can never satisfy four desires for: pleasure, power, pampering or possessions. Decide when to say, "No," and stick to your decision without excessive drama. Then your children, too, will drop the drama.
* Be patient. Character training is a long-range goal.

* Demonstrate the character traits you want your children to have, particularly loving-kindness and self-mastery.

* Children want to be grown-up. That means that they want power, which is often gotten by sabotaging adult goals. Expect it. Don't indict yourself or them over this natural tendency.

* Don't think "*Davka.* They're doing this deliberately to hurt me." This will cause you to want to take vengeance and hurt them back deliberately.

* When you discipline, have only the child's good in mind.

* Notice your children's shortcomings. Then stay objective as you plan how to help them improve themselves.

* Sandwich rebuke between love.

* Be assertive and authoritative, not dictatorial and authoritarian.

* Assume that your children are doing the best they can with the tools they have, given the passions, pressures and pains of the moment and the experiences and conditioning of their past. [Then keep saying these words over again until you calm down and can discipline them constructively.]

Anxiety

* Avoid anticipatory agony. You'll probably do just fine once the event arrives.

* Your foremost relaxant is your own breath. Throughout the day, take a deep, cleansing breath, drop your shoulders, and think, "Breathe in strength, joy, faith and wisdom. Breathe out anxiety, fear, resentment and jealousy."

* Take the overwhelming event in "part acts," bit by bit, minute by minute.

* Detach: See yourself in a comfortable, safe place watching your anxious self from that position of security. Then go to that self and provide reassurance and support.

* Drop your judgments against yourself and your family members. Your condemnations cloud your thinking and prevent you from working toward constructive solutions.

Beware the Mental Health Wreckers

When you feel stress, go through the following questions. They will help you determine whether your responses are rational and appropriate, or overdramatic and inappropriate.

1. Exceptionality: Do you think you are the only mother with this problem? The only mother who thinks or feels as you do?

2. Eclipsing the good: Are you failing to remember all the good things that you, your children and your husband have done?

3. Exaggeration: Are you exaggerating the seriousness of this situation? Are your exaggerations ("awfulizing") causing you to suffer from excessive emotionalism? Are you seeing danger in something which is really a triviality in comparison to your mental health? Is this something you will forget quickly or be able to laugh about ten years from now?

4. Extrapolation: Are you causing yourself unnecessary tension by having "anticipatory agony" about an upcoming event or by thinking that you know for sure how your children will turn out, or that you will suffer certain mental or physical illnesses or punishments? Are you playing "doomsday prophet"?

5. Erroneous judgments: Are you making blanket condemnations of yourself or others? Are you giving a negative meaning to this event when you could be looking at it from a more positive point of view?

6. Unrealistic expectations: Are you having unrealistic expectations of yourself and others regarding maturity, cooperation, communication, control or general perfection (i.e., omniscience, omnipotence and omnipresence)? Are you being respectful of your own and others' limitations, talents, past conditioning and inherent predispositions?

7. Evading responsibility: Are you denying that there is a real problem in your life and trying to run away from it by busying yourself with other matters? Are you being lazy, passive or submissive when you could be industrious, active and assertive?

8. Excessive responsibility: Are you being overly controlling of other people? Are you trying to "mother" the whole world while neglecting yourself or your family? Are you taking too much on your shoulders to the point of self-punishment? Are you crippling your children by doing too much for them and not letting them discover their own inner strengths and resources by letting them face and overcome hardships? Are you trying to "play God" and force yourself or your advice on people when it is not wanted?

Memorize these "eight Es." When you are upset, run through the list. At some point, you should feel a big sigh of relief when you realize what particular thoughts are causing you to be unnecessarily distressed. Of course, if the situation *is* actually dangerous, then your tension is appropriate and self-protective. It is meant to motivate you to take action.

APPENDIX B

Forming a Mother's Support Group

All self-help groups, such as Weight Watchers, find that group pressure and support are invaluable in helping members overcome non-constructive behavior and maintain good habits. You will find it very helpful to form a support group of other mothers. You may be enthusiastic when you read this book and want to put its techniques and principles into practice. But as time passes, you will forget much of what you have read. However, when you come to group, each mother will have used some particular technique which she found helpful, and this will reinforce it in your own mind. When you see that other mothers are using the objective "Oh . . . " response, or calm themselves down by avoiding gloomy extrapolation into the future or using some creative technique to gain cooperation from a child instead of hitting, pinching or yelling, you will feel inspired to do the same. You will also realize how normal it is to have setbacks and to lose control at times. Knowing that other mothers are struggling with similar problems and feelings is very reassuring.

A possible sign might read:

> Do you want to improve your mothering skills and bring greater joy, love and calm into your home? Come to a peer-led support group based on Torah principles. We will meet at _____o'clock on Tuesday, at the home of _____, _____(Address). Call me at _____ .
>
> Signed:_____.

Follow a disciplined format which should include the following:

1. Start on time.

2. Emphasize that everything said at the meeting is confidential.

3. State emphatically that no *lashon hara* will be allowed. Members can say, "A family member" or "A person. . . " when giving an example. If members would retain a negative attitude toward a child, then examples about that child should not be allowed. Tell members that exceptional problems should be discussed with a Rav or Orthodox therapist.

4. Let each member talk about her problem for no more than ten or fifteen minutes. Any more than this can a) make other women feel that they are being left out, b) turn the session into a coffee klatch, c) allow for too much diagnosing and advising.

5. Do not allow any advice giving. Do not allow anyone to play therapist. Advice can be a very subtle form of rejection, implying that the other person is stupid and inadequate. The group is aimed at building self-esteem, which requires that each mother develop her own resources. Of course, if practical advice is requested about toilet training, ear infections or how to get the kids to sleep, the one with the advice can say, "I have some suggestions. If anyone wants to call me, here is my phone number." Or, the leader may allow mothers to give their brief suggestions about such practical matters for a five- or ten-minute period.

6. Avoid "coffee klatching." Remember, your main goal is to learn to see all stressful events as tests of *middoth* and to increase self-mastery. This means that members are not there to gab, but to talk about how they are achieving greater self-discipline or, if they failed, how they hope to do better in the future.

7. No criticism, moralizing or diagnosing. No one is there to be preached at or lectured to. This is a lay group of non-professionals, all working together as equals.

8. No non-productive kvetching. If a member brings up a problem, don't let the kvetching go on and on. The leader should make sure that she gains insight into how she can solve the problem and how she can use it for her growth.

If at all possible, recommend that mothers find baby sitters so that they can fully concentrate on the meeting. If mothers do bring their babies, limit the group to no more than four or five women as more than that creates too much noise and distraction for serious work.

Many support groups have a "theme of the week" at the end of each session, when the leader suggests that all members give extra attention to one particular *middah*, such as acceptance: "I will it to be this way since this is the way Hashem wills it to be," or gratefulness.

If there are no noisy children present, the leader can also lead the members in a P.E.P. exercise at the end of each group, during which the members imagine themselves to be in the midst of a distressing situation and then see themselves responding in a calm, confident, constructive manner.

It is also very helpful to practice the REACH technique during sessions. Whenever a mother mentions an example which involves others, she should practice role-playing or role-reversal in the group so that she can create new neural pathways in her brain for improved communication techniques. For example, a mother gives an example about a child who says she wants to run away from home or who talks disrespectfully. The leader can play the child while the mother practices using her constructive communication skills and gets used to using phrases like: "I'm really sorry that you are in so much pain. What can I do to help?" Or, "It hurts me very much to be talked to like that. I want to hear what you have to say, and I may be willing to arbitrate, negotiate, compromise or help you find a solution, but first I want you to go out the door and walk back into this room and tell me in a respectful voice what you want." The leader can also play an oppositional child who does not want to do his homework, eat or pick up after himself. The mother can then practice the phrases she could use to gain cooperation without violence. The leader or other members can play the child, husband or mother.

[Note: Since no *lashon hara* is allowed in group, members should not give examples if the total view of the person involved is negative, for then the event is not a triviality, but is a major, life-altering distress. Since the group is run by lay people, it is not capable of handling such problems. They require expert attention. Whatever the example, members should be left with a basically good feeling about the persons involved, so as not to constitute *lashon hara*. Events involving abuse or possible danger to mental or physical health should be referred to proper authorities, rabbis or therapists.]

Sample EMETT Examples to Guide a Mothers' Group

Example 1: The Reluctant Husband

STEP 1: The Stressful Event

Last Friday afternoon things were very hectic. Then, in the middle of it all, my husband told me he wanted to go visit his parents.

STEP 2: The Temperamental Reaction

My harmful impulse was to say, "Yes," and then stew in silent hostility toward him for the rest of Shabbath for not helping me. I judged him as wanting to run away from the work and being inconsiderate of my feelings. My insecure thoughts were that he must not really love me and that I would not be able to count on him in a crisis. I wanted to put on my most miserable face to show him all that I was going through for him so he would feel sorry for me and would make my life easier. I wanted to maintain the most pitiful face possible. I had knots in my stomach and head pressure. I felt very bitter, angry and helpless.

STEP 3: The Positive Response

I took the secure thought that he didn't realize that I was so behind in my work, since I usually have everything under control and had not said anything to him. I gave him the benefit of the doubt and decided to go for peace, not power. I took the total view of the marriage, which is positive. He doesn't let me down when I really need him. He is very average in not wanting to be around the hectic pre-Shabbath chaos. Then I did what for me was the most difficult thing: I stated my feelings without anger or theatrics. I told him that I was behind with my work and that I would prefer his help, or, if he wanted to go, that he please take the two middle children who usually start fighting when they are bored. Then I smiled and admitted that I was jealous that he could go off so easily. I didn't do it with bitterness. He responded very positively and said he would go for a short while and then return.

STEP 4: Evaluation and Endorsements

Before EMETT, I would have either resentfully let him go, or angrily made him stay. I avoided the romantic expectation that my husband be able to read my mind and know what I need without my having to express it. I also avoided the erroneous conclusion that if he doesn't help as much as I want, it is because he does not love me, or that if I need help, it's a sign that I'm inadequate. I didn't have to "awfulize" the Friday afternoon preparations, which really were not all that bad. I endorse myself for speaking calmly, yet assertively, for dropping my judgments against my husband and against myself, and for not making nasty faces or *shlepping* out my resentment toward him for days. I endorse for realizing that I was having an attack of "I-can't-stand-it-itis."

Example 2: The Self-Defeating Comparison

STEP 1:

I was frantically trying to get my kids ready for *shul* when I happened to look out the window and notice my neighbor walking so proudly along, her head high, her face beaming with joy and calm satisfaction, as her eight children walked along with her, each with polished shoes and beautifully ironed shirts. That did it. I began to sink into a temperamental torrent.

STEP 2:

I began to condemn myself as totally untogether and unfit. I condemned my children for being stupid, lazy, undisciplined, wild and sloppy. I had the insecure thought that I would always be a failure, that I would never be calm and happy, and that my kids would suffer. I thought about how my neighbor has her kids in bed by half past six, while some of mine are still jumping around at ten o'clock! I thought about how well trained hers are, how they do all the ironing and most of the cooking and how well organized everything is by her. I had the harmful impulse to scream at my kids even more and smack the little ones. I felt very tense, drained, jealous and inferior.

STEP 3:

I realized that I had to get myself out of temper. I started to think of all the good that I have in my life, and that it's only when we have these stressful moments when everybody is home and there is the pressure of time that things get kind of whacky. I am basically good and loving and so are my kids. I have a weakness which is lack of order. I looked at the positive side, which is that I am really trying to work on this shortcoming. I made a promise to myself that I would sit the kids down after Shabbath and work out a chore schedule. Most of all, I dropped the judgment of inferiority and superiority against my neighbor and myself. She has different skills, conditioning and predispositions than I do. She is more self-assured and decisive. We are working with different tools, that's all. I gave myself permission to stop my past habit pattern of self-torture through condemnations.

STEP 4:

Before EMETT, I would certainly have been so anxious and depressed that I would have given up and just stayed home. I would not have known how to do something positive with my jealousy, which, in this case, meant using it to motivate myself to do something constructive to change my present behavior. I endorsed myself for not staying in negativity or "awfulizing" the differences between myself and my neighbor. It is not all that bad. We have a lot of fun in our family despite the chaos. To me, that means that we are basically healthy.

Example 3: The Critical Relative

STEP 1:

A critical relative happened to be visiting. She had brought some things for the kids and they started fighting over them. She said, "Boy, he sure is a crybaby," about one of the kids. As things got worse, she said, "They are certainly quite undisciplined, aren't they!" That's when I began to get into temper.

STEP 2:

I had the insecure thought that she was right, that my children are exceptionally undisciplined and that I am an exceptionally poor mother. I mean, they were even fighting over who was going to get the stupid little ribbons off the wrappings! I was condemning her for condemning me and condemning myself and my children. I was very tense and wanted to tell her to take her things and just leave, to leave the house myself or to scream at the kids. I felt attacked, insulted and hurt as well as hostile, vengeful and cold.

STEP 3:

That's when I thought about some creative tools. First, I thought of my "Oh . . ." response. "Oh, the kids are fighting. Instead of getting emotional, I have to find a solution." I brought some humor into my internal environment by telling myself, "I will that my children be acting so obnoxiously right now. I will that this person be so critical." It was such a downright lie, that I had to smile. That relaxed me and I was able to step in very assertively. I took all the toys, boxes and wrappings out of the room and told them that they wouldn't be allowed to touch anything until they had calmed down. Then I did the thing which I have always feared to do most, which was to tell this relative that her critical comments hurt my feelings, even though they were directed at the children. I told her that my children are really quite normal and that many other children pounce with unrestrained passion on gifts. I apologized to her and had the children apologize. Then I told them to replay the scene, this time using their best manners. It worked, *baruch Hashem*! They became more self-controlled. I bore the discomfort of the visit, knowing that it would eventually be over. I wore a mask of calm confidence in order not to let the grimaces and remarks bother me. At the same time, I recognized my need to teach my children better manners. That was the positive message in this whole event.

STEP 4:

Before EMETT, I would have been so mortified that I would have either just sat there in a stupid stupor or gotten violent with the children just to please her and show her that I do know how to be the boss. The event would have been a disaster. I would not have known that it was only distressing, not dangerous. I endorse myself for speaking up and for finding a creative solution and not sinking into self-pity and discouragement. I managed to keep my sense of self-esteem despite what was going on, which is a big accomplishment for me. It used to be that I only felt good about myself when everything was going smoothly. I endorse myself for giving up my romantic desire for everyone to love me all the time and for everything to always be in perfect control. I endorse myself for diverting my attention instead of torturing myself with condemnations or getting into one of my self-punishing moods just because I was criticized. I endorse myself for learning not to be so suggestible to others' opinions, yet for recognizing that I am not the type of person who can be unfeeling when I am criticized. It hurts. But I don't have to hurt back or dwell on it.

Example 4: The Fear of Future Discomfort

STEP 1:

Next week daylight-saving time starts and I've been *oy'veying* about it for three months already in anxious anticipation.

STEP 2:

My insecure thought is that I won't be able to get the kids to sleep at night and won't be able to get them up on time in the morning because of the time change. I keep visualizing the same awful struggles that I had last year and I keep thinking that I just can't go through this again. My harmful impulse is to talk about it to everyone, how awful it is, and to brood about it and become discouraged.

STEP 3:

I am calming myself down this year by taking the secure thought that we got through it last year and we will again this year. True, they don't want to go to bed when it's still light outside, but I've already ordered new room-darkeners to help with that problem. I am trying to remain calm and trusting. I can either work this up or work it down. My tendency is to over-dramatize difficulties. I am sure that other mothers are also going to have difficulty with bedtimes after the time change. Yes, it is distressing, but not dangerous. It is only a change. I can trust my basic strengths to pull me through.

STEP 4:

Before EMETT, I would have had a much stronger emotional response and would have complained more. I would have thought that I was exceptional, that I was the only mother who had such difficulties adjusting and coping. I don't have to "awfulize" this situation. There are certainly enough real tragedies in the world without my having to create an extra one over such a relatively trivial matter. I realize that with my anxiety-prone nature, I have to work harder at having confidence and being my own source of reassurance and strength. I endorse myself for diverting my attention and taking secure thoughts.

Example 5: Coping with Present Discomfort

STEP 1:

It was 5 P.M. I was exhausted. I had been in the house for three days with two sick children. I felt weepy and thought I couldn't go on.

STEP 2:

I had the insecure thought that I would not be able to take proper care of my children and that I would sink into total lethargy and apathy. I condemned myself for feeling so bad. I felt hostile toward the kids for being sick and resentful of their demands. I felt that I simply could not manage. I wanted to go into my room and hide there and cry and cry. All I could think of was how miserable my life was.

STEP 3:

I realized that I was in temper. I told myself that my response was really very normal for a woman who was deprived of sleep and in the house for so many days. I was average and so were my children. The whole situation was realistically very uncomfortable for all of us. However, I told myself that the situation was temporary and that I would soon feel better once I had gotten sleep and returned to my normal routine. I also noted that the total view was actually positive. We had played many games together and I had managed quite well considering the circumstances. Five o'clock is usually a low point for me. However, I could push up my will to bear the discomfort of this period until the children were in bed.

STEP 4:

I see that when my nerve resistance is low, I tend to have very gloomy thoughts and eclipse all the good in my life. I have a romantic desire that life go smoothly and that I always feel good. I don't want ups and downs, only ups! I was awfulizing the situation. After all, the children were on the mend. There was nothing seriously wrong with them, *baruch Hashem*. I endorsed myself for making so many extra meals, for trying to be cheerful and for staying functional in the midst of my distress. I really had a lot to endorse for.

Glossary

BARUCH HASHEM: Thank God!

BASHERT: it was meant to be this way

BENTCHER: the booklet from which the blessing after eating bread is said

BITACHON: trust in God

BRACHA: blessing

BRITH: "bris" circumcision ceremony

CHALLOT: special ceremonial bread for Shabbath

CHAZAL: the greatest Jewish sages of our past

CHEDER: a school where young children learn Torah

CHESED: loving-kindness

CHINUCH: education of children in spiritual values

CHIZUK: strengthening, uplifting communication

CHUPPAH: the bridal canopy

DAAVEN: pray

EMUNAH: faith in God

GASHMIUTH: the materialistic aspects of life

HACHNASATH ORCHIM: warm hospitality to guests

HAKARATH HATOV: gratefulness

HALACHA: Jewish law

HASHEM: God. (Literally, the name)

HASHGACHA PRATITH: awareness of God's personal guidance in all matters

HASHKAFA: the Jewish outlook

KADIMA: forward

KAPARAH: an atonement; a painful event which atones for past misdeeds or saves one from some greater harm

KEDUSHA: holiness

KIBUD AV V'AME: honoring one's parents

270

KOLLEL: an institution where married men learn Torah

KOL NIDRE: the name given to the opening service on Yom Kippur

LADUN L'CHAF ZECHUTH: giving the benefit of the doubt

LASHON HARA: speaking evil of another; giving people a negative view of someone

M'VATER: overlooking another's faults; giving in for the sake of peace

MADRAIGA: one's level of spiritual awareness at any given moment

MEGILLA: scroll of the Book of Esther, read in the synagogue on Purim

MENTSCH: a person who acts and thinks as a Torah-observant Jew should

MENUCHATH HANEFESH: peace of mind

MESIRUTH NEFESH: self-sacrifice

MEZUZAH: words of scripture attached to the doorpost of each door in the home

MIDDAH (pl. MIDDOTH): a good character trait

MUSSAR: morally uplifting statements

NESHAMA: spirit

NISAYON (pl. NISYANOTH): tests (any experience can be seen as a test of one's *madraiga*)

OLAM HABAH: the World to Come (also known as the World of Truth)

PISUKIM: verses from Torah

POTSCH: a slap

RASHA: an evil person

SEDER: ceremony observed in the home on the first night (outside Israel two nights) of Passover, when the story of the exodus from Egypt is recounted by reciting the Hagaddah.

SHABBATH: Shabbos, the Sabbath day

SHALOM: peace

SHALOM BAYITH: peace in the home

SHLICHIM: Godly messengers

SHMATA: literally "a rag," a doormat

SHTUP: to force-feed

SHUL: a synagogue

SIDDUR: prayer book

SIMCHA: a happy event

TEHILLIM: psalms

TRAIFE: any non-kosher food, and extended to apply to anything
    which does not comply with Torah standards (i.e., a traife book)

TIKUN: spiritual repair work

TSHUVAH: to repent of one's misdeeds

TZITZITH: a fringed garment which boys wear after the age of three

YETZER HARA: the will to do evil

YETZER TOV: the will to do good

ZCHUTH: merit, privilege

Torah terms:

BERESHITH: Genesis

SHEMOTH: Exodus

VAYIKRA: Leviticus

BAMIDBAR: Numbers

DEVARIM: Deuteronomy

MISHLAI: Book of Proverbs

PIRKAI AVOTH: Ethics of Our Fathers

Bibliography

[Full addresses are given for some of the following books so that you can write to the publishing house and order directly from them. They will send promptly to Israel. Write first to ask for price of book plus postage. Then send a money order.]

English

Ayres, A. Jean. *Sensory Integration and the Child*, Western Psychological Services (1979), 12031 Wilshire Boulevard, Los Angeles, California 90024.

Bachya, Rabbi Ibn Paquda. *Duties of the Heart*, Feldheim Publishers, Jerusalem-New York, 1962.

Brazelton, T. Berry. *Infants and Mothers*, Dell Publishing (1969), 1 Dag Hammarskjold Plaza, New York, New York 10017.

Briggs, Dorothy. *Your Child's Self-Esteem*, Dolphin Books, New York, 1975.

Dessler, Rabbi Eliyahu, *Strive for Truth!* vol. I, translated by Rabbi Aryeh Carmell, Feldheim Publishers, Jerusalem-New York, 1978, and vol. II, 1986.

Eyre, Linda and Richard. *Teaching Children Joy*, Ballantine Books (1980), Dept. TA, 201 E. 50th St., New York, 10022, *Teaching Children Responsibility*, 1980.

Faber, Adele and Elaine Mazlish. *How To Talk So Kids Will Listen and Listen So Kids Will Talk*, Avon Books (1980), 959 Eighth Avenue, New York, New York, 10019.

Ferber, Richard. *Solve Your Child's Sleep Problems*, Simon & Schuster (1985), 1230 Avenue of the Americas, New York, New York 10020.

Fraiberg, Selma H. *The Magic Years*, Charles Scribner's Sons, New York, 1959.

Hirsch, Rabbi Samson Raphael. *Horeb*, Soncino Press, New York, 1962.

—. *Yisodoth HaHinnuch*, vol. II, translated by A. Wolf, Netzach Publishers, B'nei Brak, 1968.

273

Johnson, Spencer. *The One Minute Mother*, William Morrow & Co. (1983), 105 Madison Avenue, New York, 10016.

Keirsey, David and Marilyn Bates. *Please Understand Me*, Prometheus Nemesis Books (1978), POB 2082, Del Mar, Calif. 92014.

Levy, Miriam. *Effective Jewish Parenting*, Feldheim Publishers, Jeusalem-New York, 1986.

Lopian, Rabbi Eliyahu. *Lev Eliyahu*, translated by Rabbi B.D. Klein, published by Rabbi Kalman Pinski (1975), 53 Hapisgah, Jerusalem, Israel.

Luzzatto, Rabbi Moshe Chaim. *The Path of the Just*, translated by Shraga Silverstein, Feldheim Publishers, Jerusalem-New York, 1966.

Maimonides, Rabbi Moshe. *The Book of Knowledge*, translated by Moses Hyamson, Feldheim Publishers, Jerusalem-New York, 1974.

McCullough, Bonnie and Susan Monson. *401 Ways to Get Your Kids to Work at Home*, St. Martin's Press (1981), 175 5th Avenue, New York 10010. Also see, *Bonnie's Household Organizer* and *Bonnie's Household Budget Book*.

Pliskin, Rabbi Zelig. *Gateway To Happiness*, Aish HaTorah (1983), 1742 E. 7th St. , Brooklyn, New York 11223, 1983.

—. *Love Your Neighbor*, 1977.

Sears, William, M.D. *Creative Parenting*, Dodd Mead and Co., New York, 1982.

—. *The Fussy Baby,* La Leche League, Chicago, 1985.

Shreeve, Caroline. *The Premenstrual Syndrome*, Thorsons Publishers, London, 1983.

Young, Pam and Peggy Jones. *Sidetracked Home Executives*, Warner Books, New York, 1977.

Hebrew

Levenstein, Rabbi Yechezkail. *Ohr Yechezkail*, B'nai Brak, 1976.

Lichtstein, Rabbi Mordecai. *Mitzvoth Hal'vovoth*, Jerusalem, 1967.

Munk, Rabbi Meir. *Schar V'ha'anasha B'chinuch,* B'nai Brak, 1982.

Papu, Rabbi Eliezer. *Pele Yoetz*, Kushtandia, 1824.

Rosenstein, Rabbi Moshe. *Ahavath Maishorim*, New York, 1958.

Yadler, Rabbi BenTzion. *B'Tuv Yerushalyim*, Netzach Publishers, B'nai Brak, 1976.

Yosef, Rabbi Yaakov, of Polonoyne. Peterkov, 1884.

Author Unknown

Alai Shur, B'air Yaakov, 1968.
Erev Shabbath Newspaper, Jerusalem, 1986.
HaYom Yom, Kehot Publication Society, Eastern Parkway, New York, 1976.
Kuntres Ahavas Yisroel, Kehot Publication Society (1977), 770 Eastern Parkway, Brooklyn, New York, 11213.

Index